T0327927

MANGIA

To my family, particularly my parents,
for your love and encouragement and for
always putting food on our Italian table.

And heartfelt thanks to the city of Urbino.
For profound reasons known only to me,
I quote the prince of painters Raffaello:

*'I, however, have always seen – and still do see –
things differently.'*

MANGIA

How to eat your way through Italy

Maria Pasquale

Smith
Street
Books

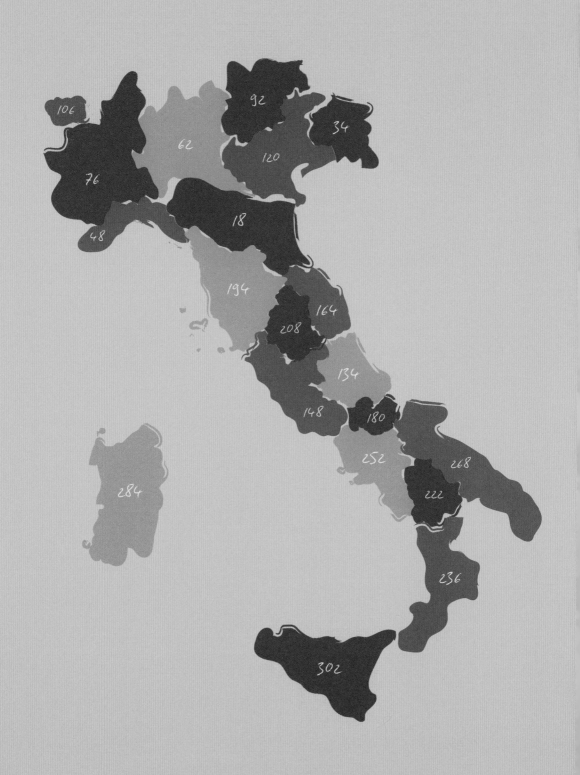

Contents

I 've known Italy my whole life and have loved it for just as long. You could say it's an obsession, which I've indulged by slowly eating my way through the entire country. *Mangia* is the mouth-watering culmination of this journey, over 40 years in the making. It's a distillation of a lifetime's worth of meals and conversations with chefs, vintners, olive growers, cheesemakers, caper farmers, fishermen, restaurateurs, culinary journalists and the many others who work with food, or who just love it.

What better way to understand Italy than through its kitchens? *Mangia* means 'eat', and I guarantee that is exactly what you'll want to do after diving into this book that weaves a tale of Italy's culinary heart. But while people from around the world might arrive here on an empty stomach, ready to overindulge in la cucina italiana, what if I told you an Italian cuisine doesn't actually exist? That there's no such thing?

The truth is, Italy doesn't have a homogeneous menu or culture: both are regional and dynamic. In fact, you could almost describe Italy as 20 different countries in one, each with its own food, customs, dialect and geographic make-up. Their individual cuisines are guided by local seasons, produce, traditions and the constant pull of innovation. But no matter where you are in the country, food in Italy is united in *convivialità*: conviviality, or the art of being together and sharing special moments.

The cuisine of Italy is not just about pizza, pasta and gelato (although there's plenty of those to go around). And it's not just washed down with wine or an Aperol spritz. It's so much more.

For instance, did you know that risotto will never taste as good as it does in the North? That spaghetti is never served with a bolognese sauce, and couscous is a staple dish in parts of Sicily? That the Tuscans bake their bread without salt? That apple strudel is Italian too, or that tiramisù originated in Veneto?

While art galleries and archaeological sites may dominate Italian itineraries, I'll bet that long after your trip is over, you won't recall the height of the Pantheon or the year Florence's Duomo was built. But by gosh will you remember how you felt biting into your first ever pizza in Naples, licking ricotta off your fingers after devouring a cannolo in Sicily, the saltiness of the guanciale in that Roman carbonara you never wanted to end and the experience of devouring cicchetti sitting on the Venetian lagoon's edge. Moments like these make me feel alive, privy to an insight into history, heritage and culture.

Yes, food nourishes us. But it's so much more than that. Food feeds the soul, and memories of it are some of the most powerful. A taste or a scent can take us right back to a moment, and Italy has no end of memories to offer.

When I travel, the experiences that combine food, history, people and culture are the ones that remain with me years later; I'll never forget watching Luna the dog run through the woods and kick up dirt to find a truffle in the hills of Piedmont. The eggplant parmigiana I still make to this day (with fried – not baked! – eggplant, because everybody knows fried is better): well, Luca taught me that over 15 years ago at a cooking class in Amalfi. In nearby Vietri sul Mare, Patrizia and Alfonso treated me to a wine tasting with views of the vineyards, and I still remember the locally produced cheese and lemon jam we ate. I made my first torta caprese with my friends Holly and Gianluca at Michelangelo, their cooking school on the isle of Capri. And in Pescara, Rosy taught me to make ravioli teramani and pallotte cacio e ova in her home.

Yes, food nourishes us.
   But it's so much more than that.
Food feeds the soul, and memories
   of it are some of the most powerful.

These experiences are the tip of a very delicious iceberg, but the point is, food makes the soul sing. It makes memories. When we travel, it helps us learn about a place. Beautifully, it also helps us learn something about ourselves.

I've come to know Italy, not just by travelling around and living here, but through food. I've had the good fortune of working in the food sector as a writer and dining at the country's best restaurants, including those housed in former monasteries, farmhouses and trattorie. I've dined on rooftops, on the street, at markets, in homes and on boats. And after all these meals, I can confirm: food is the way to Italy's heart.

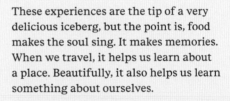

This book is intended to guide you to that heart and to inspire you to explore on your next visit. It's intended to nurture your curiosity and encourage you to think about what you're eating, where it came from and how it's tied to the place you're in. To me, that's what food is about: connecting people and places across ages. It's about the past, the present and even the future.

Mangia is divided into 20 chapters, covering each Italian region. I've visited them all, and these are my musings and knowledge, collected over decades. These chapters are designed to make your mouth water, to pique your curiosity and then – while you're travelling – to prompt you and inspire you to keep uncovering, to keep eating and to keep loving Italy. As you travel, you'll come across even more dishes and items that haven't been covered in these pages, because that's the beauty of Italy's regional cuisine: it's boundless.

Each chapter will introduce you to the geography and food culture of a region, lay out the primary produce you should be on the lookout for, and outline the must-eat dishes – including a quick Top 10 of my personal favourites. Drinks are covered too, and not just the alcoholic varieties: think almond milk in Sicily, hot chocolate with whipped cream in Turin and coffee in Naples.

More than just what to eat and drink, I'll also tell you *when*, with a list of *sagre* (food festivals) to mark on your calendar. These festivals are ingrained in Italian culture, providing meaningful moments where communities unite. From celebrating mushrooms to olive oil, alpine yoghurt to chocolate, getting involved in a town sagra is a full Italian immersion you won't soon forget. There will be hundreds more than the ones I've selected, and dates change from year to year, so use this as a reminder to research what's on when you travel.

I've also included a curated collection of unique and memorable culinary experiences, such as foraging and forest bathing in Umbria, liquorice and bergamot tasting in Calabria and cheesemaking in the hills of Molise. If those aren't to your taste, there's also truffle hunting in Piedmont, glamping in an ancient Sardinian olive grove and taking a cocktail masterclass on the island of Ischia. My tips take you to farms and farmhouses, restaurants and markets, wineries and breweries, workshops and factories: the places and moments that will take you deep into Italy's gastronomic DNA.

Additionally, there's an introduction to dining etiquette, *le feste* – those Italian feast days and holidays that, of course, revolve around food – and a guide to navigating markets. These tips and tricks will no doubt come in handy as you travel through Italy, virtually or physically. And for good measure, I've included a carefully selected recipe from each region, courtesy of cooks from across the country, including Michelin-starred chefs: a regional repertoire of 20 dishes that you can try at home.

Of course, this is not an all-encompassing, exhaustive guide, but rather a large slice of the products, ingredients and delicacies that you'll find on your travels. In Italy, there are countless street foods and flatbreads, cured meats and sweets and pastries: a list that could go on and on and on, because the food here is never ending. Italy's kitchens transcend borders, sharing history, tradition, innovation and lessons in art, sustainability and transformation. Food is nourishment, yes, but it also provokes thought, feeds curiosity and inspires new ideas.

For Italians, eating is one of the great pleasures of life and their enthusiasm is wildly contagious. I hope that this book shares that enthusiasm with you, and that you'll treasure these pages. That *Mangia* will serve as a reminder to ask, to taste, to explore. And now, I invite you to come along on a delectable journey with me through my Italy: a country whose love language, without a doubt, always has been and always will be food.

So, get dreaming, get planning, get travelling and *mangia*!

Baci, Maria

DINING ETIQUETTE

Table manners in Italy really come down to *la bella figura*, which is fundamental to the Italian DNA: that is, to make a good impression, be well mannered and always on your best behaviour. Essentially, it is a set of unwritten rules, and the ones listed here will guide you through some of the dos and don'ts of Italian dining.

DO

- Follow the order Italians eat in. A meal typically starts with an *antipasto*, such as bruschetta, cheese and salumi or fried treats. Then comes the *primo,* which is your pasta or rice course. The *secondo* can be considered a main course and is usually a meat or fish dish (or a vegetable dish for vegetarians). It is served with a *contorno* (a side dish that's normally a vegetable or salad) of your choice. There's *dolce* (dessert) to finish, followed by coffee. Very last comes a *digestivo* or *amaro*, a liqueur to aid digestion.

- Ask your wait staff what dishes are local or typical to the area. They'll be more than happy to help and, if you're in a group, to guide your ordering.

- Leave a tip, especially for good service. If you're charged *coperto* (cover charge), a round up to the nearest euro or some coins are appreciated. If you've been charged *servizio* (service charge) too, tipping is up to you. In any case, it's not obligatory and should never be automatically applied to a bill (but it sure is welcome). Note: many EFTPOS machines in Italy still don't allow for tipping, so keep some cash on you.

- Feel free to wipe up sauce on your pasta plate with bread, depending on your location. This action is affectionately known as *la scarpetta* (little shoe). It's more than welcome at casual restaurants, trattorie and in the home, but less so at formal or fine-dining venues.

- Expect to be in for the long haul. Dining in Italy is an indulgent pastime, never to be confused with eating as a function. I'd say hurrying off is okay if you're in a casual outlet, travelling solo or at an airport. Otherwise, it can be considered rude to rush wait staff.

- Have the sommelier help choose wine to perfectly match your meal, or at a more casual restaurant, ask the wait staff for something local.

- Expect to head to a bar for a post-meal coffee as some trattorie and enoteche don't have coffee machines.

- Pay for your coffee at the bar register before heading to the *bancone* (counter) to have your order made. The barista will always happily have a chat, but this is not a leisurely affair. It's social, yes, but you should have your coffee and then get out.

DON'T

- Order an Aperol spritz with your meal. This now-seen-everywhere cocktail is for aperitivo, before dinner or even after, but is not meant to match your pizza and pasta.

- Have pizza and pasta together. Ever. These are discrete meals and not to be eaten in the same sitting.

- Ask for cheese when you're eating pasta with seafood. Unless the dish comes with cheese or it's offered to you, it means it can do without.

- Ever cut your pasta. Unless it's, say, a large lasagne or cannelloni. Short pasta and especially spaghetti shouldn't have a knife in sight. You *can* use a spoon to help twirl your spaghetti, but most Italians do without and leave spoons for kids.

- Order a cappuccino with food unless it's breakfast. The problem is less about time and more what you're mixing it with. It is inconceivable to an Italian to have a lasagne followed by a big, frothy milk drink. In their view, it will ruin digestion: a no-no. *Caffè* (espresso) or a *caffè macchiato* (espresso with a dash of milk) is the go-to at any time.

- Expect a big breakfast. Hotels will serve up American-style breakfast with eggs and other savoury dishes but this isn't typical for locals, who enjoy a sweet breakfast. (Note: compared to breakfast pastries from many western countries outside the Mediterranean, Italy's contain less processed sugar.) To start the day, Italians usually have a caffè or cappuccino with a *cornetto* (Italian croissant) or, at home, coffee with warm milk and biscuits.

- Ask for tap water, unless you're at a bar where it's commonly served so you can cleanse your palate before a coffee. Buying water as part of your meal is the cultural norm.

- On the topic of water – don't *cin cin* with it. It's considered bad luck and the Italians are superstitious. Same goes for plastic cups. However, it is okay to clunk another plastic glass as long as you use your hand as a buffer.

LE FESTE

One of the things I love most about Italy is that at any
given time of year there is a reason to try a particular dish,
thanks to *le feste* (the festivities): a chance to celebrate,
reflect and spend time with loved ones.

Depending on where you are in the country, the dishes will change, but one thing that stays the same is the Italian love for conviviality. Sitting at the table to share a moment and a meal with loved ones is the cornerstone of the boot.

During Carnevale, bakeries and pasticcerie are filled with sugar-dusted, fried frappe and doughnuts (castagnole or zeppole included). The idea is to gorge before Lent begins in the lead-up to Easter. It's my favourite time of year.

Then comes the feast day of San Giuseppe on 17 March: Father's Day in Italy. In many regions, that means *zeppole di San Giuseppe*, which are fried or baked doughnuts filled and/or topped with custard and sour cherries.

At Pasqua (Easter) and Natale (Christmas), traditional dishes change from region to region. Yes, there are many similarities, particularly where borders are shared, but each town has its own way of celebrating, and each specialty and dish reflects towns' histories and identities. They are commonly tied to religion; for example, lamb is widespread at Easter and symbolises the 'lamb of God', new life and rebirth. Many dishes eaten on Easter feature cheese and eggs, from *pastiera* (a sweet tart) in Naples to breakfast spreads in Rome. Lasagne is also quite the common scene on Italian tables on Easter Sunday, as is *colomba* (Easter dove bread). And across the country, you'll find panettone, pandoro and varieties of torrone and panforte at Christmas.

It's very common to eat *fave e pecorino* (broad/fava beans and pecorino) on 1 May for Labour Day, while depending on what part of the country you're in on Ferragosto, the warm August temperatures usually call for watermelon.

On the feast day of San Silvestro (New Year's Eve), you'll find most Italians eating lentils in some form or another. They believe that their round shape, thought to resemble Roman coins, symbolises money and prosperity, and that eating them will bring good luck and fortune to the family for the upcoming year.

No matter what time of the year, or what occasion, the best part about all of these traditions is that festivities are a time to indulge! And I'm always up to the task – I wouldn't dare to break with tradition.

Region by region, here are some iconic delicacies to look out for. If you're travelling through Italy during le feste, be sure to ask locals at restaurants, bakeries and markets what to sample, because each town will have something memorable for you to try.

ABRUZZO
- **Carnevale:** Chiacchiere, Cicerchiata
- **Christmas:** Caggionetti, Torrone
- **Easter:** Fiadone, La pupa e il cavallo

BASILICATA
- **Carnevale:** Taralli al naspro
- **Christmas:** Panzerotti dolci, Pettole
- **Easter:** Scarcedda, Torta di ricotta

CALABRIA
- **Carnevale:** Pignolata
- **Christmas:** Cuddrurieddri, Nacatole, Turdilli
- **Easter:** Cuzzupe/Cudduraci, Scalille

CAMPANIA
- **Carnevale:** Graffe
- **Christmas:** Capitone, Struffoli
- **Easter:** Casatiello, Pastiera

EMILIA-ROMAGNA
- **Carnevale:** Intrigoni, Sfrappole
- **Christmas:** Spongata, Tortelli di Natale
- **Easter:** Ciambella ferrarese o brazadela,
  Torta tagliolina

FRIULI VENEZIA GIULIA
- **Carnevale:** Chifelini, Crostoli
- **Christmas:** Brovada e muset, Gubana putizza
- **Easter:** Pinza triestina, Pistùm, Presnitz

LAZIO
- **Carnevale:** Castagnole, Frappe
- **Christmas:** Fritto misto, Pangiallo
- **Easter:** Corallina, Pigna dolce,
  Torta al formaggio

LIGURIA
- **Carnevale:** Bugie, Schiumette
- **Christmas:** Natalini, Pandolce
- **Easter:** Torta pasqualina, Quaresimali genovesi

LOMBARDIA
- **Carnevale:** Chiacchiere, Tortelli
- **Christmas:** Bossolà, Torrone di Cremona
- **Easter:** Bussolano, Resta

MARCHE
- **Carnevale:** Pesche dolci, Scroccafusi
- **Christmas:** Frustingo, Lu serpe
- **Easter:** Calcioni, Ciambelle strozzose

MOLISE
- **Carnevale:** Caragnoli, Scorpelle
- **Christmas:** Ostie ripiene, Rosacatarre
- **Easter:** Casciatelli/Fiadoni

PIEMONTE
- **Carnevale:** Frici, Bugie
- **Christmas:** Pan d'Natal, Torta di Nocciole,
- **Easter:** Ciambella Pasquale, Salame del papa

PUGLIA
- **Carnevale:** Farinella, Pettole, Purcidduzzi
- **Christmas:** Cartellate, Pesce di pasta
  di Mandorle
- **Easter:** Dita degli Apostoli, Scarcella

SARDEGNA
- **Carnevale:** Acciuleddhi, Arrubiolus
- **Christmas:** Pabassinas, Pane saba
- **Easter:** Casadina, Pardulas/Formaggelle

SICILIA
- **Carnevale:** Cartocci, Pignolata
- **Christmas:** Buccellato, Torrone
- **Easter:** Cassata, Cuddura

TOSCANA
- **Carnevale:** Berlingozzo, Cenci, Fritelle di Riso
- **Christmas:** Befanini, Copate, Panpepato
- **Easter:** Pan di Ramerino, Pasimata/Crescenza

TRENTINO-ALTO ADIGE
- **Carnevale:** Krapfen, Smacafam, Strauben
- **Christmas:** Zelten
- **Easter:** Corona, Pane di Pasqua/Forchaz

UMBRIA
- **Carnevale:** Cicerchiata, Crescionda
- **Christmas:** Pampepato, Pinoccate
- **Easter:** Ciaramicola, Torta al Formaggio

VALLE D'AOSTA
- **Carnevale:** Panzerotti alla marmellata, Tortelli
- **Christmas:** Mécoulin, Pandolce di Cogne
- **Easter:** Crescia mécoulin

VENETO
- **Carnevale:** Galani, Mammalucchi, Megiassa
- **Christmas:** Mandorlato, Zaleti
- **Easter:** Fugassa Pasquale

Le Feste

MARKET GUIDE

The market in Italy is not just about buying food. It's a true cultural experience linked to the Italian way of life.

This hallmark of the community descends on the piazza or the outskirts of the town centre. It's here that you build relationships with stall holders, fishmongers and cashiers. If you are a local, they often know your name, where you live and definitely what you're cooking. In Italy, markets transcend the mere act of purchasing food. They are a profound cultural immersion intertwined with the very essence of Italian existence. These vibrant settings across towns and cities are the backdrop for relationships with market characters, familiarity their undisputed heart and soul.

I like to say Italian cuisine starts in the market, while French cuisine starts in the kitchen. That's not to take anything away from French food, which I love, but France's dishes are more technical. Very often, food is less elaborate in Italy – seasonality and quality produce are what's paramount.

At any given fresh food market, you'll generally find everything from vegetables to cheese, salumi, seafood and meat. Locals always have 'their' *fruttivendolo* (fruit and vegetable seller), and if you speak to one, you'll learn a lot. Among the sights, tastes and sounds of a market, there's always someone willing to share which variety of tomato is best for the dish you're making or to show you how to prepare artichokes or how best to cut watermelon. Locals and store holders at any market will also be more than happy to indulge in a conversation with you about what's in season. An hour spent at a market is an immersive introduction to the real backbone of Italy's cuisine and food heritage.

As the Italian diet is led by seasonality, you'll be hard pressed to find summer vegetables on the menu in winter. When I pass by markets, even at a distance, I can tell what season we are in just by looking at the shades of fruit and vegetables on display. At the end of summer, the vibrant reds, yellows and pinks start to make way for the warmer browns and oranges of autumn. In Rome, I know that winter is near when I see puntarelle on menus across the city. I love eating this type of chicory, but what I love more is seeing buckets of iced water at markets as the puntarelle are left to soak after they're shaved so that they curl up.

Seasonality in Italy is not just about the fruits and vegetables, though, but about seafood too. The Mediterranean alone boasts almost 40 fish species, and while they are generally available all year round these days, Italian fishmongers consider fish to be in season in the stages either before or after their reproductive phase. So check with fishmongers to ensure you're getting your fish at its very best.

When visiting supermarkets, you can find most produce all through the year, but keep seasonality in mind as you shop. The produce that is in season is what will really shine on your plate.

Markets really are a true feast for all the senses. No matter where or when you find yourself in Italy, visiting one will be among the most authentic things you'll do. The sights, sounds and smells will give you a real taste of local life, which will stay with you long after your holiday has ended.

TIPS

AT THE MARKET

* Check the schedule, as some markets are open daily, others one or two days a week. Almost always, the markets run from early morning until around lunchtime.

* Respect vendors' preferences. Unless given permission, avoid touching the fruit and vegetables. Some vendors prefer to handle the bagging themselves for safety reasons. Look for bags left out in front of the food as a sign that you can select produce. Confirm with a simple '*Posso?*' (Can I?) if unsure.

* Learn numbers 1–10. Since you may not be able to bag the produce yourself, knowing how to say the numbers in Italian is helpful. Food is usually purchased by the gram or kilogram.

* Build vendor loyalty. Establishing a relationship with a specific stall is key to being treated like a local. Vendors will recognise you over time and may offer discounts or extras. However, avoid bargaining as prices are clearly displayed, and you will receive a receipt. Food markets in Italy are not for bartering!

* Discuss your menu and share your story. Engage in conversations with the vendors about what you plan on cooking. Don't be afraid to ask about ingredients you've never seen before.

Market Guide

AT THE SUPERMARKET

* Always wear the provided plastic gloves when handling produce to maintain hygiene and avoid stern looks from employees or other shoppers.

* After selecting your items, locate the associated number displayed on signs in the produce section. You'll need this to weigh your selection.

* Find the scale and weigh what you're buying by selecting the item's price code on the keypad and taking the sticker that is printed. There are no scales at check-out, so don't forget to do this.

Emilia-Romagna

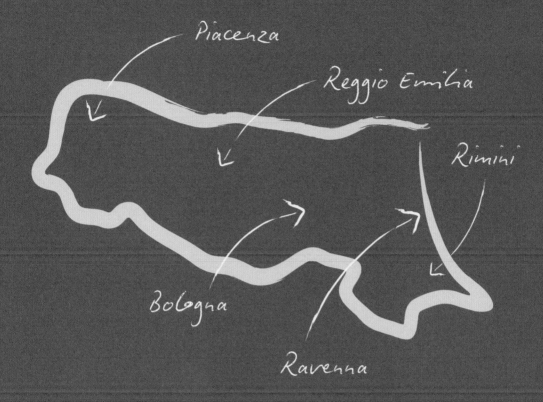

Piacenza

Reggio Emilia

Rimini

Bologna

Ravenna

Regional produce

Much of Emilia-Romagna is known as Italy's 'food valley': a centre of abundant agriculture since ancient times. Stretching from the Apennines to the Adriatic, with the fertile Po Valley running through its centre, the region nurtures a staggering amount of produce, from world-renowned cured meats and cheeses to flavoursome fruit and vegetables.

- Altedo's green asparagus
- Beef
- Casciotta d'Urbino cheese
- Chestnuts
- Eel from Comacchio
- Modena's balsamic vinegar
- Mortadella Bologna
- Parmigiano Reggiano
- Peaches
- Prosciutto di Parma
- Rice from the Po Delta
- Sogliano's Formaggio di Fossa cheese
- Squacquerone cheese
- Vignola cherries
- Zibello's culatello

Cathedral of Ferrara

N o stranger to big names, Emilia-Romagna is home to none other than Ferrari, Lamborghini, Maserati and Ducati, while Luciano Pavarotti, Federico Fellini and Giuseppe Verdi were all born here. The region has been a playground for the food-obsessed for centuries, and its culinary specialties enjoy worldwide fame: one only need mention products like Prosciutto di Parma, Parmigiano Reggiano and Aceto Balsamico Tradizionale di Modena.

I've not had a bad meal in this region, and when you think about the excellence it has in its blood, it's easy to understand why.

It's home to dishes that are imitated all over the world like tortellini, lasagne and ragù alla bolognese (page 21). But in Emilia-Romagna, where they were born, they're the real deal. I can say, with much confidence, that if you haven't eaten these quintessential delicacies here, you just haven't eaten them ever!

The region has a distinguished culinary and engineering heritage, and no one has described its culture more aptly than the famed Massimo Bottura – Italy's best chef and one of the world's finest. He says that

here, they like their cars fast, their food slow. With his unique talent, Bottura marries Emilia-Romagna's defining traits in a true art form – one that honours his upbringing, his beloved region and Italian regional nuances in a quirky, cutting-edge way. Food across Italy is about historical ties and ancient customs. It's about tradition. But, as Bottura says, contemporary cuisine needs not revolution but *evolution*. He has brought this in spades to the culinary world. You just can't have a conversation about food in Emilia-Romagna without mentioning Massimo Bottura.

He is nothing short of a celebrity in Modena, having transformed food tourism in this small city. My meal at his Osteria Francescana is still the best of my life – and I've been around the traps! Comprising 12 perfectly executed dishes, with wines and cocktails to match, it was a journey through Bottura's creative mind and an ode to dishes that evoke childhood. Take 'the crunchy part of the lasagne': it captures that quintessential Italian childhood wish for mamma or nonna to cut the corner slice of the lasagne for you – the piece with a crisp, charred edge. I will cherish that meal forever.

Emilia-Romagna

To this day, Emilia-Romagna is famous for its egg pasta, thanks to the period's wealthy families who began adding eggs to their pasta to create a richer and more luxurious dish.

It sits with so many other luscious moments of time spent in this rich, gastronomic slice of Italy. I first visited as a six-year-old, because the theme parks and nightlife of the Riviera Romagnola (the region's coast) are a rite of passage for Italian families. I've returned multiple times to the resort towns of Riccione and Rimini and eaten my share of *piadine* (the traditional flatbread, similar to pita; page 24) stuffed with squacquerone cheese and prosciutto or *rucola* (rocket/arugula). This part of Emilia-Romagna is often overlooked by foodies, but away from the beach clubs (and nightclubs), the area has a rich gastronomic tradition that combines wine, cheese, salumi and, not least, one of my favourite pastas to eat here: the delicately twisted strozzapreti (page 26).

In Emilia-Romagna, I've feasted on *tortellini in brodo* (in broth; page 24), the ultimate in Italian comfort food; luscious layers of green *lasagne* (page 24), because yes, the traditional local lasagne is made with spinach-infused sheets of egg pasta; and I had my first *tagliatelle alla bolognese* (page 24) – the closest thing you'll find

to the international spaghetti bolognese, which is not Italian! *Ragù* here is a rich tomato sauce made with both beef and pork and it's only paired with tagliatelle or lasagne. My first time in Bologna, I practically rolled out of the city that, among many nicknames, is known as *la Grassa*, which means 'the fat one'. If you're not planning on eating day and night, the city might just not be for you.

I'll never ever forget my Parmigiano Reggiano factory tour on the outskirts of Bologna, where I watched artisans handcraft this golden king of Italian cheeses. These factory experiences make for an early start, and so, by 9:30 am we were done, our guide serving up sandwiches with local mortadella and sparkling Lambrusco!

There are so many other firsts in this region that I've lost count: my first aperitivo under the porticoes of Bologna; my first *gnocco fritto* (fried pastry strips; page 24) in Modena; my first slice of culatello in Parma; my first *cotoletta alla bolognese* (veal with prosciutto and cheese; page 24) promptly followed by

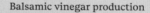

Balsamic vinegar production

my first delicious *zuppa inglese* (a trifle-like dessert; page 24) in Bologna; and, not least, dining for the first time at the Ferrari and Bottura collaboration, Cavallino (named after the small black horse, the symbol of Ferrari). Here, the energy of Italian pride and legacy is almost palpable. Collaborations like these and figures like Bottura – in the most beautiful of ways – capitalise on the region's rich and diverse make-up.

Geographically, the region that's home to all these gastronomic hallmarks extends from the Adriatic coast to Liguria, with the Po River to the north and the Apennines along most of the southern border. It consists of two historical regions: Emilia and Romagna, each with its own distinct cuisine. Emilia is located between Florence, Venice and Milan and is known for its dairy and meat dishes containing beef, veal and pork. Romagna, which includes the Adriatic coast and the mountains, is closer to central Italian cuisine, with more olive oil, herbs, seafood and wild game. The region's capital, Bologna, is located in Emilia, along with the famous foodie cities of Parma and Modena, while the smaller Romagna is home to Ravenna and the seaside resort of Rimini.

The fertile soil and temperate climate of the Po Valley provided ideal agricultural conditions for the Etruscan and Roman civilisations. During the Middle Ages, the region became a crossroads for trade and cultural exchange. When the Renaissance arrived, it brought innovation and refinement to the local cuisine, as well as the introduction of new ingredients, such as tomatoes, potatoes and corn. It also introduced a new ingredient to pasta-making – eggs! To this day, Emilia-Romagna is famous for its egg pasta, thanks to the wealthy families who began adding eggs to their pasta during this period to create a richer and more luxurious dish.

Each of the region's eight provinces boasts its own distinct pasta dishes. For instance, in Bologna, one can savour lasagne, gramigna (page 25) and tortellini pasticcio (page 26), while Parma and Piacenza are known for their anolini pockets, usually served in broth (page 25). In Ferrara, cappellacci stuffed with pumpkin (winter squash; page 25) are a local specialty, while Reggio's signature dish is cappelletti with minced (ground) meat (page 25). Romagna, on the other hand, offers a wide range of delights, such as garganelli with various fillings (page 25) and passatelli dumplings served in meat broth (page 24).

It's not all pasta, though: meat and dairy products, primarily produced in Emilia, have a long and illustrious history. One of Italy's earliest known culinary traditions is the production of Parmigiano Reggiano. This hard, salty cheese dates to at least the 13th century and remains a cornerstone of the region's food culture. The renowned Prosciutto di Parma has been produced in the area for over 2,000 years, while Culatello di Zibello (cured pork made from the hind, whereas prosciutto is the made from the leg) has been made in the Po Valley since the 15th century. Finally, Emilia-Romagna is known for its certified Aceto Balsamico Tradizionale di Modena, which has been made in Modena and Reggio Emilia since the Middle Ages. Around 300 artisans produce the thick, syrupy vinegar with grape must and age it in barrels for anywhere between 12 and 25 years. The real deal is a far cry from what's commonly called balsamic: an imitation made of grape must and caramel colouring.

These landmark products are the pride of the region. Emilia-Romagna's cuisine is a testament to the region's rich agricultural heritage and long-standing food traditions, which have produced some of Italy's most famous products. This heritage, which is still evolving to this day thanks to figures like Bottura, continues to inspire and delight food lovers around the world.

MARIA'S TOP 10 DISHES OF EMILIA-ROMAGNA

1 BOLLITO

Boiled meat comes in many guises across Northern Italy. In Bologna, it is traditionally served in restaurants from a trolley, accompanied by salsa verde or *mostarda* (candied fruit in a mustard syrup). The meat is actually the same as that used to make broth served with tortellini and can include beef, veal, capon, the local *zampone* (pig trotter stuffed with sausage) and cotechino.

2 . COTOLETTA ALLA BOLOGNESE

Taking its other name, *Petroniana*, from Bologna's patron saint, Petronius, this is a signature dish of the city. A veal cutlet is coated in breadcrumbs and fried in butter. It's then covered with prosciutto, parmigiano and stock and cooked until the cheese melts. During truffle season, some white truffle may be added.

3 GNOCCO FRITTO

Also known as *torta fritta*, this bread, made with flour, lard and water or milk, is deep-fried until golden and puffy. It's commonly served with local cured meats and cheeses.

4 LASAGNE

Emilia-Romagna is home to the definitive version of this dish. Sheets of pasta – usually green thanks to spinach – are layered with ragù alla bolognese, bechamel and parmigiano, then baked to achieve a crunchy top and flavourful, slightly burnt edges.

5 PASSATELLI

With a wrinkled, worm-like appearance, *passatelli* date to medieval times. Made with breadcrumbs, parmigiano, egg, nutmeg and sometimes bone marrow, they may be flavoured with lemon. The dough is passed through a tool known as a *ferro per passatelli* to create small, cylindrical strands that are often added to a broth, commonly made with chicken or beef, for a warming winter meal.

6 PIADINA

From the Romagna half of the region come these large, circular flatbreads that are cooked in a flat pan. Kiosks often sell them as a street food, usually filled with meat, cheese or vegetables.

7 SPOJA LORDA

Also known as *minestra imbottita* (stuffed soup), this dish's name comes from a dialect term for scantly filled ravioli. These small parcels were created to use up left-over egg pasta made in abundance for special occasions. Stuffed with cheese, parmigiano and nutmeg, they're added to meat broth or simple sauces.

8 TAGLIATELLE ALLA BOLOGNESE

While spaghetti bolognese might be known around the globe, connoisseurs know that Bologna's authentic version is served with the more robust tagliatelle. The thicker, flatter strands have more surface area to hold the weight of the slow-cooked meat sauce, and the egg they're made with adds a richer, more luxurious flavour.

9 TORTELLINI IN BRODO

Venus, one legend has it, stayed at an inn in Castelfranco Emilia, where the innkeeper spied her through the keyhole. He could only see her belly, which inspired him to create tortellini: the reason the pasta is also known as *ombelico di Venere* (Venus' navel). Legends aside, a cold day cries out for the fresh, meat-stuffed pasta swimming in a hot beef or chicken broth, dusted with parmigiano.

10 ZUPPA INGLESE

This 'English soup' layers *savoiardi* (ladyfingers), softened in alchermes liqueur, with a chocolate and a vanilla cream. It recalls English trifle, which the Este family may have recreated after their trips to the Elizabethan Court.

Other dishes to look out for

In Emilia-Romagna, the birthplace of so many of Italy's greatest food hits, it is almost impossible to have a bad meal. From a simple fried snack to ribbons of silken yolk-yellow pasta, the local cuisine is as lush as it gets.

Pane

Borlengo

As wafer-thin as a crepe, *borlengo* is a crispy flatbread that is often cooked outdoors on a large flat pan. The traditional filling is *cunza*, also known as *pesto modenese*: a mixture of finely chopped pancetta, lardo, rosemary and garlic. It's spread across the borlengo, which is folded and eaten hot.

Tigelle / Crescentine

Modena's small flatbreads are cut into circles and cooked on the stove in a special embossed pan called a *tigelliera*. They are often served with cunza.

Primi

Anolini

Little circular buttons of fresh pasta, *anolini* are stuffed with meat – usually stewed beef – and traditionally served with a broth of beef and capon. They are typically made for special occasions due to the long prep time – the beef filling is cooked for up to 36 hours to create a thick gravy and maximum flavour.

Cappellacci

Hailing from the town of Ferrara, these rectangles of egg pasta are filled with pureed butternut pumpkin (squash) flavoured with nutmeg and folded to create their distinctive hat shape (*cappellacci* means 'little hats'). They are usually served tossed in melted butter with crisp sage leaves.

Cappelletti

Similar to tortellini, *cappelletti* are larger in size, made with a thicker dough and sealed differently. They can be filled with cheese or meat and are served bobbing in broth or with a meat sauce.

Erbazzone

A savoury pie from Reggio Emilia, *erbazzone* (or *scarpazzone* in dialect) has a pastry crust made with lard and a filling of fresh chard that uses both the green leaves and the white ribs, along with onion, pancetta, parmigiano, ricotta and sometimes spinach.

Garganelli

Similar in looks to penne, *garganelli* are made with squares of egg pasta dough that are rolled around a rod, closing two opposite ends over each other to create a flap. They are then rolled over a *pettine* (comb) to create ridges for the sauce to stick to.

Gramigna

This quirky pasta shape found around Bologna and Modena is a curved tube with a hole running through, like a shortened version of bucatini. They are made with egg and typically combined with a sauce of sausage meat and tomato.

Panzerotti piacentini

Crespelle (savoury crepes) are spread with a filling of ricotta and spinach and rolled up, then cut into smaller cylinders and placed upright in a dish. They are covered with butter and plenty of Grana Padano or parmigiano, then finally baked. Tomato sauce or bechamel may be added.

Pasticcio di tortellini

In this alternative way to prepare tortellini, they are layered in a dish, coated in ragù and bechamel, topped with parmigiano and then baked, creating a kind of pie. The same technique can be used with different sauces and varieties of tortellini.

Pisarei e fasö

This famous recipe from Piacenza has origins that trace to the Middle Ages, when pilgrims heading to Rome along Via Francigena stopped at monasteries for meals. Today, pisarei e fasö features small, bean-sized gnocchi made of breadcrumbs, flour and water that are served with a sauce of borlotti (cranberry) beans and tomatoes, which is enriched with pork fat.

Strozzapreti romagnoli

There are multiple theories about the origin of this pasta's name, the first half of which translates to 'priest stranglers'; one attributes it to the former anti-clerical feelings of the region's adzore (housewives). Made from just flour and water, these twists are traditionally served with a rich ragù of beef or sausage, but can also be paired with fish, seafood or a basic tomato sauce.

Tagliolini con culatello

Culatello di Zibello is a prized cut of pork leg that's stuffed into the pig's bladder and aged for 10–14 months. Here it is given a starring role, cooked in butter until crunchy. After a dash of meat stock is added, the culatello is tossed with tagliolini and plenty of grated parmigiano, to thicken the sauce.

Tortél dóls

This filled pasta from the Parma area plays with sweet and savoury flavours, thanks to its filling of mostarda. The tortelli are usually simply tossed in melted butter and finished with grated parmigiano to allow the filling's flavours to take centre stage.

Tortelloni

Tortellini's larger cousins are shaped the same but are usually sealed slightly differently and, instead of a meat filling, feature ricotta (and sometimes spinach). They are served simply with melted butter and sage, or tossed with a little tomato sauce.

Secondi

Brodetto di pesce

The Adriatic-facing regions of Italy's east coast each boast a local version of brodetto. The Romagnan take varies from town to town, but tradition states there should be at least seven different types of seafood, which can include gurnard, scorpionfish, eel, squid, monkfish, clams, mussels and many others. The seafood is added to a sauce of rich stock, garlic and tomato in stages to ensure everything is perfectly cooked.

Cavàl pist

Parma's *pesto di cavallo* (horse pesto) dates to 1881 when the first horse butcher opened in the city. The meat is squashed to a thick paste using a fork, then seasoned with garlic, olive oil and sometimes lemon juice. It's eaten either by itself or used as a filling for panini.

Coniglio in porchetta

A rabbit dish found in both Emilia-Romagna and neighbouring Marche, this recipe shares a preparation method with pork – hence the name (*in porchetta*). The rabbit is deboned, flattened and filled with a stuffing of sausage meat flavoured with garlic and herbs, such as rosemary and wild fennel. It's then tightly rolled with pancetta and roasted in the oven.

Faraona arrosto

Roast guinea fowl is a common sight in this region, often prepared for Sunday lunch or special occasions. With a flavour between chicken and game, the guinea fowl is usually marinated with red wine, garlic and herbs including rosemary, juniper and sage before roasting. It can also be prepared *alla creta*, wrapped in baking paper and coated with a layer of clay to keep all of the flavours, juices and aromas inside.

Giambonetto / Vitello al latte

This easy roast ensures a tender, juicy result. A large cut of veal is tied with string and browned in butter and oil. Milk is added along with rosemary and bay leaves, and the meat is cooked gently for an hour. Once tender, it's removed and the sauce is blended until creamy to serve with the sliced meat.

Rosa di Parma

A celebration of Parma's products, this 'rose' is made with a beef fillet cut to lie flat. It's rolled with a filling of parmigiano and Prosciutto di Parma, and cooked in Lambrusco. The meat is set aside and rested, and the sauce is reduced with a splash of cream that's served with the rose-pink fillet.

Stracotto alla piacentina

A large cut of beef is cooked for around five hours with red wine, tomatoes, stock and *pistà ad gràss* (a kind of Piacenza pesto of lardo, parsley and garlic). The time ensures the meat will fall apart when it's served as a stew with polenta or pureed potatoes, as a pasta sauce or chopped up to fill anolini.

Dolci

Bensone

Also known as *ciambella romagnola*, this sweet, oval-shaped bread from Modena is a symbol of its birth city. The original recipe calls for just flour, butter, eggs, milk and honey, but there are now versions filled with jam or chocolate. It is often eaten after a meal, dipped in a glass of Lambrusco.

Bustrengo

This cake is made with a mixture of cornmeal, milk, sugar, flour and breadcrumbs, which give it a moist, creamy texture. Dried fig, raisins, apple and citrus zest stud each piece.

Spongata

A Christmas staple, *spongata* traces its roots to ancient times. A shortcrust (pie) pastry base is packed full of hazelnuts, walnuts and pine nuts as well as raisins, candied fruit, honey, spices and crumbled cookies like amaretti. It is topped with another layer of pastry and baked until the surface appears undulating and pinched, like a sponge.

Torta di tagliatelle

With its topping of fine, yellow strands of pasta, this cake from Ferrara, which dates to the Renaissance, is said to recall the golden hair of Lucrezia Borgia. Under the tagliatelle top lies a cake of soft shortcrust pastry filled with candied fruit, almonds and Modena's aniseed liqueur, Sassolino.

Torta nera

Sassolino finds a home in this local 'black cake'. A simple shortcrust pastry case holds a dark, dense filling of almonds, dark chocolate, espresso and liqueur.

Torta tenerina

Ferrara's mouthwatering dark chocolate cake is devilish and decadent, with a slightly hard exterior giving way to a soft, sticky interior that melts in the mouth. Made with just a small amount of flour, it's flat and dense, with a brownie texture that pairs well with Chantilly cream or mascarpone.

... and to drink

Emilia-Romagna's vineyards, which span the entire width of the region, date to the 7th century BCE, when the Etruscans introduced vines to the area. Today, wine production here is roughly even between whites and reds, with Lambrusco as the star varietal. The sparkling red is unique to Emilia-Romagna and is known for its fresh, fruity flavour that pairs well with the region's hearty cuisine. In total, there are five Lambrusco DOCs: Salamino di Santa Croce, di Sorbara, Grasparossa di Castelvetro, Modena and Reggiano.

Emilia-Romagna is also home to several other quality wines, such as Albana, a white that's sweet and fragrant with a golden colour and full-bodied taste. Sangiovese is popular throughout Italy, but here you'll find the Sangiovese di Romagna; considered one of the finest examples of the varietal, it has a medium intensity, with a complex aroma and a full-bodied taste. Trebbiano is a crisp, refreshing white often used in the production of balsamic vinegar, while Emilia-Romagna's malvasia grape is commonly used to make sweet wines, such as the famous Malvasia di Candia Aromatica. Known for its floral and fruity aroma, this wine is usually enjoyed as an aperitif or paired with desserts. Barberas are medium-bodied locally, generally low in tannins and have notes of red and dark fruits. And finally there's bonarda – not to be confused with the Argentinean bonarda grape. Also known here as croatina, it is often used as a blending grape to add colour, acidity and tannins to wines, but it can also be found as a medium-bodied varietal with notes of red and dark fruits.

In addition to these local varieties, international grapes such as pinot blanc, chardonnay and cabernet sauvignon are grown, used for both varietal wines and blends.

When it comes to spirits, liqueurs and digestifs, the region is home to one of Italy's most popular amari: Amaro Montenegro. First produced in Bologna in 1885 by Stanislao Cobianchi, it is named after Princess Elena of Montenegro, who wed the future king of Italy. It is made of 40 different herbs, fruits and botanicals, and the recipe has remained unchanged since its inception.

The region is also quite well known for many types of grappa, sambuca and nut-infused liqueurs like *nocino* and Nocello. Biancosarti is a distinctly yellow spiced liqueur used in long drinks and Zabov is an eggnog-like liqueur that hails from Ferrara.

Emilia-Romagna

Culinary experiences

Whether you'd like to dine at Italy's first restaurant to make it to world number one, tour Bologna's bars, try your hand at pasta-making or enjoy local produce in the shadow of Roman monuments, Emilia-Romagna will keep your itinerary and stomach full.

Eat and drink Bologna

Experience Bologna's markets and independent food artisans on a privately guided food tour. Learn about Bolognese cuisine and Emilia-Romagna's gastronomic specialties while exploring historical and modern markets. Casa Mia Food Tours specialise in the area, and their food experts will introduce you to small, family-run businesses and share intimate historical details – all while you savour the local lifestyle and learn about the region's food traditions and trends. They also run an aperitivo experience where you can indulge in local drinks and delicacies at the many bars in Bologna that locals frequent.

CASAMIATOURS.COM

Fast cars, slow food: the full Bottura experience

Nothing says Emilia-Romagna more than Massimo Bottura! Get organised well in advance and book a lunch or dinner at Osteria Francescana: you won't regret it. In addition to being a local institution and boasting the coveted three Michelin stars, it's the first Italian restaurant to *ever* make it to the number one spot on the World's 50 Best Restaurants list. Can't get a booking? Try Franceschetta58, Bottura's casual bistro, which never disappoints. Stay at Casa Maria Luigia, the Botturas' plush boutique countryside estate where walls are swathed in Gucci wallpaper, and jazz, art and antique lovers will rejoice. Breakfast and dinner are world-class affairs at this chic property where you can feast on Osteria Francescana's classics at their outpost, as well as visit the sustainable Al Gatto Verde, helmed by Chef Jessica Rosval. In nearby Maranello, enjoy a contemporary trattoria meal at the Ferrari–Bottura venture, Cavallino, and breathe in the real Made in Italy with a visit to the Ferrari museum.

OSTERIAFRANCESCANA.IT, CASAMARIALUIGIA.COM
FRANCESCHETTA.IT, FERRARI.COM/EN-EN/MUSEUMS

Cooking classes and wine tasting

Why not take a professional-led cooking class in Parma
to delve into the local culture? Learn to make pasta and
other Italian classics with an expert chef, then enjoy an
aperitivo followed by a leisurely meal of all the dishes
you made. If wine is more your thing, embark on a day
trip in the Emilia-Romagna countryside to visit wineries
and try Lambrusco. Meet the winemakers, learn about
the grapes and enjoy unique wine tasting experiences
in historic cellars. For lovers of wellness and wine, the
Civardi Racemus agriturismo and winery in the Piacenza
area is a one-stop immersive experience. Here you can stay
and enjoy a year-round program of events, from cooking
classes and olive- and wine-tastings to grape harvests and
vineyard dinners.

CASAMIATOURS.COM, CIVARDIRACEMUS.COM

Taste Parma through its renowned products

There's nothing like a day spent in the Parma countryside
on a delicious gastronomic journey. With Casa Mia Food
Tours, you'll meet the local producers who are proudly
preserving time-honoured traditions by creating iconic
regional foods, such as Parmigiano Reggiano, Prosciutto
di Parma and Aceto Balsamico Tradizionale di Modena.
They will take you to a local dairy and prosciutto producer
for tastings, followed by a relaxing lunch with traditional
cured meats, homemade pasta and local desserts.

CASAMIATOURS.COM

Piadina and street food in Ravenna

Local company Italian Days runs a variety of cultural and
gastronomic tours in Ravenna, the city of mosaics and well-
preserved Roman and Byzantine architecture. Its cuisine is
just as fascinating and layered, so in addition to uncovering
Ravenna's impressive monuments, such as the Church of
San Vitale and the Mausoleum of Galla Placidia, indulge in
local specialties, such as the famous piadina, squacquerone
cheese and semi-sparkling white wine Pagadebit.

ITALIANDAYS.IT

SAGRE

FEBRUARY
Slow Wine Fair, Bologna

AUGUST
Sagra del Porcino,
Porcini mushrooms festival,
Castel del Rio

SEPTEMBER
*Festival del Prosciutto di
Parma*, Parma ham festival,
Parma

*Sagra dell'Uva e del
Lambrusco*, Wine festival,
Grasparossa, Castelvetro

Festa della Piadina,
Piadina festival, Bellaria

Sagra del Tortellino,
Tortellini festival,
Castelfranco Emilia

OCTOBER
Mortadella Please,
Mortadella festival, Bologna

Sagra dell'Anguilla,
Eel festival, Comacchio

*Fiera Nazionale del Tartufo
Bianco*, White truffle fair,
Sant'Agata Feltria

Caseifici Aperti, Parmigiano
Reggiano festival, Parma

NOVEMBER
Tartófla, Truffle festival,
Savigno

Il Pesce Fa Festa,
Fish festival, Cesenatico

I passatelli di Nonna Ancella

Grandma Ancella's breadcrumb pasta in broth

What an honour to have Massimo Bottura share a recipe with me, and not just any recipe but a family treasure and a rite of passage in the Modenese household. This is his grandmother's recipe, and with breadcrumbs as the star of the dish, it marries perfectly with the 'waste not, want not' food ethic Massimo so fervently promotes. He says, 'If there is an important lesson we have learned from the Italian kitchen, and one that we can pass on to future generations, it's never let edible food go to waste! We share this message in the shape of my grandmother Ancella's recipe for passatelli in broth. This classic Emilian recipe has been passed down from generation to generation in the Bottura family.' Massimo's daughter, Alexa, learned how to make passatelli from her grandmother Luisa, while he learned the art from his grandmother Ancella. And so from his family, to mine, to yours, here is nonna Ancella's recipe – I know it will become a favourite.

Emilia-Romagna

NORTHERN ITALY

SERVES 4

1 litre (4 cups) chicken or vegetable broth

150 g (5½ oz) fine fresh breadcrumbs

100 g (1 cup) finely grated Parmigiano Reggiano

pinch of freshly grated nutmeg

pinch of lemon zest

3 small eggs

Bring the broth to a low simmer in a large saucepan.

Meanwhile, place the breadcrumbs, parmesan, nutmeg and lemon zest in a bowl. Break in the eggs and mix into a uniform ball of firm dough.

Fit a potato ricer with a 4 mm (¼ in) hole disc. Place the dough in the ricer and press it, squeezing the passatelli directly into the simmering broth. If you do not have a potato ricer you can push the dough through the large holes of a cheese grater or food mill to create a similar shape. Cook the passatelli for about 1 minute, until they rise to the surface. Divide the broth and passatelli among bowls and serve.

Friuli
Venezia
Giulia

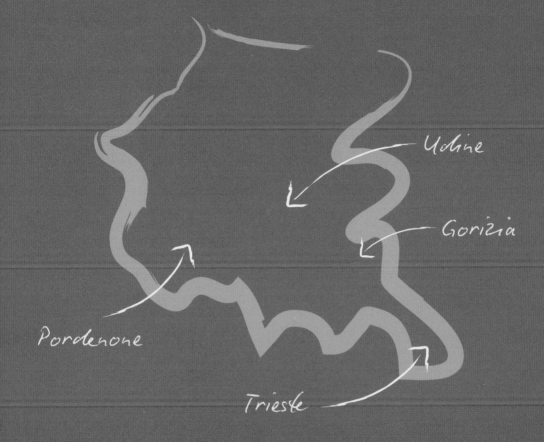

Udine

Gorizia

Pordenone

Trieste

Regional produce

Friuli Venezia Giulia's mountains and hills provide a selection of homegrown products that range from alpine cow's cheeses and world-famous prosciutto to wild game and fresh vegetables, while fish from the region's lakes, rivers and coastline are abundant. These merge with the cooler climate and culinary influences from neighbouring Austria and Slovenia to create a robust cuisine.

- ◆ Ajvar
- ◆ Brovada fermented turnips
- ◆ Cherries
- ◆ Cuincir ricotta
- ◆ Formadi frant cheese
- ◆ Goose salami
- ◆ Montasio cheese
- ◆ Pestat di Fagagna
- ◆ Pitina
- ◆ Polenta
- ◆ Rosa di Gorizia radicchio
- ◆ Prosciutto di San Daniele/Sauris
- ◆ Scuete fumade cheese
- ◆ White asparagus
- ◆ Wild game

Piazza Unità d'Italia, Trieste

I have sweet memories of my time spent in Trieste, the capital of Friuli Venezia Giulia, and not just because it bewitched me with the local mille-feuille filled with custard cream: the *pasta crema Carsolina*, known in Trieste dialect as the *zavatta*.

The first thing you notice about this bustling seaport that once belonged to Austria's Habsburg Empire is its magnificent waterfront: it's lined with impressive Neoclassical buildings that rival those of London or Paris. But the city's real charm lies in its breathtaking views: the sparkling blue bay, the bustling marina filled with elegant white yachts, the inviting lidos on long sandy beaches, and the lush vineyards that carpet the surrounding hills. If it makes any sense to put these two words together, there's a feeling of relaxed grandeur in Trieste. Here, life unfolds at a leisurely pace, tempting you to linger.

Once a humble border town on the fringes of the Balkans, the magnificent Italian port has bloomed into a dynamic centre of culture, pulsing with life and creativity. Tumbling down to the Adriatic from il Carso, a steep limestone plateau that follows the Gulf of Trieste and the Slovenian border, this city stands apart from the rest of Italy both physically and culturally. Its isolation has allowed it to maintain a distinctive border town atmosphere, reflected in the Triestine dialect which blends Italian, Austrian-German, Croatian and Greek.

On arrival, you can't help but feel Trieste's alluring pull (even with its alpine winds that sometimes blow): it delivers such a unique Adriatic experience with spacious piazze, charming coffeehouses and intimate seafood restaurants. But it's Trieste's history that's the real charm. The city's fascinating past spans from dinosaurs and Neanderthals to the Roman and Byzantine Empires. It has welcomed an array of notable figures over the centuries, like 20th-century Irish novelist James Joyce, who lived in Trieste for 16 years.

... a feast where pork reigns supreme and marble counters groan under the weight of succulent roast hams, boiled pork loin, smoked sausage and enormous mortadellas.

Most notably, centuries of Austrian rule under the House of Habsburg left an indelible mark on the city's architecture and cuisine. From its grand buildings to traditional dishes like sauerkraut and strudel, Trieste's Austrian influence is palpable, but the city has its own unique identity. Its vibrant nightlife, contemporary photography museum and the nearby marina in Portopiccolo add modern flair to a rich heritage. From this neighbouring village's idyllic location overlooking castles, the Gulf of Trieste and the Croatian coast, you can enjoy a beach club, luxurious accommodations, boutique shopping and fine dining.

And no one should visit Trieste without experiencing an authentic buffet, a tradition dating to the city's Austrian rule; it's a feast where pork reigns supreme and marble counters groan under the weight of succulent roast hams, boiled pork loin, smoked sausage and enormous mortadellas. Meats are accompanied by various sauces and horseradish, and you'll find professionals rubbing shoulders with students and construction workers at communal tables, eating away and washing it all down with locally sourced wine straight from the barrel.

Friuli Venezia Giulia

NORTHERN ITALY

Beyond Trieste, Friuli Venezia Giulia is captivating with its jagged alpine mountains and a cultural fusion with neighbouring countries, Austria and Slovenia. Nowadays, the region is divided into four provinces, with Pordenone and Udine located in the area known as Friuli, while Gorizia and Trieste are in Venezia Giulia. By population, the region is Italy's sixth smallest, the majority of its residents of Italian origin, with a sizeable Slovenian community in the east. The region's name is also an amalgam of culture; Friuli comes from Forum Iulii, the port thought to have been established by Julius Caesar. Venezia Giulia on the other hand is said to reflect the area's historical ties to the Venetian Republic throughout the Middle Ages and the Renaissance, along with its geographical features which include the Julian Alps, also named after Caesar.

Beyond these mountains, the region's names combine to comprise a land that includes the Carnic Alps, the Adriatic and a river plain, with a cuisine that's also the sum of distinct identities, sitting at the intersection of hearty mountain and Mediterranean dishes.

Like other alpine areas, Friuli is renowned for its exceptional cheese, along with its cured meats: in particular Montasio, a semi-hard cow's milk cheese with a delicate taste that is mainly crafted in the mountain areas of Udine. Meanwhile, *formadi frant* is prepared by blending offcuts of various cheeses with black pepper: the result is soft and pungent. Its name, which originates from Friulan dialect, translates to 'crushed cheese'.

The prized Prosciutto San Daniele is produced in the commune of San Daniele del Friuli in the Udine province. Then

Piazza Unità d'Italia, Trieste

there's Speck di Sauris, the popular smoked cured pork, and *muset*, a spiced pork offal sausage flavoured with cinnamon, nutmeg, black pepper, coriander and cloves. Ćevapčići (page 40), meanwhile, is a minced (ground) beef and lamb sausage and a delicious example of the region's Slavic influence.

Polenta is also a staple, forming the basis of many dishes, while *jota* (page 40), a bean soup prepared with sauerkraut, is probably one the most famous winter dishes. There's *frico* (page 40), a kind of flat cake made from Montasio, while *ajvar*, a sauce made of red bell peppers (capsicums) and eggplant (aubergine), is eaten as an accompaniment to meats and cheeses. Seeing this red sauce appear together with ćevapčići on the region's menus felt like such a familiar return to my many trips through the Balkans– a beautiful example of how food traditions transcend borders.

Within the region, there are two significant rivers, the Tagliamento and the Isonzo, which are sources of freshwater fish, such as trout and carp. As for seafood, thanks to the region's access to the Adriatic and a lagoon, it has a similar offering to Veneto: this includes sardines, octopus, calamari, scallops, crab and mussels.

Among the region's popular dishes with Venetian influence is *sarde in saor*, made of sardines in sweet and sour onion sauce. Meanwhile, *capesante gratin*, a dish of scallops baked in breadcrumbs and parsley butter that's popular in many Italian coastal areas, originated in Trieste.

Of course, what is a visit to this region without a stop in the local *pasticcerie*? Trieste's pastry shops were a travel highlight for me because this part of Italy knows its way around a sweet, and each one reflects different cultural influences. Apple strudel, which you can find made with walnuts or cherries, is one of the most common. Locals claim tiramisù is from here, rather

Carnevale parade in San Pietro al Natisone

Friuli Venezia Giulia

than Treviso, and you'd be wise not to argue with them. *Presnitz* is a puff pastry cake with Germanic origins, while *gnocchi di susine* (prune-stuffed gnocchi; page 41) originated in Bohemia. *Gubana* (page 40), which is of Slovenian origin and especially popular in Gorizia, is a sweet dough dessert filled with nuts, raisins, grappa and lemon peel, while *strucchi*, also of Slovenian origins, has a sweet nut-based filling between two layers of dough that are either boiled or fried and dusted with icing (confectioners') sugar.

Friuli Venezia Giulia is a testament to the beauty and diversity that can be found in a region. Its history, geography and cultural influences have come together to create a unique and remarkable place: one that has made a significant impact on Italy's cuisine and culture, despite its size. Let this region serve as a reminder that our differences should be celebrated and that they can come together to create something truly beautiful.

NORTHERN ITALY

MARIA'S TOP 10 DISHES OF FRIULI VENEZIA GIULIA

1 ĆEVAPČIĆI

A result of the region's Balkan influence, these long, cylindrical meatballs are made with paprika-spiced minced (ground) beef and lamb. They are usually cooked over a fire and served with ajvar. Often found as a second dish, they're also eaten as a street food.

2 CHIFELETTI DI PATATE

Deep-fried crescents made from a dough of potato, flour, eggs and butter, *chifeletti di patate* are served as a side dish. but their similarity to gnocchi means they may also be paired with sauce and eaten as a first course.

3 CROSTINI

Often accompanied by a *taj* (glass) of wine during the local aperitivo ritual of *tajùt*, *crostini* are topped with local cured meat, cheeses and vegetables. One of the most popular combinations is smoky roasted ham and freshly grated horseradish.

4 FRICO

Cheese (usually a mix of different ages of Montasio) is melted in a pan and topped with potato and sometimes sliced onions. Once the underside is browned, the cheese is flipped like an omelette and then served piping hot on a bed of polenta.

5 FRITTATA ALLE ERBE

Friuli's host of wild herbs are brought to the fore in this simple frittata. Among others, locally foraged chives, wild fennel pollen, dandelion leaves, dill, marjoram and nettles are cooked with spinach, onions, eggs and cheese for an aromatic result.

6 GNOCCHI ALLA FRIULANA

A common way to prepare gnocchi in the region is to substitute the usual potato with roasted pumpkin (winter squash). They're delicious served with melted butter and sage and also pair well with the region's cheese sauces.

7 GUBANA / PUTIZZA

Two similar cakes from two separate parts of the region, *gubana* and *putizza* both consist of rolled dough with a filling of walnuts, raisins, pine nuts, lemon and grappa. Gubana, from the Natisone Valleys, is rolled tighter with less filling, while putizza, from Gorizia and Trieste, is looser and has more filling, which features chocolate.

8 JOTA FRIULANA

Ingredients for *jota* vary, but almost all agree that this thick Friulan soup should contain beans and sauerkraut along with potatoes, garlic and cumin. It can be served by itself or eaten along with cuts of pork, pancetta or sausage.

9 POLENTA

Used extensively across the whole region, polenta provides the perfect partner to rich stews and flavourful cheeses. Both yellow and white polenta are common, the latter lighter and finer. A popular way to serve polenta is *alla concia* (with butter and cheese). In Friuli, *tosella alla panna* (with tosella cheese and cream) is popular.

10 SCAMPI ALLA BUSARA

Trieste is the home of this quick recipe. Fresh scampi are cooked with a tomato sauce flavoured with garlic, parsley and a hint of chilli. The term *busara* is thought to refer to the large iron cooking pot that sailors used on board, but may derive from the Trieste dialect term *busiara* (to lie), as the scampi are hidden by the sauce.

Other dishes to look out for

From alpine cow's cheeses and world-famous prosciutto to wild herbs and seafood fresh from the Adriatic coastline – you can't go wrong with this multifaceted and vibrant cuisine.

Primi

Blecs

These irregular shapes of pasta, similar to maltagliati, are made with buckwheat and wheat flours. They're accompanied by many sauces, most commonly one made with butter and Montasio cheese.

Cjalsons / Cjarsons / Cjalzòns

Friuli's ravioli are characterised by their sweet and savoury filling. Ingredients vary but are usually a combination of spinach, ricotta, raisins, cookies, cinnamon, herbs and chocolate. They're served tossed in melted butter and covered in smoked ricotta.

Gnocchi di susine / prugne

In this twist on regular potato gnocchi, each ball of dough hides a filling of sweet plum and brown sugar. Once boiled, they are drained and topped with melted butter, sugar and cinnamon-infused breadcrumbs. They can be a first course or a dessert.

Minestra di bobici

A soup from the area of Carso, mainly eaten in August and September when the bobici (grains of new corn) are in season. They're combined with potatoes, beans and sometimes pancetta.

Paparot

This dense soup from Pordenone is made with spinach and polenta or flour. It's eaten with crostini or served as an accompaniment to cuts of meat or sausages.

Risotto agli scampi

The fish of the Adriatic and the extensive rice production of Friuli's neighbouring regions meet in the delicious seafood risottos of Trieste. In this version, fresh scampi are served with rice cooked in a rich, fish-based stock: a perfect comfort dish.

Toc' in braide

Golden, buttery polenta and a tangy cheese fondue come together in this typical antipasto dish. The fondue, made with milk and either a mix of cheeses or a heap of Grana Padano, is served poured over the polenta. The finishing touch is a drizzle of melted, nutty brown butter in which some of the polenta grains have been toasted.

Secondi

Baccalà alla cappuccina

In this recipe from the Capuchin friars, baccalà (salt-dried cod) is cooked with anchovies, raisins, onions, pine nuts, milk, cinnamon, bay and nutmeg to create a salty sweet sauce. The fish and sauce are then placed on top of polenta and baked.

Boreto alla graisana

Born of humble origins in the town of Grado, this simple seafood stew has just a handful of ingredients. Cheap fish and seafood are cooked in vinegar and water with salt and lots of ground black pepper. Historically, the dish was served with white polenta, which was less costly than its yellow counterpart.

Contorni

Patate in tecia

For this dish from Trieste, sliced onion and pancetta are fried in butter. Roughly pureed potato and stock are added and everything's cooked until the edges are crunchy. A similar dish, *bisi in tecia*, uses peas, not potatoes.

Verze alla carnica

To create this hearty side for meat, shredded and boiled savoy cabbage is tossed with pancetta and a bechamel-style sauce.

Dolci

Colaz

Made to celebrate the rite of confirmation, these doughnut-shaped cookies were once affixed to the clothes of the confirmed. They're flavoured with cinnamon, cloves and vanilla and may contain grappa or white wine.

Pinza triestina

Enjoyed at Easter, *pinza triestina* is a sweet brioche flavoured with lemon and orange. Eaten as part of Easter Sunday breakfast with cured meats and cheese, it can be covered with chocolate spread or jam.

Pistùm

These sweet gnocchi from the town of Pordenone are made from stale bread and flavoured with raisins, pine nuts, candied citrus, cinnamon and herbs. Cooked in broth, they're served sprinkled with icing (confectioners') sugar.

Sbreghe

A close cousin of cantucci (page 200), these hard almond cookies are shaped to look like small slices of bread. They're usually served with a glass of sweet wine after a meal.

Brovada e muset

Two typically Friulian products come together for Christmas. *Brovada* is made from thinly sliced white turnips fermented in red grape pomace, which gives them a pink tinge. It is served hot with slices of boiled *muset* (a fatty pork sausage).

Gòlas

As a result of Austro-Hungarian influences, *gulasch* (or *gòlas* in Gorizia) has been made in Friuli Venezia Giulia for so long, it's been adopted by the region. The local version of the beef stew with red wine and sweet paprika adds cumin and marjoram.

Lepre in salsa

A whole hare is cut into pieces and marinated for 12–24 hours in red wine and herbs. It is then slow-cooked, the left-over marinade added for a rich, aromatic sauce. They're served together on a bed of polenta.

Rambasicci

Leaves of savoy cabbage are rolled around a filling of minced beef and pork, garlic and paprika. The parcels are cooked in a pan with onion and stock and served with a topping of parmigiano and breadcrumbs.

... and to drink

Italy's northeastern corner isn't a household name when it comes to viticulture, but it produces some exceptional wines. Friuli Venezia Giulia has captivated enthusiasts around the world with its range that showcases a diverse terroir and the expertise of local winemakers. Many of its vineyards are sustainable, relying on organic and biodynamic farming, safeguarding the land for future generations.

Bordered by the sea and mountains, the region enjoys a moderate maritime climate: ideal for viticulture. Warm days and cool nights allow grapes to ripen slowly, preserving their acidity and allowing complex flavours to develop. Among the most celebrated local wines are whites that include exceptional expressions of Friulano, Ribolla Gialla and Malvasia Istriana.

Friulano, the flagship grape, creates aromatic and full-bodied wines with notes of ripe peach and almond, their undertones floral. Ribolla gialla, on the other hand, yields zesty and mineral-driven wines that are perfect for refreshing summer sipping. Lastly, malvasia istriana produces wine with luscious, honeyed lavours and hints of tropical fruits: a delightful companion for seafood.

Friuli Venezia Giulia is also recognised for its pioneering mastery of skin-contact wine. Often dubbed 'orange' or 'amber' wine, this style dates back thousands of years. Despite a fall in popularity, in the last 25 years Friulian winemakers like Joško Gravner (who doesn't define his wine as orange) have rekindled the method. Produced from white grapes that undergo extended skin contact during fermentation, these unique wines are characterised by an amber hue and distinctive flavour profiles, ranging from dried fruits and spices to floral and herbal notes. Local orange wines have a remarkable balance of tannins, acidity and texture, making them a great choice for adventurous wine enthusiasts.

In recent years, Friuli Venezia Giulia has also gained recognition for its high-quality sparkling wines – particularly those made using the *metodo classico* (traditional method). These wines, often crafted from chardonnay and pinot noir, exhibit finesse and complexity, offering an alternative to the more renowned Italian sparkling wines like Franciacorta and Prosecco.

And the region produces some quality reds, too. The most notable grape variety is the indigenous refosco dal peduncolo rosso, which yields wines with deep colour, vibrant acidity and a bouquet of dark berries, violets and spices. Others, such as merlot, cabernet and sauvignon, also thrive in the region's terroir.

Friuli Venezia Giulia has only a few liquors, but what it makes, it makes well. Among the most traditional are *cjariei* (herbs and spices digestif), *crema di pera* (pear and cream infusion), *maraschino* (cherry liqueur), *mirtillo* (blueberry liqueur), *nocino* (walnut liqueur), *sliwovitz* (plum spirit) and *pino mugo* (mountain pine liqueur).

And if you're looking for a wake up in Friuli Venezia Giulia, you're in luck: Trieste is a city of coffee. As such, it boasts literary cafes with a nostalgic charm, once frequented by renowned writers like Umberto Saba and James Joyce. A visit to one is a must – two of the famous spots are Antico Caffè San Marco and Caffè degli Specchi.

Culinary experiences

Immerse yourself in the food of this spectacular region by visiting a pop-up tavern, cooking in a castle or checking into a luxurious wine resort.

Eat in an osmiza, pop-up taverns in the Trieste area

When in the Trieste province, make sure to experience *osmiza*! With a name derived from the Slovenian *osmica*, these pop-up taverns are a blend of culture and cuisine. Operating only on particular days, these culinary havens showcase local farmers' homemade delights – think wines, cured meats, cheeses and traditional desserts. They are a chance to immerse yourself in vibrant, local community spirit while you savour the authenticity of regional flavours. There are about 50 in operation across Friuli Venezia Giulia, with around 20 in the Trieste area, so keep an eye out for these gems that connect you with rich cultural heritage. Visit the online portal for daily updates on what's open.

OSMIZE.COM

Cook, eat and drink in a medieval castle

Indulge in the wine and culinary delights of Friuli Venezia Giulia's south at the 13th-century Castello di Spessa near Gorizia. This historic castle, nestled among vineyards, offers a majestic blend of luxury accommodations, a day spa and gastronomy. Step into a world of elegance as you explore the beautifully restored grounds and discover a rich heritage. Marvel at the medieval architecture, stroll through manicured gardens and indulge in exquisite local flavours as you savour the renowned wines produced here at the castle's vineyards. In addition to a guided wine tasting, you can visit the on-site apiary and learn about honey-making, or try your hand at pasta-making with the chef. Beyond the castle's walls, a treasure trove of attractions awaits, with charming villages, vibrant local markets, historical landmarks and beautiful countryside all nearby.

CASTELLODISPESSA.IT

Sip and stay at a wine resort

Slow right down at Venica & Venica wine resort. Here you can do as much or as little as you like – go wine tasting in the cellar, take a local tour or just laze away by the pool. This sprawling estate, located deep in wine country by the Slovenian border, is home to one of Friuli's most famous winemaking families. As there are only a few rooms and apartments (but all the modern amenities you need), you'll feel as though you're staying at a friend's farmhouse.

VENICA.IT

Cook with a local in Pordenone

Teresa grew up in her grandmother's kitchen in central Italy. After moving to Pordenone, she began running cooking classes to show off the best of this region. You can learn just the basics or enrol in a more elaborate lesson that covers meat dishes, spectacular seafood pastas, the classic frico and even risotto. She also offers guided market tours and takes you into a grocery store to learn the art of Italian shopping. Teresa can organise cheese farm visits as well, in which you head to the heart of Friuliano cheese – particularly Montasio, caciotta and the local ricotta. See the cheesemaking process and then try some samples too.

COOKINITALYWITHTERESA.COM

Indulge in a spa hotel, cheese and prosciutto

Udine is an overlooked gem where history lives and gastronomy thrives. Located just out of the city, Fagagna is officially one of Italy's most beautiful *borghi* (villages), known for a cheese of the same name that's been produced there since the 1860s. Nearby you have the town of San Daniele del Friuli, home of the famous Prosciutto di San Daniele. The official consortium, Il Consorzio del Prosciutto di San Daniele, has a full list of producers who offer guided factory visits. Villaverde Hotel & Resort is the perfect base from which to explore it all. This wellness oasis has a golf course, spa and a region-focused restaurant. The team can create a program for you with visits to local wineries, prosciutto tastings and more.

VILLAVERDERESORT.COM, PROSCIUTTOSANDANIELE.IT

SAGRE

APRIL

Festa degli Asparagi, Asparagus festival, Fossalon

JUNE

Festa del Pane, Bread festival, Ampezzo

Festa dei Cjarsons, Feast of the Cjarsons, Sutrio

JULY

Festa del Prosciutto di Sauris, Sauris prosciutto festival, Sauris

AUGUST

Sagre del Frico, Frico festival, Carpacco

Festa da Polenta, Polenta festival, Prato Carnico

SEPTEMBER

Friuli DOC, Wine festival, Udine

Easy Fish, Fish festival, Lignano Sabbiadoro

OCTOBER

Ein Prosit, Food and wine festival, Udine

Risotto di scampi

Scampi risotto

Harry's Trieste sits within the boutique luxury hotel Grand Hotel Duchi
d'Aosta and has a coveted two Michelin stars, thanks to the culinary prowess
of its chefs, Matteo Metullio and Davide De Pra. The remarkable duo are
at the helm of all the hotel's dining, and together have amassed numerous
prestigious awards. They kindly shared this recipe with me that combines their
expertise and passion for locally sourced fish. This risotto is a contemporary
version of the local classic and an ode to scampi, usually cooked in a tomato
sauce (busara-style). It's a testament to Matteo and Davide's artistry and the
flavours will no doubt transport you to Trieste. Matteo, a local, says it reminds
him of day trips his family took to the Istrian coast when he was a child.

Friuli Venezia Giulia

SERVES 4

300 g (10½ oz) sashimi-grade
scampi or tiger prawns (jumbo
shrimp) per person, heads and
shells removed and set aside,
deveined

extra virgin olive oil

zest and juice of 1 lemon

320 g (11½ oz) carnaroli rice

1 teaspoon fine salt

300 ml (10½ fl oz) white wine

olive oil, for drizzling

1 tablespoon butter

handful of grated parmesan

handful of chopped parsley,
to serve

Scampi stock

heads and shells of your
scampi or prawns

1 celery stalk, trimmed and
cut in half

1 carrot, roughly chopped

½ tomato

Cut the scampi into pieces, cover with olive oil, add the
lemon zest and juice and a sprinkle of salt and pepper.
Cover and leave to marinate in the fridge for 1–2 hours.

To make the scampi stock, put the scampi or prawn heads
and shells in a large stockpot with 1.5 litres (51 fl oz) of cold
water, along with the remaining ingredients. Bring to the
boil, then reduce the heat to a simmer and cook for 1 hour
or until the stock has reduced by about one-third. Strain and
set aside, discarding the solids.

Preheat a large saucepan over medium heat, add the
rice and salt and toast for 2 minutes. Pour in the wine and
cook until the alcohol has burnt off and the liquid has
reduced slightly, then add 675 ml (23 fl oz) of the strained
scampi stock and stir well.

Cook the rice, stirring constantly and adding more
stock as the previous amount is absorbed, for 13 minutes
or until al dente. When the risotto is ready, add a drizzle
of olive oil, the butter and grated parmesan, and stir to
thicken. Season to taste with salt and pepper.

Remove the pan from the heat, cover with a clean, dry
cloth and allow the risotto to rest for 2–3 minutes.

Reheat the rice over medium heat until simmering,
then add another ladle of stock. At this point the rice
should be a light orange colour. Add a little chopped
parsley and serve the risotto with the marinated scampi
placed on top.

Liguria

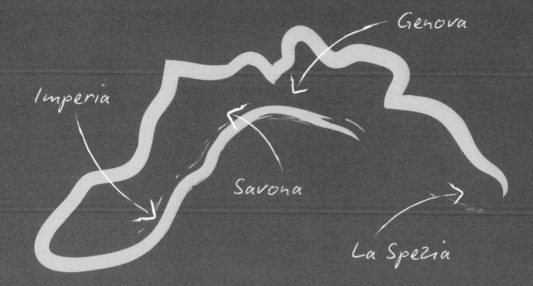

Genova

Imperia

Savona

La Spezia

Regional produce

Liguria's kitchens rely heavily on
the region's mountainous and coastal
areas: there is only one section of flat,
open land, around Albenga. Seafood is
abundant here, as are produce and game
from the woodlands and forests. Liberal
use of wild herbs and aromatic olive
oil gives Ligurian cuisine its signature,
fresh flavours, enjoyed alongside baked
goods that have a long tradition thanks
to sea trade that historically brought in
produce, including flour.

- Albenga's trumpet
  zucchini (courgette)
- Anchovies
- Basil
- Belendina onions
- Chinotto oranges
- Grapes
- Pine nuts
- Purple asparagus
- Preboggion mixed wild herbs
- Prescinsêua cheese
- Rabbit
- Stracchino cheese
- Taggiasche olives
- Vessalico's garlic
- Violet artichokes

Portofino

This small, crescent-shaped region is home to the Italian Riviera and one of the country's biggest cities: Genoa. Because of its glorious past and impressive landmarks, the city is nicknamed *la Superba*, which means 'the proud one' but also 'the arrogant one'. The locals have a slight haughtiness about them, but when you visit, you'll understand why. I mean, this city has grandeur in its DNA. It was, after all, one of the medieval world's greatest trading powers, and the legacy of that wealth can be seen in the city gates, fine palazzi and churches with austere edifices and lavish interiors.

In a sense, the hilly city has two faces. You have the old working port, with its steep, narrow lanes, Baroque churches and vacant lots, which served as the foundation for Genoa's growth. And then you have the bustling modern city, full of avenues, arcades, palaces, theatres and cafes that spread to the nearby hills. Anywhere in the region's capital, though, you have food. Oh, Ligurian food.

On my first trip to the region, I ate an excessive amount of pesto, and so should you! I tried it on bread, focaccia, pasta – I'll never forget a quick lasagne I grabbed on the run for a train, made with luscious pasta sheets lathered in the sauce. And, of course, I ate pesto served on the traditional *trofie* (page 54), a short and twisty durum wheat pasta that the basil clings to perfectly.

Basil in this small region is serious business. Its history dates to Ancient Rome, when it was believed to have healing powers. The Romans were fond of a green sauce called *moretum*, which was spread on bread and made by crushing cheese, salt, olive oil and herbs in a mortar: a clear predecessor of modern pesto, which was developed in Genoa at the start of the 19th century.

Regular basil pales in comparison to Genovese basil, unique among other varieties because it lacks the hint of mint in its delicate smell. It's grown on a narrow strip of land between mountains and sea using a technique called *raccolta volante* (flying harvest), whereby the basil is handpicked in high-density farming by farmers balancing on planks to ensure they don't damage the plants. Granted DOP status by the European Union in 2005, Genovese basil is in high demand as Italy's most exported herb, with most sent to the United States.

The other culinary staple in the region is focaccia. Known in Ligurian dialect as *fugassa* (very similar to the French *fougasse*), focaccia is a hallmark of Ligurian cuisine and can be enjoyed at any time of day, by itself, with a meal or, as the locals do – dipped into their morning cappuccino!

Focaccia genovese (page 54) is the original and most popular focaccia in Italy (well, according to the Ligurians at least), easily recognised by its thinness, soft interior, golden crust and seasoning of salt and olive oil. Other regional variations include the *focaccia di Recco* (which is stuffed with cheese; page 54) and the *sardenaira* (page 55) from Sanremo, best enjoyed in one of the Cinque Terre – a collection of five cliffside towns along the Riviera. This variation is topped with anchovies, which are delicious enjoyed on a focaccia, though worth trying by themselves among the Cinque Terre's vivid, seafront buildings.

Liguria produces some of the country's best seafood, thanks to its coastline that spans nearly 300 km (185 miles). This stretch produces an incredible bounty, which the region's culinary history can't be told without, given that Genoa was one of the most important ports in the Mediterranean for centuries. All the usual fare can be found in the markets, but the Ligurians particularly love their sea bass, mussels and *seppie* – tiny cuttlefish that are cooked simply and eaten as a snack or main meal.

Included in this seafaring history is Genoa's Boccadasse neighbourhood, a former fishermen's village with pastel houses and a small, pebbled beach. There on a recent trip and on the hunt for street food, I tried some of the *torte salate* (savoury pies) stuffed with zucchini (courgette) and *pansotti* (triangular ravioli) stuffed with wild herbs and greens and topped with another regional classic: *salsa di noci* (a creamy walnut sauce).

Beyond pansotti and trofie, some of Italy's most unique pastas come from Liguria. This is the home of ravioli, flattened *trenette* (which sits somewhere between linguine and fettuccine) and the rare, highly unusual *mandilli de saea* – a veil-thin pasta sheet named after the Genovese term for a silk handkerchief. But by far the most intricate pasta are the coin-shaped *corzetti* (page 54), which were once impressed with nobles' family crests.

Geographically, Liguria sits between Piedmont to the north, Emilia-Romagna to the east, Tuscany to the south and France to the west. Comparatively small, the region manages to retain its own cultural and culinary identity, but there are quite a few similarities between the Italian and French Rivieras – you only need look at the gentle pace of life and love of simple cuisine. Their shared history is visible in dishes like Ligura's *condiglione*; this salad usually features onion, tomato, anchovy, salted olives, boiled egg, tuna and plenty of Ligurian olive oil. Sound familiar? It's literally just a border crossing away from being a salade niçoise!

No matter what you call it, though, no version of this salad (or pesto and focaccia, for that matter) would be the same without olive oil. Liguria's terraced farms produce some of the best in the country. You can find fantastic drops all over Italy, but the sweet and delicate oil made in Liguria boasts a reputation that outstrips many of its peers.

Camogli

The farms that produce the region's superb olives are nestled among its hills and mountains. This undulating landscape means large-scale meat farming isn't prevalent in this area of Italy. However, mountains bring snowy, winter months, and the need for filling, warming stews to keep villagers happy means meat is on the menu. Rabbit is particularly popular, as it's abundant and doesn't require acres of farmland to rear; it appears alongside veal on most restaurant menus.

Liguria's mountains are reflective of Northern Italy, which tends to have a colder, more alpine climate than the South. However, the region's unique blend of mountains and coastlines creates the perfect environment for 'southern' vegetables to grow in abundance. While meat does appear on tables, the region is home to copious amounts of tomatoes, olives, garlic, artichokes and more, all of which contribute to a diet that leans heavily

Basil harvested via the raccolta volante method

on vegetarian dishes, including pesto made with broad (fava) beans, a legume which is considered a lucky charm in the region, and *torta pasqualina* (page 55), in which eggs are baked, symbolising rebirth – traditionally, it is served at Easter. To finish a meal, locals may enjoy a *castagnaccio*, a chestnut cake often topped with honey, ricotta or orange.

Growing alongside the sweeter oranges used for desserts is a sour variety: Savona's myrtle-leaf orange, also known as the chinotto orange. If that variety sounds familiar, it's likely because of the popular Italian soft drink Chinotto. While the evergreen tree used to make the drink is native to China, the species was transplanted to the Ligurian coast in the 1500s, where it thrived and improved in quality. The bitter, dark-coloured beverage produced with it has a fresh aftertaste: the perfect drink to enjoy while taking in Liguria's vistas.

This beautiful slice of Northern Italy offers panoramic views of striking mountains and mild seas, all at the same time! Its warm climate, its beautiful fishing villages turned beachside resorts and its love for Italian staples like focaccia and olive oil make it a truly fascinating culinary stop. You'll no doubt eat your body weight in pesto, and I don't think you'll regret doing so!

Regular basil pales in comparison to Genovese basil, unique among other varieties because it lacks the hint of mint in its delicate smell.

MARIA'S TOP 10 DISHES OF LIGURIA

1   ALICI RIPIENE

These Ligurian-style anchovies feature a flavourful filling of capers, breadcrumbs, eggs and herbs, mixed with salt-preserved anchovies. Once stuffed, they're dipped in flour and fried to a crunch.

2   BACCALÀ ALLA LIGURE

Cheap and accessible, *baccalà* (salt-dried cod) is popular across Italy, each region introducing its own unique flavours. The Ligurian version marries the fish with potatoes, olives and pine nuts in a tomato sauce. This local favourite is enjoyed all year round but is a Christmas Eve staple.

3   BACI DI ALASSIO

To make these 'kisses' from Alassio, a light, airy dough of hazelnut and cocoa is piped into delicate rosettes and baked. Once cooled, a decadent chocolate ganache is used to sandwich two cookies together in a delicious union.

4   CORZETTI

The beautiful *corzetti* pasta medallions from the Riviera di Levante trace their history to medieval times. The discs are decorated with a *corzetto*, a wooden stamp which was traditionally embossed with a coat of arms. Corzetti are usually accompanied by a pesto-style sauce made with walnuts or pinenuts.

5   CONIGLIO ALLA LIGURE

This slow-braised rabbit marries flavours of the Italian Riviera. It is cooked with red wine, pine nuts, herbs and the prized local taggiasche olives, until the meat is soft and falls off the bone. There is almost always enough sauce to warrant some bread served on the side to mop it all up.

6   FARINATA DI CECI

It is said that when Genovese ships hit a storm, barrels of chickpea (gram) flour and olive oil spilt across the deck. In an effort to save the goods, sailors dried the slurry in the sun and discovered an early form of *farinata*. Today's recipe mixes chickpea flour, water and olive oil, which is poured into a wide, flat copper pan and baked until the outside is golden and the inside is creamy. Sold in slices, farinata is a popular street food.

7   FOCACCIA DI RECCO

When the farmers of Recco were forced inland by Saracen invasions in the Middle Ages, they found themselves with just flour, water and cheese, which they transformed into this bread. While the authentic recipe calls for the local *prescinsêua* cheese, this cross between yoghurt and ricotta can be substituted with stracchino or crescenza. It is spread between two thin layers of dough, which are then baked and cut into rectangles to serve.

8   FOCACCIA GENOVESE

The aroma of Genoa's focaccia wafts through the port. Golden slabs of dough, glistening with olive oil, are made in every bakery, toppings varying between onion, olives and rosemary: once the perfect solution to sate sailors' appetites.

9   FRITTELLE DI BIANCHETTI

Whitebait is the star of this fried antipasto typical of Liguria. A batter of egg, flour, garlic and parsley is left to rest before fresh whitebait is added to the mix. Spoonfuls of the mixture are fried in oil until golden, then served piping hot with a dash of salt. Concern over sustainability means, in some cases, that whitebait is replaced by the similar ice or noodle fish.

10   TROFIE AL PESTO

Liguria's biggest export features the very best of the region's produce. The aromatic blend of basil, garlic, salt, pine nuts, parmigiano and olive oil is strictly pounded by hand using a pestle and mortar to release the most flavour. Pesto is traditionally served here with *trofie* (small twists of pasta), combined with green beans and cubes of potato.

Other dishes to look out for

Thanks to its unique landscape and history of maritime trade, Liguria blends traditions, making its kitchens a worthwhile place to have a meal (or two).

Street food

Frittelle di cipolle / baccalà

These golden, fried puffs of dough (called *friscieu* in dialect) are much-loved in Genoa, where *sciamadde* (fry shops) churn out different versions like *frittelle de cioulette*, which incorporate thin slices of onion into the dough, and *frittelle di baccalà*, which are made with chunks of salt-dried cod.

Sardenaira

Liguria's border with the Côte d'Azur is evident in this dish from Sanremo that echoes the flavours of the French pissaladière. It's a tomato-topped foccaccia, adorned with the punchy flavours of anchovies, taggiasche olives, capers, garlic and oregano.

Sgabei

Typically made in Lunigiana, *sgabei* are strips of dough that are fried until crisp and dashed with salt. Heartier versions are filled with cured meat, cheese or, in the sweet variant, chocolate or cream custard.

Torte rustiche

Savoury pies are a quintessential Ligurian favourite, often filled with vegetables, such as pumpkin (winter squash), and the local prescinsêua cheese. The most famous version, *torta pasqualina*, is enjoyed at Easter. It has a puff pastry crust, traditionally made of 33 layers – one for each year of Jesus' life – and a creamy filling of ricotta, whole boiled eggs and spinach or chard.

Antipasti

Capponada

Not to be confused with Sicily's caponata (page 308), this easily prepared salad was once eaten by sailors while they passed their time at sea. The *gallette del marinaio* (a dried, long-lasting bread) is softened under a mix of tuna, anchovies, capers, olives, tomatoes and boiled eggs. Everything is dressed with olive oil, vinegar and a sprinkle of salt.

Gattafin / Ravioli fritti

Workers near Levanto would bring home foraged herbs, prompting their wives to create these delicious, fried ravioli that are stuffed with an aromatic egg and cheese filling. When seasonal herbs aren't available, they're made with local greens, such as chard and spinach.

Frittata di patate / di trombette

The abundance of vegetables in Liguria often finds a home in frittata. Common versions include *frittata di patate*, made with sliced potatoes and parmigiano, and *frittata di trombette*, which utilises the celebrated trumpet-shaped zucchini (courgette) of Albenga.

Panissa

This straightforward mixture of water and chickpea flour is heated until thickened and served immediately with a crack of black pepper, a drizzle of olive oil and a squeeze of lemon. Alternatively, panissa can be left to cool, then cut into sticks that are deep-fried.

Secondi

Buridda

This stew is one of the region's principal fish dishes. While the simplest version uses just soaked stockfish, any combination of seafood – from dogfish and conger eel to octopus – can be added to a base of stock, tomato, onion and garlic.

Cima ripiena

To avoid waste, a cut of veal stomach is sliced to create a pocket, which is stuffed with a blend of meat, vegetables and cheese. The pocket is sewn up and boiled in stock for three hours, then rested under a weight in the fridge overnight before being sliced like a terrine and eaten cold.

Trippa in umido

Almost every region has a recipe for tripe. In Liguria, it is cut into strips and cooked in a tomato-based stew with potatoes. There is also a version that substitutes the potatoes for *fagiolane* (locally grown white beans).

Primi

Bardenulla

White polenta, made from finely ground white cornmeal, has a lighter, more delicate taste than its more common yellow counterpart. It's found across Northern Italy, including the port of Savona, where it's cooked until creamy and paired with a sauce of leeks, dried mushrooms, milk and cream to create a thick soup.

Mesciua

Originally from La Spezia, *mesciua* is a rustic soup of three ingredients – spelt, cannellini beans and chickpeas (garbanzo beans) – which were once gathered for the dish from spoiled or open bags arriving in the town's port. They are united with a generous dose of broth, olive oil and a dash of salt and pepper.

Zemin

A warming, inviting soup that is cooked for hours over a low flame, *zemin* features chickpeas and chard. For an extra depth of flavour, dried mushrooms, beans and pork rind are sometimes added.

Dolci

Gobeletti di Rapallo

These famous pastries have been made in Rapallo, a town on the Italian Riviera, since 1862. They are small, circular tarts of shortcrust (pie) pastry with quince jam hidden inside. Other towns make similar gobeletti (or *cubeletti*, meaning 'little hat' in dialect) filled with apricot jam.

Pandolce

Genoa's Christmas fruitcake, also known as Genoa Cake, consists of a light batter combined with raisins, candied citrus, nuts, aniseed, sweet wine and fennel seeds. There's a taller version that's left to rise and requires a longer prep time, or a shorter version which is denser and quicker to make.

... and to drink

Liguria's wines are delicious, but the region's production is limited despite a viticultural history stretching back to the Etruscans and Greeks. Vineyards are difficult to cultivate here: Liguria is Italy's second-smallest wine-producing region, and many of its vineyards are planted in scattered, challenging locations like steep cliffs – some are only reachable by boat. Inland, the hillsides offer only marginally less vertical inclines.

Most wine in Liguria is produced by small, artisanal winemakers who grow their vines on compact terraces carved from the rocky slopes. These steep elevations require many winemakers to cultivate grapes by hand, but the slopes do protect vines from the Alps' winter winds.

The local soil's high limestone content is ideal for white grapes, imparting minerality to the region's wine. Unfortunately, these wines are as difficult to find abroad as the land is to cultivate, with very few making their way across international borders.

Liguria

Despite these difficulties, the region is home to dozens of grape varieties, including some rare gems like buzzeto and granaccia. Liguria is well known for its white wines made from vermentino and the similar pigato. These grapes produce wines with a fragrant nose reminiscent of the Ligurian landscape, with notes of pinewood and sea salt. The standout red varieties are rossese, which creates subtle, fruity and spicy wines generally found in the west, and ormeasco, a similar variety to the Piedmontese dolcetto.

Rossese di Dolceacqua was the only regional DOC/DOP in the past, but the number has recently expanded. The largest DOC in Liguria is the Riviera Ligure di Ponente, which is famous for its white wines made from pigato and vermentino grapes, and its red wines made from ormeasco and rossese.

While some wines from Liguria have become known internationally, the local spirits and liqueurs fly under the radar. However, the region has a host worthy of trying. Thanks to the aromatic herbs grown here and other local ingredients, such as the basil of Pra and the chinotto of Savona, Ligurian spirits offer a real taste of the land. A few to look out for include Basanotto, made with basil, sage and chinotto, and various brands of rose and basil aperitifs and digestifs.

For beer lovers, Italy's first breweries are said to have opened here. Names like Savona's 019 and El Issor are among the most famous.

Culinary experiences

Blow your mind – and your appetite – in Liguria as you get lost in Genoa's magical food market, stroll pretty fishing villages and discover how the region's famous pesto is made.

Take a food tour in a colourful fishing village

Step into the vibrant world of Camogli with an exclusive food tour, led by renowned and award-winning author Laurel Evans. You'll discover the true essence of this charming fishing village as you taste your way through local shops and street food stands, with the option to add on a Ligurian wine and spirits tasting. Laurel's energy and stories transport you to the heart of this picturesque town's culture and flavours, her tour winding through its colourful houses lining the pebbled beach cove.

LAURELEVANS.COM

Eat your way through the streets of Genoa

Embark on an unforgettable culinary journey through the charming alleys and historic shops of Genoa's old city with Laurel Evans. Immerse yourself in the vibrant and diverse food culture of this bustling port town and uncover its fascinating maritime history. With Laurel leading the way, you'll get to taste some of the most authentic and mouth-watering local dishes while discovering the secrets behind their preparation. And, because no visit to Genoa would be complete without a trip to its famous covered food market, Laurel includes a visit to this feast for the senses, with its array of fresh and delicious offerings. In addition to food tours, Laurel runs a week-long food and wine retreat on the Italian Riviera every year.

LAURELEVANS.COM

Lose yourself in stunning coastal vineyards

Experience the magic of Cà du Ferrà's elegant vineyards in Bonassola, often dubbed the Sixth Cinque Terre. Here, sun-kissed slopes produce the finest grapes, carefully cultivated using ancient knowledge. Owners Davide and Giuseppe's guided tours begin in their cellar, offering breathtaking sea views. You're then taken to explore their organic vineyards while learning about local culture and history. Discover ancient grape varieties and how Davide and Giuseppe have restored them. Finally, indulge in a tasting of their exquisite wines accompanied by seasonal snacks.

CADUFERRA.WINE

Let Ligurian locals Emanuela and Anna feed your soul

You don't need to look further for bespoke, Ligurian culinary experiences than Emanuela Raggio and Anna Merulla. Their agency, Beautiful Liguria, can make your foodie holiday dreams come true, from a focaccia tour of Genoa and cooking classes in Rapallo to wine and organic farm days in Portofino with olive oil tastings. You can learn how to make pesto or hike the Cinque Terre on the hunt for secret food trails. Whatever you're craving, Emanuela and Anna are your local and passionate foodie go-to team, with unique, multi-day food itineraries on offer.

BEAUTIFULIGURIA.COM

Visit Liguria's historic greenhouses and delve into the world of basil

Uncover the pride of Genoa and discover all there is to know about pesto, the region's most famous delicacy. In this authentic field-to-table experience, you get to visit one of the historic family-owned greenhouses in Serre di Pra', where basil has been grown since the 1830s. See the cultivation process and then join a cooking lesson to make pesto the traditional way – with a mortar and pestle. You'll get to eat what you prepare with a sumptuous Ligurian lunch to close.

BEAUTIFULIGURIA.COM

SAGRE

MARCH
È Tempo di Carciofi, Artichoke festival, Ospedaletti

APRIL
Vin per Focaccia, Wine and focaccia festival, Celle Ligure

MAY
Sagra del Pesce di Santo Fortunato, Fish festival of Saint Fortunatus, Camogli

Festa della Focaccia di Recco, Focaccia of Recco festival, Recco

Meditaggiasca & Expo Valle Argentina Armea, Taggiasca olives and olive oil event, Taggia

Campionato Mondiale di Pesto Genovese al Mortaio, Pesto World Championship, Genoa and surrounds (every two years)

JULY
Sagra del Bagnun, Anchovy soup festival, Sestri Levante

SEPTEMBER
Sagra del Fungo, Mushroom festival, Masone

Sagra della Lumaca, Snail festival, Molini di Triora

Sagra dello Stoccafisso, Stockfish festival, Badalucco

NOVEMBER
Pane & Olio, Bread and olive oil festival, Sestri Levante

Pesto genovese

Basil pesto

If Liguria was a dish, it would undoubtedly be trofie al pesto, and
I'm so glad Executive Chef Corrado Corti at the luxurious Splendido,
A Belmond Hotel, Portofino, chose to share his version with me.
His isn't a contemporary instalment but is prepared the classic way.
He says that the dish is a Ligurian love story, and considering the Latin
origin of the word 'basil' means 'king', you could say the love story
is a regal one. The traditional pesto around these parts has these five,
and only these five, ingredients. The difference in flavour will depend
on the quality of the produce and the amount of love you put into it.

Stir your pesto through trofie pasta (or whichever short pasta you have
on hand) or use in sandwiches or on crostini. This recipe makes a large
batch that can be stored in airtight jars or containers in the fridge for up
to a week. (Pour a layer of olive oil over the top to keep the oxygen out.)
Alternatively, the pesto can be frozen for up to three months. For a
smaller amount simply halve or quarter the quantities below. Enjoy!

Liguria

NORTHERN ITALY

MAKES ABOUT 750 G
(3 CUPS)

200 g (7 oz) basil leaves
(the best quality you can find)

125 g (4½ oz) pine nuts

2–3 garlic cloves, cut lengthways,
inside germ removed

200 ml (7 fl oz) extra virgin
olive oil (preferably from Liguria),
plus extra if needed

150 g (5½ oz) Grana Padano,
finely grated

150 g (5½ oz) Pecorino
(preferably Fiore Sardo),
finely grated

Rinse the basil leaves and pat dry carefully.

Blend the pine nuts, garlic and olive oil in a food
processor or blender until the pine nuts are finely
chopped. Add the basil and process or blend on high
until creamy and evenly mixed. Add the cheeses and
pulse the mixture until combined. With the machine
running, add a little more oil to thin the consistency,
if you like. Season with salt, to taste.

Lombardia

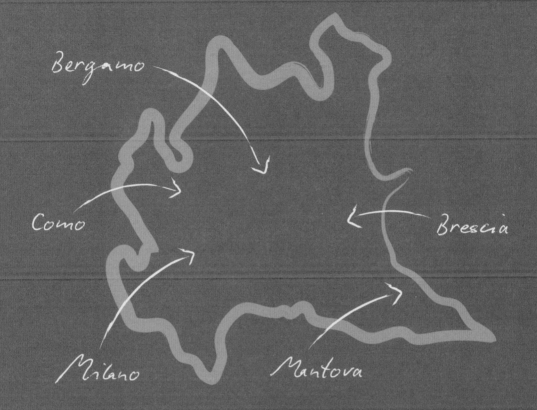

Bergamo

Como

Brescia

Milano

Mantova

Regional produce

In this historically wealthy region, many dishes feature rich ingredients including butter, eggs and cheese, as well as lots of slow-cooked and stewed meat. Although Lombardy is landlocked, there are plenty of lake and river fish, such as perch and trout, along with vegetables – particularly pumpkin (winter squash) and cabbage. As the region is one of Italy's biggest producers of rice, risotto is king here, along with polenta and fresh, stuffed pasta.

- ◆ Arctic char fish
- ◆ Asparagus
- ◆ Bresaola
- ◆ Cotechino and zampone
- ◆ Formai de Mut cheese
- ◆ Gorgonzola
- ◆ Mantua's melon, pears and pumpkin
- ◆ Polenta taragna
- ◆ Rice
- ◆ Silter cheese
- ◆ Taleggio
- ◆ Valtellina apples
- ◆ Veal

Galleria Vittorio Emanuele II, Milan

I'm not sure you ever forget your first *risotto alla milane*se (page 68). Flavourful and creamy, it is a rich, comforting indulgence cooked with bone marrow and an aromatic note of saffron. Golden perfection on a plate, it reflects the cuisine of Lombardy's capital, Milan: as cool, confident and refined as the city itself.

But there's so much more to this region than its capital. Think Lake Como with its native lake fish; Bergamo, where polenta reigns supreme; regal Mantua, with its pumpkin (winter squash); and of course, Brescia and surrounds, where Franciacorta – the premium Italian sparkling wine – is produced.

This northern region is the nation's industrial powerhouse, and its fertile plains, rolling hills and lakes have allowed it to prosper agriculturally since ancient times. Thanks to this wealth of resources, Lombardy's cuisine is characterised by fresh, local ingredients, such as corn, meat, butter and other dairy products, with rice as one of its key features: hence Milan's golden risotto.

Another key feature – and one which defines the region as a northern one – is the use of butter, which is virtually non-existent in the South's olive oil–rich cuisine. The North has a strong tradition of dairy farming, and in Lombardy, high-quality butter made from cow's milk is readily available: a staple for generations.

The region's dairy farming goes hand-in-hand with meat-forward dishes. The Lombardi are famous for many, including the oh-so-tender ossobuco (page 68) and my personal favourite: the *orecchia di elefante* (elephant ear), which is an oversized crumbed veal cutlet, different from the classic *cotoletta* (page 68) in that it doesn't have a bone.

These dishes are rooted in a history rich with diverse cultural influences. The Celts were the first to settle the region in the 5th century BCE, while the Romans conquered it in the 2nd century BCE, bringing with them new ingredients (like olive oil) and culinary traditions that still feature prominently in Lombardy. During the Middle Ages, noble families like the Visconti and Sforza clans began their rule of the region, introducing their own ingredients and influences, including saffron.

In the 20th century, Lombardy became a hub of industrialisation, which had a profound impact on the food industry. Producers and manufacturers began innovating and adopting modern techniques to enhance their products' quality and consistency. But throughout this period, their devotion to high-quality ingredients and traditional cooking methods never wavered.

For instance, you'll find a wide range of high-quality cured meats, such as salumi, bresaola and prosciutto. One of the most famous is the *salame Milano*, made with pork and flavoured with spices and herbs. Cheese is also a significant staple, with some of the most famous Italian varieties hailing from the region, including the prized Gorgonzola – often paired with honey or figs to balance its pungent tanginess – the hard, part-skimmed Grana Padano and the semi-soft Taleggio, perfect stirred through risotto.

The richness and diversity of Lombardy's cuisine run deeper than the dishes and traditions it's famous for, though: take Milan. Italy's fashion and design capital is home to sophisticated and elegant fare that marries fresh, local ingredients and global influences. Milan has embraced international cuisine, particularly from Japan, as a result of globalisation; in fact, the running joke of the last decade is that sushi is the quintessential Milanese dish because of its significant presence in the city. It's no coincidence that after the 2015 World Expo, Milan's culinary offerings became even more expansive and quality-driven as a result of the huge investment the event injected into the local economy.

Villa del Balbianello on Lake Como

The city has always been one of migrants, with people from all over Italy – particularly from the South – drawn to its commerce and industry. It's dynamic and always transforming – just like its food. With a recent increase in arrivals from Apulia, Milan has become home to a host of new street food outlets selling *panzerotti* (fried pastries stuffed with tomato and cheese): a recent addition to the capital's diverse, rich fabric. It's heart-warming to think the traditions and flavours of many Italian regions have a home in this northern city, where they continue to thrive and inspire new generations of Milanese residents and visitors. Walking through the streets, you can feel the warmth and vitality of this multicultural melting pot.

Just as Milan has imported many traditions, though, it has also exported its own: take the famous Italian apertivo. Said to have originated in Turin, this social hour truly took off in 19th-century Milan, where cafes and bars began serving a variety of snacks with drinks. The city's vibrant nightlife included the Camparino bar (still there today): the home of the Campari spritz. The liqueur was developed in the mid-19th century by Gaspare Campari in Novara, near Milan; in 1915, Davide Campari served it up with soda water at Camparino, creating a new signature drink that eventually took hold around the world.

For those looking for a non-alcoholic offering at aperitivo, Milan also created a great answer: the Campari brand's Crodino. Such a dark orange that it's almost red, this carbonated drink is made with herbal extracts and comes in the cutest little glass bottle.

Lombardy is not all bustling streets, however. You can head north to the quieter Valtellina, a valley located along the Swiss border. This area is known for its rugged mountains and alpine scenery, as well as its traditional cuisine that loves buckwheat, even in polenta; on my first visit to the area, friends made a dish that I fell in love with – *pizzoccheri della Valtellina* (page 68), a rib-sticking buckwheat pasta served with, among other ingredients, melted cheese. The latter is common within the Valtellina, which is known for its local cheeses, including Bitto and Casera. When they're not melted on pasta, you can often find them on top of polenta dishes like *polenta taragna*, which has a characteristic brown, speckled appearance and nutty flavour, thanks to its mix of cornmeal and buckwheat.

To the south in cultured Bergamo, you'll find *casoncelli alla bergamasca* – a stuffed pasta similar to ravioli, filled with breadcrumbs, sausage, cheese and spinach. East in Mantua, *tortelli di zucca* are a Christmas eve staple; these pumpkin tortelli have been around since at least the Renaissance and celebrate the flavours of their hometown, stuffed with pumpkin, crushed amaretti and local *mostarda mantovana* (candied fruit in a mustard syrup) for a signature sweetness.

The cuisine differs again as you approach Lake Como, Italy's third largest lake, with an eco-climate of its own. It's characterised by crystal-clear waters, stunning mountain scenery and charming villages. Menus here feature freshwater fish like perch and dishes like *missoltini*, which is made from salted and dried fish and typically served with polenta.

At least in my experience, Lombardy as a food destination is sadly and grossly underrated, perhaps because it's overshadowed by Milan's international reputation for fashion and design. However, among the region's verdant valleys, crystalline lakes and breathtaking mountains, you'll find a dynamic and bountiful land. If you come looking to eat well, rest assured that you'll have absolutely no problem in Lombardy.

... home to sophisticated and elegant fare that marries fresh, local ingredients and global influences.

MARIA'S TOP 10 DISHES OF LOMBARDIA

1   BIGOLI CON LE SARDELLE

This light dish from Mantua signals the beginning of Lent. It comprises *bigoli* (thick spaghetti also popular in neighbouring Veneto) served with a simple sauce of fresh sardines, garlic and olive oil.

2   BOLLITO MISTO ALLA MILANESE

Boiled meats are widespread across Northern Italy, each region preparing them with particular ingredients and accompaniments. In Milan, beef, veal, chicken and pork rind are boiled in stock along with a calf head and tail. The bollito is served at the table with horseradish, salsa verde or the local mostarda on the side.

3   COTOLETTA ALLA MILANESE

In this dish, cutlets of veal loin are left on the bone, tenderised to an even thickness and dipped in flour, then beaten egg, and finally breadcrumbs. The crumbed cutlets are fried in clarified butter until glossy, crisp and golden.

4   OSSOBUCO

Cross-cut shanks of veal, complete with prized bone marrow, are slowly braised with broth and onions until the meat is meltingly tender; contemporary versions may add a tomato sauce. A common accompaniment to risotto alla milanese, ossobuco is most often served with a topping of *gremolata* – a sauce of chopped parsley, garlic and lemon zest.

5   PANETTONE

Known globally as Italy's Christmas cake, *panettone* was invented in Milan, where it's sold in beautiful pastry shops. The signature domed, brioche-like sponge takes several days to make, the cake hung upside down after baking to prevent it collapsing as it cools. The result is a tall, fluffy treat, jewelled with dried and candied fruit.

6   PIZZOCCHERI ALLA VALTELLINESE

Bringing warmth to the mountains of the Valtellina, this sturdy dish uses *pizzoccheri* – a short, flat tagliatelle with a rustic texture and flavour, thanks to the buckwheat it's made with. The pasta is baked with savoy cabbage, chunks of local Casera cheese, potatoes and plenty of butter.

7   RISOTTO AL PESCE PERSICO

Lombardy's beautiful lakes provide much more than gorgeous scenery: they are also home to fish used extensively in the region's cuisine, including in this risotto. To make it, perch is fried in butter and sage, and then stirred into the lush rice.

8   RISOTTO ALLA MILANESE

This golden risotto is a symbol of Milan. The rice is cooked with beef marrow, meat broth, parmigiano and saffron, to which it owes its vibrant colour. Served *all'onda* (wave-like), the risotto is reduced to the exact point that it's creamy but still liquid enough to move around on the plate. The recipe is relatively simple, but the execution requires attention and expertise.

9   TORRONE DI CREMONA

One of Italy's most famous producers of *torrone* (nougat), the Po Valley city of Cremona has been linked to the dense Christmas sweet for centuries. To make it, honey, almonds, egg whites and sugar are combined and cooked gently in a bain-marie to form a thick mixture. This is shaped into bars and packed between rice paper to set.

10   TORTA SBRISOLONA

Mantua's 'crumble cake' is made with unpeeled almonds, flour, sugar, butter, cornflour (corn starch) and maraschino liqueur. The mixture is lightly patted into a tin and baked. Due to its crumbly texture, the cake is broken into pieces and served with cream.

Other dishes to look out for

With meaty mains, generously stuffed pastas and dishes that turn scraps into a hearty feast, Lombardy is a food lover's dream.

Antipasti

Mondeghili

Milan's meatballs were created to use left-over meat (usually beef) and stale bread. After soaking the bread in milk, it's combined with boiled or braised beef, sausage, mortadella and egg. The meatballs are flattened and coated in breadcrumbs before frying in butter.

Rane fritte

Nowadays just the plump thighs are used, rather than the whole frog. These nuggets of meat on the bone are often dipped in a beer batter, deep-fried and served hot and crisp.

Primi

Casoncelli

A stuffed pasta from Brescia and Bergamo, whose fillings differ slightly: the first mixes meat with breadcrumbs and Grana Padano, while the latter adds a sweet note to the meat with the addition of raisins, pears, amaretti, cinnamon and nutmeg.

Marubini cremonesi

Cremona's stuffed pasta is filled with braised beef, roasted pork and veal brains. They're shaped like ravioli or tortellini and served in a broth of boiled beef, pork and chicken.

Risotto con la luganega / alla monzese

The local Luganega sausage stars in this simple risotto from Monza, which uses just a little onion, butter and parmigiano.

Zuppa alla pavese

Slices of stale bread are fried in butter and placed in a bowl. An egg is cracked onto each piece of bread, the yolk kept intact, and grated Grana Padano is sprinkled over. Hot meat broth is then poured into the bowl, the heat gently poaching the egg.

Secondi

Brüscitt

This dish gets its name from the word briciole (crumbs) and was originally made using small pieces of meat still attached to the bone to prevent them going to waste. Today, it's more common to find it made with small pieces of beef, separated from the bone, cooked in butter with fennel seeds and red wine.

Cassoeula

A traditional winter stew, cassoeula was created to use the less desirable cuts of a pig. Alongside the ribs, head, tail and rind, it features savoy cabbage as well as local verzini sausages.

Rostin negàa

Milan's traditional way of preparing veal, with a name that's dialect for 'drowned roast'. Knots of veal, on the bone, are floured and fried in butter with rosemary and pancetta. They're then covered in white wine and stock and cooked in the oven until tender.

Spiedo bresciano

Brescia's signature kebabs are a meat lover's dream. Pieces of pork, chicken, rabbit and sometimes game or goat are threaded onto wooden skewers, alternated with potato and sage leaves. The *spiedi* are then slowly cooked on a spit for four to five hours, brushed in liberal amounts of butter.

Stùà in cunscia

A beef stew that is prepared for the Feast of the Immaculate Conception on 8 December. The beef is marinated for two days in red wine and herbs, including bay and juniper, then cooked with butter and pancetta and served with potatoes.

Trippa alla milanese

Also known locally as *busecca*, this is the Milanese take on tripe. The cow stomach is cooked in a thick soup with carrots, celery, onion, passata (pureed tomatoes), white beans and warm notes of juniper and cloves.

Dolci

Biscotti ambrosiani

These buttery cookies are traditionally made and eaten on 7 December, the feast day of Milan's patron saint, Saint Ambrose; this date kicks off the beginning of the city's Christmas festivities. Made with a simple dough of flour, butter, sugar, eggs and vanilla, these cookies may be decorated with chocolate and nuts.

Bossolà bresciano

With a texture similar to pandoro (page 123), Brescia's large, ringed Christmas cake requires multiple proving stages and a long preparation time to achieve its airy, cloud-like texture. It is liberally doused in icing (confectioners') sugar before serving.

Caviadini

These simple vanilla cookies from the Valsassina date to the 1600s and are instantly recognisable by their unique shape: elongated rectangles with a hole in the centre. They're covered in fat grains of sugar.

Pan dei morti

Made for All Saints Day and All Souls Day on 1 and 2 November, the 'bread of the dead' are actually dark, dense oval cookies flavoured with dried fruit, nuts, cocoa, nutmeg and cinnamon.

Torta del Donizetti

Dedicated to composer Gaetano Donizetti and made in his hometown of Bergamo, this ring-shaped sponge cake is studded with dehydrated pineapple and apricot. It is flavoured with vanilla and maraschino.

Tortionata / Torta di Lodi

An almond cake from Lodi named after the *tortijon*, a wire once used to slice it. Made with a simple mix of eggs, flour, sugar, almonds and lemon zest, it's light and crumbly.

... and to drink

When it comes to drinking, you won't leave this region thirsty. Lombardy has a long and rich history of winemaking that dates to the Etruscans, with the Romans who followed them establishing vineyards in the Po Valley. During the Middle Ages, monastic orders furthered viticulture in the region, with many of Lombardy's vineyards owned and operated by the Church in this era.

During the Renaissance, Lombardy's wines gained popularity and were exported to other parts of Italy and Europe. In the 20th century, the region's winemakers focused on improving production methods and quality, resulting in the creation of the DOC and DOCG certifications that guarantee the authenticity and quality of wines. Today, Lombardy is home to several well-known and highly regarded wine styles, including Valtellina Franciacorta and Oltrepò Pavese Metodo Classico, with unique and popular offerings like Bergamo's Moscato di Scanzo.

Among these, Franciacorta is king. This bottle-aged sparkling wine is produced with hand-harvested grapes and adheres to the stringent regulations and quality standards set by both the DOC and DOCG certifications. Despite being relatively new to the world of sparkling wines, Franciacorta has gained recognition for its high quality. It is different from Prosecco in that it's more complex and drier, and is produced with different methods (Franciacorta requires the traditional method, which is used to make Champagne). The other popular sparkling to look out for here is Oltrepò Pavese Metodo Classico from the Pavese area.

While in Lombardy, also keep an eye out for Nebbiolo from Valtellina or a dry, Amarone-style wine called Sforzato, made from dried nebbiolo grapes. The fizzy Lambrusco Mantovano with red-ruby tones is also quite popular, as is the Moscato di Scanzo: a red wine passito.

If you're looking for a cocktail, try stopping in at the Camparino bar in Milan. It is the birthplace not only of the Campari spritz, but of the Milano-Torino cocktail as well. It was invented here in the 1860s, and was named after its two main ingredients: Campari (Milan) and sweet vermouth (Turin). Eventually, sparkling water was added to create the Americano.

Beyond Campari, other liqueurs that call this region home include Fernet Branca, Amaretto Disaronno and Ramazzotti. And while popular globally, the Peroni beer brand was established here in Lombardy in 1846.

Culinary experiences

From wine to wellness, markets to Michelin stars and local food tours to lakeside lounging, these experiences will stay with you for a lifetime.

Go wine tasting and stay at a boutique Franciacorta hotel

A wine tasting tour is a great way to explore the Franciacorta wine region in the province of Brescia. Journey through the area's vineyards and sample their famous sparkling wine made using the *metodo classico* (traditional method). Winedering offer a number of different itineraries for all tastes and budgets, or you can stay and play at the chic L'Albereta, a vine-wrapped boutique hotel right by Lake Iseo. This haven in the Franciacorta heartland comes complete with gourmet restaurants, a first-class spa and top wineries right on your doorstep.

WINEDERING.COM, ALBERETA.IT

Savour Milan's culinary delights on a walking food tour

Milan is a food lover's paradise, and a walking food tour is a great way to explore the city's culinary scene; they typically include a visit to local markets, specialty food shops and traditional trattorie. Context Travel offers a three-hour walking tour that will guide you through the most cherished traditions of the city, from coffee to aperitivo, led by food writers, chefs or culinary educators. Secret Food Tours offers small-group tours that delve into the diverse nature of the Milanese dining scene, with the chance to taste regional snacks. Do Eat Better takes small groups on a Milan Patisserie Tour or Milan Aperitivo and Street Food Tour.

CONTEXTTRAVEL.COM, SECRETFOODTOURS.COM
DOEATBETTEREXPERIENCE.COM

Join a cheese tasting tour in the Valtellina

The Valtellina is a valley in the province of Sondrio known for its cheeses, such as Bitto and Valtellina Casera. Take a tour with Lake Como for You and explore the different varieties, learn about the production process and meet the hard-working locals who strive to preserve ancient cheesemaking traditions. Tours include visits to cheese factories with plenty of tastings and a full-day Valtellina cheese tasting tour with wine.

LAKECOMOFORYOU.COM

Enjoy your pick of Michelin-starred restaurants

Italy boasts almost 400 restaurants with a star in the Michelin guide, and Lombardy – with almost 60 of those restaurants – is the region with the most. Dine at one to experience the full culinary prowess of this region. In Milan and beyond, you'll find starred establishments with tasting menus to suit all preferences and budgets. Chefs like Carlo Cracco and Enrico Bartolini are household names in the capital, but no matter where you are in the region, you're bound to find a restaurant that's right for you.

GUIDE.MICHELIN.COM

Indulge on Lake Como

Known for its picturesque scenery and luxurious villas, Lake Como is unforgettable. The area has a unique culinary tradition because of its geographic make-up, which Do Eat Better can help you explore with a three-hour walking tour in Como town. This typically includes a visit to local markets, specialty food shops and traditional restaurants. Base yourself at one of the area's glamorous properties – Grand Hotel Tremezzo, with its famous pool that floats on the lake, or Passalacqua, which was crowned Best Hotel in the World by World's 50 Best in 2023. Here you step into another time, where the old Italian concept of *villeggiatura* (spending a long summer holiday steeping yourself in the landscape) comes alive. With sprawling gardens, lake views and a chef ready to teach you how to make pasta, you won't want to leave.

DOEATBETTEREXPERIENCE.COM, GRANDHOTELTREMEZZO.COM, PASSALACQUA.IT

SAGRE

JUNE

Festa del Melone, Melon festival, Mantua

SEPTEMBER

Sagra del Bitto, Bitto cheese festival, Gerola Alta

Sagra Nazionale del Gorgonzola, Gorgonzola festival, Gorgonzola

Festival Franciacorta, Franciacorta wine festival, Franciacorta territory

OCTOBER

Festa del Salame, Salami festival, Cremona

Sagra della Mela e dell'Uva, Apple and grape festival, Villa di Tirano

Festa del Riso, Rice festival, Carpiano

Sagra della Zucca, Pumpkin festival, Mezzago

Milano Wine Week, Milan

Mostra del Bitto, Bitto cheese festival, Morbegno

Sbrisolona & Co, Sbrisolona almond cake festival, Mantua

NOVEMBER

Festa del Torrone, Torrone festival, Cremona

Valtellina Wine Trail, Running race through vineyards, Valtellina

Risotto allo zafferano con foglia d'oro

Saffron risotto with gold leaf

Widely regarded as the grand maestro of modern Italian cuisine, Gualtiero Marchesi lives on at the Grand Hotel Tremezzo on Lake Como. The hotel's La Terrazza Gualtiero Marchesi serves up his signature dishes, and I've had the good fortune of trying this one. It blew me away, and to this day, I maintain it's the best risotto I've eaten. Ever. And there have been a few! (I confess, the gold leaf did make it feel extra special.) It's the world's only restaurant that offers the dish, but now you can try your hand at it.

Lombardia

NORTHERN ITALY

SERVES 4

1 teaspoon saffron threads

1 litre (4 cups) chicken or beef stock (or use vegetable stock for a vegetarian risotto), heated

20 g (¾ oz) butter

320 g (11½ oz) carnaroli rice

175 ml (6 fl oz) white wine

20 g (¾ oz) grated parmesan

4 edible gold leaves (optional)

Butter mixture

80 g (2¾ oz) butter, at room temperature

1 onion, chopped

175 ml (6 fl oz) white wine

To make the butter mixture, melt 20 g (¾ oz) of the butter in a small saucepan over medium heat. Add the onion and cook until softened, then pour in the white wine and simmer for 5–6 minutes, until the alcohol evaporates and the liquid reduces by about one-third. Turn off the heat and let the mixture cool to room temperature. Strain the liquid, discarding the onion. Gradually stir the liquid into the remaining butter until combined, then set aside.

Place the saffron threads in a small heatproof bowl and add enough of the stock to generously cover the saffron. Set aside to steep.

Melt the butter in a large saucepan over medium heat, add the rice and cook for 2 minutes or until it is semi-translucent and toasted. Add the wine and cook for a few minutes to allow the alcohol to evaporate, then add 100 ml (3½ fl oz) of the remaining stock.

Cook the rice, stirring often and adding more stock each time it begins to dry out, for about 15 minutes, until the rice is almost al dente. Add the saffron liquid, reduce the heat to a gentle simmer and cook until the rice is al dente.

Stir in the butter mixture and parmesan and cook gently until the consistency is *all'onda* (like a wave): neither too liquidy nor too thick. It should move slowly as you tilt the pan. Season with salt to taste.

Divide among plates and add a gold leaf on top of each. Leave to rest for a couple of minutes before serving.

Piemonte

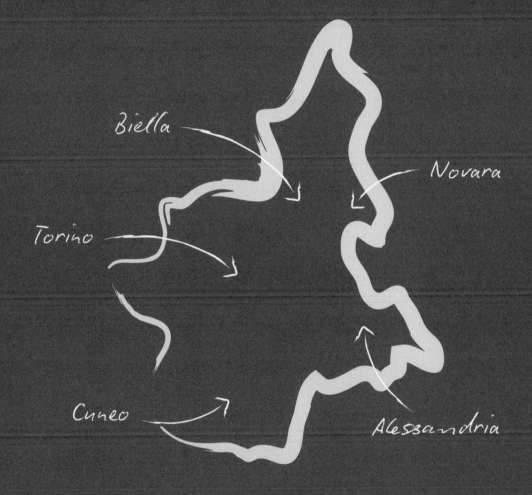

Biella

Novara

Torino

Cuneo

Alessandria

Regional produce

The cows of Piedmont, which are
famous throughout Italy, ensure that
beef and cheese are ever present in
this alpine region. Situated next to
France, Piedmont lacks access to the
sea, but its foothills are replete with
vegetables, beans and truffles. Hazelnuts
and chestnuts feature extensively in
its cuisine – especially in the region's
sweets and desserts.

- Bra's veal sausage
- Carmagnola's peppers
- Castelmagno cheese
- Chestnuts
- Chocolate
- Cuneo beans
- Doctor fish/tench
- Hazelnuts
- Murazzano cheese
- Novara's Gorgonzola
- Piedmontese beef
- Red apples
- Rice
- Toma Piemontese
- White truffles

View of the Mole Antonelliana, Turin

I n Australia as a teen, I took geography classes that positioned Turin as a dull, grey city in Italy's industrial North. 'Industrial' never really sounds that sexy, so it didn't seem like much of a contender for my bucket list. Boy, was I wrong.

Turin was Italy's first capital and remains one of the country's most beautiful, refined cities. Historical museums and galleries are housed in Baroque-style buildings reminiscent of Paris or Vienna. The city's grand squares, elegant shopping arcades and cobbled streets offer glimpses of the surrounding snow-capped Alps, adding to the charming ambience. There are bustling cafes where you sit and indulge (unlike shots of coffee taken standing in Rome and Naples), bars full of locals with bold red wines in hand at aperitivo hour and restaurants serving up traditional Piedmontese fare.

So, you can imagine my surprise when I visited Turin as an adult, those geography classes still echoing. I'd been duped! There was nothing grey and ugly about this city. Under the porticoes of Piazza San Carlo, Caffè Torino's neon Martini sign filled me with awe, and I fell in love with my first *bicerin* (the local hot chocolate layered with a shot of espresso and whipped cream) in one of the city's grand cafes where aristocrats and writers once gathered. I am a renowned sweet tooth, and this region, with its abundance of chocolate and hazelnuts, is praline heaven. I went into a reverie when I tasted chocolate bonet (page 82), and I couldn't get enough of the famed *baci di dama* (lady's kisses), which traditionally feature chocolate cream sandwiched between two hazelnut cookies.

Every one of my meals in Piedmont has been unforgettable: this northwestern region packs a culinary punch. It boasts award-winning wines, from Barolo and Nebbiolo to the sweet Moscato d'Asti, and a high concentration of Michelin-starred restaurants, and it is the birthplace of the 'slow food' movement, which honours local produce and promotes heritage and culture. What Piedmont produces it exports to the world, from its *grissini* (bread sticks) to its fine chocolate, including the praline-like *gianduiotto* (page 82), along with Ferrero Rocher and Nutella; these two household names sit alongside other brands with local origins like Fiat, Lavazza, Eataly and Martini. This region wears quality and international success like badges of honour.

Over the years, Piedmont's cuisine has been shaped by other cultures, including French, Swiss and Austrian: take *bagna cauda* (page 82), a dip made with garlic, anchovies and olive oil. It originated in the Piedmontese countryside, yet the technique used to prepare it reflects the region's close ties to France.

Within Piedmont's borders, its cuisine is shaped by the Alps to the north, the Po River to the south and between them, an abundance of fertile plains and rolling hills with a rich tradition of farming and agriculture. This geography has given rise to many dishes featuring meat, mushrooms and polenta, the last of which is made with local cheese and butter in Biella. In Novara, they top their polenta with *tapulon* (donkey meat), while in Borgomanero, they serve it under *taupone* (donkey stew), which is made by cooking the meat in lardo, butter, herbs and Nebbiolo until tender and juicy.

The areas of Vercelli and Novara are famous for their rice fields, which produce arborio, carnaroli and other varieties that are exported globally: hence the famous *risotto alla piemontese* (page 84). This creamy risotto is typically served as a first course and is a staple in many households.

Personally, I've never quite gotten over my crush on *agnolotti del plin* (page 82), the little pinched and stuffed pasta. They can be found everywhere now, but the tradition hails from Monferrato and the Langhe. In fact, the whole of Piedmont is famous for its stuffed pasta. Throughout, you'll find different fillings, such as donkey meat in the Asti area. Across the region, agnolotti are served in a few traditional ways, with butter, sage and Grana Padano; in broth; with a meat ragù; and – in some parts of Monferrato wine territory – braised in wine.

Meanwhile, the town of Alba is home to the food world's most coveted treasure – *tartufo bianco* (white truffle). Piedmont is also known for its abundance of black truffles, but it's the white truffle of Alba that chefs from Tokyo to Manhattan pay upwards of 4,000 euros per kg (2.25 lb) for. It is harvested from late September to December, its scarcity and high demand making it one of the world's most expensive ingredients.

If I close my eyes, I can still taste my first *tajarin al tartufo bianco* (tagliolini topped with white truffle) in Alba, the luxurious butter sauce paired with the delicate flavour of the truffle. And I'll never forget watching Luna the dog run through the woods to hunt for the delicacy in the hills of the Langhe, the hunter yelling out coordinates in dialect, our muddy boots kicking up dirt.

Also vivid in my recollections is my first visit to Piedmont's wine regions. It blew my mind travelling through namesake towns like Asti and Barolo; you never forget your first glass from either or, for that matter, your first Nebbiolo, Barbera or Barbaresco. In Piedmont, these wines find their way from glass to plate in dishes like *risotto al Barolo*. Cooked with butter, leeks and bay, this risotto is a ruby red, thanks to the wine that's added.

Even without the wine mixed into dishes themselves, every Piedmontese delicacy perfectly matches with the local varietals; this includes the cheeses, such as Castelmagno and Robiola di Roccaverano, which both reflect the particular flavours of the region's pastures and forests.

Truffle hunting in the Langhe hills

... it is the birthplace of the 'slow food' movement, which honours local produce and promotes heritage and culture.

Within those forests, hunting has been an important activity for centuries. As a result, many traditional dishes feature game, such as wild boar, rabbit and pheasant. Given the famously long alpine winters, the region's meats historically needed to be preserved, leading to the development of cured products, such as bresaola and salami. In turn, there is a local prevalence of meat dishes, such as the *brasato al Barolo* (page 82), a beef stew slow-cooked in Barolo, and the *bollito misto* (page 82), a mix of meat cuts cooked in broth.

Quite simply, this is a region that just can't put a foot wrong when it comes to food and wine. However, despite the reputation the region's cuisine and its high-quality ingredients have garnered, the Piedmontese never boast. With a history of industry and agriculture, they are quietly confident as they work with their sleeves rolled up and their heads down, producing some of the world's finest dishes, wine, truffles and chocolate. Despite what high school classes may tell you, Piedmont really is a gastronomic paradise.

MARIA'S TOP 10 DISHES OF PIEMONTE

1 AGNOLOTTI

The region's signature stuffed pasta are bite-sized parcels filled with left-over roasted meats, cheese or vegetables. Although usually served in broth or with butter and fresh sage, there are countless variations, from stuffing them with donkey meat to dousing them in red wine. *Agnolotti del plin*, typically from southern Piedmont and distinct in their shape, are the most popular. Thanks to how they're made, their name comes from the local dialect word for 'pinch': *plin*.

2 BAGNA CAUDA

A creamy sauce of anchovies and lots of garlic, *bagna cauda* is served over a flame like fondue. Raw and cooked vegetables are provided to dip, while slices of bread are used to catch the drips.

3 BOLLITO MISTO

Many regions have a traditional dish of boiled meat, with variations in meats, accompaniments and sauces. The local version follows the rule of seven: there are seven cuts of beef, seven types of offal and poultry, seven accompanying vegetables and seven sauces, including the requisite salsas, bagnet verd and bagnet ross. You can play around with the sauces or be guided by your waiter's tips on what pairs best with what.

4 BONET

Known as *bunet* in the local dialect, *bonet* is a dessert from the Langhe area with a dense, lush texture. A thick cream of eggs, sugar and milk is flavoured with cocoa, coffee, rum and crushed amaretti, then poured into small rectangular tins lined with caramel. The *bonet* are cooked in a bain-marie and left to cool before they're decorated with whipped cream and amaretti.

5 BRASATO AL BAROLO

Piedmont's *brasà* brings together the region's celebrated Fassona beef and Barolo. A large piece of meat is marinated in wine overnight with a soffritto of carrot, onion and celery, along with herbs and spices. It is then cooked gently for two to three hours. The beef is sliced and served with the strained Barolo sauce and a side of polenta or pureed potato.

6 FRICIULE

Little squares of dough that are fried until crisp, puffy and golden, *friciule* are often served with lardo or prosciutto and are best eaten hot.

7 GIANDUIOTTO

After Napoleon made luxury goods like cocoa expensive to import into Europe, the chocolatiers of Turin began adding hazelnuts from the Langhe into their mixtures. *Gianduiotto* was invented by Caffarel in 1865, making it the world's oldest wrapped chocolate. Named after Gianduja, a mask of the *commedia dell'arte* (a form of theatre) and a symbol of Piedmont, the ingot-shaped treat takes its shape from the character's hat.

8 MONT BLANC

This chestnut-based dessert is prevalent in Piedmont, Lombardy and France. Chestnut puree is flavoured with cocoa and rum, then squeezed through a potato ricer to form strands that are arranged into a mountain shape. It is then decorated with whipped cream and white meringue to evoke its snow-topped namesake.

9 TAJARIN

Tajarin is very thin angel hair pasta with an intense golden colour, thanks to egg yolks. It's sometimes served with ragù, but it's best tossed in butter and topped with shavings of white truffle.

10 VITELLO TONNATO

A marinated and boiled piece of veal is cooled, sliced and served with a thick mayonnaise-like sauce made with tuna and flavoured with anchovies and capers.

Other dishes to look out for

Creamy risottos, hearty peasant-style soups, street snacks and prized beef: the food of Piedmont has a dish for every occasion.

Street food

Gofri

These waffles made from flour, water and yeast were once a substitute for bread. Today, they are frequently eaten as street food, with a sweet or savoury filling sandwiched between two crispy waffles.

Torta verde

An Easter dish from the town of Nizza Monferrato in the Asti province, *torta verde* is a savoury cake made from spinach, rice, eggs and herbs. It is often cut into squares and eaten as a snack or at springtime picnics.

Antipasti

Bagnet

Two of the most common sauces in Piedmont, *bagnet* are served with boiled meats or on top of tomino cheese. There are two types: *verd* (green) and *ross* (red). The first is made with parsley, garlic and anchovies, while the second combines tomato, carrot and onion with a kick of red chilli pepper.

Battuta al coltello

The prized meat of Piedmont's Fassona cows does all the talking in this tartare-style dish. The meat is chopped finely so it stays tender, then dressed with olive oil and lemon juice and seasoned with salt and pepper. In truffle season, it's finished with a final flourish of shaved white truffle.

Carpione

A summer dish, *carpione* unites vegetables, meat, fish and eggs in endless variations. The carpione is pickling liquid, made with vinegar and flavoured with sage. Chosen ingredients are left in the liquid for 12 hours, then served cold.

Insalata russa

The centrepiece of many antipasto tables, this cold starter features cubes of cooked potato, carrot, peas and chopped boiled egg, all mixed with mayonnaise and vinegar. The thick mixture is shaped into a dome and decorated with pieces of raw and pickled vegetables, including slices of gherkin.

Uovo al palet

In Piedmont, one of the favourite antipasto dishes is a simple fried egg topped with shavings of black truffle and served with bread to mop up the runny yolk: heavenly.

Primi

Cagliette

These potato dumplings, similar to gnocchi, are from the alpine peaks of the Susa Valley. A basic mix of grated potato, egg, flour and onion, they are sometimes enriched with crumbled sausage, cheese or pieces of salami. The cagliette are boiled in water or stock and often served in a creamy sauce of butter and Grana Padano.

Risotto al gorgonzola

The town of Novara is famous for its Gorgonzola. In this dish, a simple risotto is prepared, the cheese stirred through at the end with parmigiano and parsley.

Risotto alla piemontese

The simplest yet best way to celebrate local rices, this *risotto in bianco* adds just onion, white wine, stock and parmigiano to create a creamy, comforting texture.

Zuppa mitonata

This soup is similar to nearby France's onion soup. Sliced onions, cooked in butter until dark and sweet, are divided, with half placed on top of slices of stale bread in a dish. Cheese follows, such as Toma, along with a ladle of beef stock. This is repeated, then topped with a final layer of bread and cheese. Everything is baked until the top bubbles.

Secondi

Baccalà alla piemontese

The local version of *baccalà* (salt-dried cod) sees it soaked and cut into pieces. The fish is then pan-fried in butter with anchovies and garlic. Once the anchovies dissolve, a little stock is added to make a sauce.

Finanziera

Made from the offcuts and offal of beef and chicken, including sweetbreads, crests and livers, this stew has sweet and savoury notes, thanks to its use of pickled vegetables, chicken stock and Marsala. It's served by itself or used in pasta or risotto.

Fritto misto alla piemontese

This feast of deep-fried snacks was originally an antipasto but is now enjoyed as a second dish of individually fried meat, vegetables and sweets. The meats include veal brains, pork and lamb. The vegetables are often zucchini (courgette), artichokes, mushrooms and cauliflower, while amaretti, apples and prunes cover the sweet element.

Rane fritte

Fried frogs are a historic staple in the region's rice-growing areas. After soaking, they're left to marinate overnight in vinegar, wine or lemon juice, along with parsley, onion and olive oil. Once ready, they're dusted in flour or dipped in batter and fried until golden.

Dolci

Marrons glacé

Cuneo's candied chestnuts are made with the marron variety, which are plumper and more flavourful than other varieties. The process to candy them is lengthy: they are boiled several times in sugar syrup and cooled for a day each time. They're finished with a glaze of water and icing (confectioners') sugar.

Tirulën

These cookies from Isola d'Asti are made with hazelnuts and lemon zest, and rolled in sugar. They're often paired with sweet wine, but their slightly bitter aftertaste makes them the perfect partner for reds.

Torta di Pere Madernassa

Madernassa pears are a rare, hard variety from Roero in Piedmont's hills, primarily used for cooking. In this recipe, they're grated, cooked until soft and baked in a mixture that includes almond flour, sugar, cocoa, spices and lemon juice and zest.

Torta di nocciole

From the hazelnut-rich area of the Langhe, this dense, flour-free sponge was historically prepared with harvest leftovers for Christmas. Today it's made with toasted hazelnuts, eggs, sugar and butter all year round.

... and to drink

This part of Italy is home to some of the country's – and the world's – most sought-after wines. While they're produced throughout the region, the most prestigious vineyards are in the Langhe, Roero and Monferrato areas, which are now UNESCO World Heritage sites.

Piedmont's winemaking tradition, which dates to the Celts, is defined by a terroir of rolling hills, mild climate and rich soils. This combination creates ideal conditions for producing wines of exceptional quality and complexity. The region is particularly renowned for its red wines – especially those made from the nebbiolo grape. Barolo is the most famous of these, often referred to as the 'king of wines' due to its complex aromas, rich tannins and longevity. Other notable reds from the region include Barbaresco, Barbera d'Alba and Dolcetto d'Alba.

In addition to reds, Piedmont produces some exceptional whites like Moscato d'Asti, a sweet sparkling wine made from the moscato grape; Timorasso, made with a grape that was on the verge of extinction before revival in the 1980s; and Gavi, a dry wine made from the cortese grape.

But while Piedmont is defined by wine, what would a discussion about this region be without mentioning vermouth? The spiced fortified wine, which originated in Turin in the 18th century, is made by infusing a variety of botanicals, such as herbs, spices and fruits, into a base of white wine. The results are complex, with a herbaceous flavour that is both bitter and sweet. Within Piedmont, vermouth brands of note include Carpano Antica Formula, Martini & Rossi, Cocchi and Cinzano.

The abundance of quality grapes across Piedmont also means quality spirits, Liquore di Genziana del Piemonte and Arquebuse del Piemonte among them. If you'd like to try grappa, look out for Grappa Piemontese and Grappa di Barolo.

The region isn't just known for alcohol, however: it is also home to companies that produce artisanal flavoured soft drinks, including *spuma*, which has an aromatic flavour with a caramel aftertaste, and *cedro* (citrus). Molecola has gained popularity in recent years, with its secret blend of spices and botanicals, and the Lurisia brand from the Cuneo province produces flavours including *gazzosa* (a classic lemon soft drink), *aranciata* (an orange soft drink) and the famous *chinotto*, which is made from the fruit of the myrtle-leaved orange tree.

Piemonte

NORTHERN ITALY

Culinary experiences

Learn to mix cocktails from the masters, experience the thrill of hunting for elusive truffles and finish off a day in this food paradise with some well-deserved sweets.

Head into the Langhe woods for a truffle hunt

There is nothing more 'Piedmont' than hunting for truffles. At various times of the year, you can experience the real deal with a hunter and trained dogs in the woods, with simulated hunts on offer the rest of the time. The hunters will guide you through the process and explain the nuances of finding these rare delicacies. There are many providers in the area, such as Giuseppe – a third-generation hunter – and his adorable dog.

TRUFFLEHUNTINGALBALANGHE.EU

Take a cocktail masterclass at Casa Martini

Dive into the world of bartending with expert guidance from a brand ambassador at the Casa Martini Bar Academy. Catch the Martini shuttle bus to the company's headquarters a short distance from Turin, and uncover insider tips and tricks for crafting the ideal Negroni, Americano and Martini Fiero and Tonic. Armed with your newly acquired tricks of the trade, you'll get to create your very own signature cocktail.

MARTINI.COM/CASA-MARTINI

Learn to make Piedmontese classics like agnolotti del plin

Discover the secrets of Piedmont's culinary heritage and learn how to make traditional dishes, such as agnolotti del plin, risotto and bagna cauda. Casa Mia Food and Wine offer a number of cooking classes for all levels, along with food experiences like cheese tastings where you can visit producers and taste varieties, such as robiola, Castelmagno and Toma.

CASAMIATOURS.COM

Immerse yourself in world-class wine

Visit the wineries and vineyards in the Langhe and Monferrato regions to taste Barolo, Barbera and Nebbiolo, among many others wines, while you learn about their production. For accommodation, book a stay at the exclusive wine resort Nordelaia in Monferrato and indulge in spectacular views, fine food and wine. The former farmhouse is now a 12-room boutique property set on 12 acres with its own vineyards on the grounds. Relax in the spa, soak in the infinity pool or cycle around the vines.

NORDELAIA.COM

Join a sweets and chocolate tour in Turin

Don't miss some of my favourite cafes and chocolate spots, including the historic caffès Torino, San Carlo, Baratti & Milano and, of course, the resplendent Mulassano. Visit some of them and other secret sweet spots on a chocolate tour of this famously sugar-loving city. You'll learn about the history of artisan chocolate makers and visit chocolate shops for tastings of traditional treats, such as gianduiotto and bicerin.

DOEATBETTEREXPERIENCE.COM

Agnolotti del plin al sugo d'arrosto

Plin agnolotti filled with roasted meat sauce

Stuffed agnolotti really are the pride of Piedmont, particularly in the hills of the Langhe, and I will forever treasure this recipe supplied by Chef Enrico Crippa of Piazza Duomo. The lauded restaurant in Alba, owned by the Ceretto family, has held three Michelin stars for more than a decade and continuously makes the World's 50 Best Restaurants list. In addition to the fine-dining establishment, this iconic dish of the Piedmontese tradition can be savoured at the family's bistro outpost La Piola (also in Alba). Beyond the silkiness of the pasta, the flavour here lies in the rich notes of all the roasted meats.

SERVES 6–8

extra virgin olive oil

butter

50 g (1¾ oz) pork sausage meat, crumbled

250 g (9 oz) capocollo (pork neck), cut into 5 cm (2 in) chunks

250 g (9 oz) veal belly, cut into 5 cm (2 in) chunks

250 g (9 oz) veal osso bucco

300 g (10½ oz) bone-in rabbit legs

2 onions, diced

5 carrots, diced

2½ celery stalks, diced

1.2 litres (41 fl oz) fragrant white wine

2 cloves

3 juniper berries

1 fresh bay leaf

1 small bulb of garlic, halved horizontally through the middle

3 tablespoons tomato paste (concentrated puree)

100 g (3½ oz) baby spinach leaves

1 head (about 200 g/7 oz) of escarole, roughly chopped

80 ml (2¾ fl oz) cream

2 eggs

50 g (½ cup) grated parmesan

handful of sage leaves

Preheat the oven to 180°C (350°F) fan-forced.

Heat a heavy-based frying pan over medium heat and add a drizzle of olive oil and a small knob of butter. Brown the sausage meat for 3–4 minutes, until the fat is released. Drain off and discard the excess fat and place the sausage meat in a small baking dish.

Season the capocollo with salt. Reheat the same pan over high heat, add a little more butter and another drizzle of oil, then add the capocollo and cook, turning to brown each side, for 5 minutes. Add to the dish with the sausage meat.

Season the veal belly with salt and brown this, also in butter and oil, over high heat for 5 minutes, sealing each side, before placing it in a separate baking dish. Season the osso bucco with salt and pepper, brown in the same way, and add this to the dish with the veal belly.

Finally, sprinkle the rabbit legs with salt and brown all over in butter and oil over high heat for 5–6 minutes. Transfer to a third separate dish.

Reduce the heat to medium, add 2 tablespoons of olive oil to the pan and cook the onion, carrot and celery for 7–8 minutes, until starting to soften. Add half to the dish with the veal and half to the dish with the rabbit legs.

Add the white wine to the pan, bring to the boil and cook for 2 minutes, eliminating the alcohol by setting fire to the wine with a long match. Add the cloves, juniper berries, bay leaf, garlic halves and tomato paste, then reduce the heat to low and simmer for 5–10 minutes, until reduced slightly. Remove the pan from the heat and strain, discarding the solids.

Pour 50 ml (1¾ fl oz) of the strained liquid into the dish of sausage and capocollo and divide the remainder between the veal and the rabbit. Cover all the dishes securely with foil, then transfer to the oven and roast, basting occasionally, for 1–1½ hours, until all the meat is tender. (Remove meat from the oven as it becomes tender.)

Transfer the roasted meats to a plate. Discard the left-over pork juices from the dish and strain the left-over juices from the veal and rabbit into the same small saucepan. Bring to the boil over medium–heat and cook for 10–12 minutes, until reduced and thickened slightly.

Pasta

500 g (1 lb 2 oz) flour (preferably 00 but you can use plain/all-purpose flour), plus extra for dusting

400 g (14 oz) egg yolks

Some of the liquid will be used to flavour the agnolotti filling, while the rest will be used to coat the agnolotti before serving.

Remove the meat from the bones and leave to cool. Meanwhile, heat a little olive oil in a frying pan over medium heat, add the spinach and cook for 2–3 minutes, until wilted. Repeat with the escarole, cooking until wilted.

Once cooled, place the meat, spinach and escarole in a food processor. Pulse the mixture until finely shredded and combined, then add 100 ml (3½ fl oz) of the reduced cooking liquid, the cream, eggs and parmesan. Season with salt and pepper and pulse until combined. The consistency of the filling should be creamy but not too wet. Transfer the mixture to a piping bag.

To make the pasta, place the flour on a clean work surface and make a well in the centre. Add the egg yolks and use your finger to gradually mix the ingredients together, then knead until you have a smooth and elastic dough – this will take about 10 minutes. Cover with a cloth and leave to rest for 30 minutes.

On a lightly floured work surface and working in batches, roll the pasta through a pasta machine until you have thin sheets, about 1.5–2 mm (⅛ in) thick and 30 cm (12 in) long. Pipe small balls of filling (about ½ teaspoon each), 2 cm (¾ in) apart, along one pasta sheet. Fold the bottom edge of the pasta over the filling to enclose it, then use your fingers to pinch and seal the dough around each ball of filling to remove any air. Use a fluted pasta cutter to cut along the top edge of the dough, then cut between each ball of filling from the edge closest to you, using a firm rolling motion to encourage the dough to fold over the top of the filling slightly, creating a small pleat. Repeat with the remaining dough and filling.

Working in two batches, cook the agnolotti in salted boiling water for 2–3 minutes, until the pasta is cooked through.

Meanwhile, melt 20 g (¾ oz) of butter and 60 ml (¼ cup) of the remaining meat cooking liquid per serve in a large frying pan over medium heat. Add the sage leaves and cook, swirling the pan to emulsify the sauce. Drain the pasta, toss in the buttery sauce and serve.

Trentino-Alto Adige

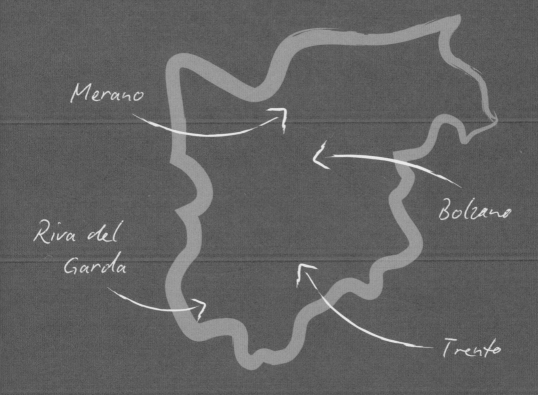

Merano

Bolzano

Riva del Garda

Trento

Regional produce

The mountainous pastures of Trentino-South Tyrol are some of Italy's best, with livestock happily grazing in large expanses of wild grasses, herbs and flowers. There's an endless number of cheeses, cured meats and dairy products in this region, and lamb, pork and beef feature heavily in the traditional stews and sauces. The fruits, vegetables and herbs of the alpine terrain all contribute to the regional cuisine which also boasts fresh fish from icy streams, and wild game and mushrooms from woodlands.

- Arctic char fish
- Asiago
- Barley
- Carne salada
- Graukäse cheese
- Luganega sausage
- Plums
- Polenta
- Puzzone di Moena cheese
- Sauerkraut
- Speck
- Spressa delle Giudicarie cheese
- Trout
- Val di Non's apples

Lake Braies in the Dolomites

I only have one regret when it comes to Trentino-South Tyrol: that it took me over 40 years to get there.

This dynamic region in Northern Italy shares borders with Lombardy and Veneto, as well as Austria and Switzerland. Personally, I find it remains one of the most fascinating and beautifully diverse parts of Italy. The area has such a unique cultural identity, which includes street and shop signs that often feature both Italian and German, while locals also speak Ladin, a regional language.

Exploring the major cities of Bolzano and Trento and the smaller towns dotted across the Dolomites was enriching and thought provoking. It took me a while to get my head around the geography and street names, not to mention the local history; among Italy's border regions, Trentino-South Tyrol shows some of the most obvious signs that it was once a part of another country. Look no further than its other name in Italy, Trentino-Südtirol, to spot the Germanic influence. When you're on the ground you can feel this blend of cultures, from the architecture to the customs and food.

As the region's names indicate, the lie of this land is complicated. While it's a single region, it's run like two – Trentino and South Tyrol. It only became part of Italy in 1919: prior to that, it was part of the Austro-Hungarian Empire. So today, you're as likely to hear German in some parts as you are Italian.

Whatever name you call it by, this region is a true melting pot. If you had to slice it clinically and culturally, further north you have Bolzano, which feels like a trip to Germany, while Trento (which lies further south) feels a little more 'Italian'.

In both these cities, and across the wider region, I've eaten my little heart out, enjoying freshly baked pretzels (page 98) and speck on the streets of Bressanone, while in Bolzano I tried flavoured *canéderli*

(bread dumplings; page 98). Here, I also sacrificed my stomach to an endless number of bakeries in search of the best custard-filled *krapfen* (page 98), my preferred variety of the delicious, sugar-dusted doughnut.

I experienced my first raclette (page 98) high up in the mountains above Merano at a typical *stube* (a wood-lined, alpine restaurant), and life was never the same again after this Swiss extravaganza of melted cheese. In Trento, there was lots of polenta and a dish whose name I love: *strangolapreti* (priest strangler). This pasta varies from region to region, but here, it is a type of gnocchi made with stale bread and spinach, served with butter and sage.

And the desserts! Strudel (page 98) reigns supreme here. Yes, strudel. Just one of the many traditional specialties of this region that proves Italy isn't simply pizza and pasta territory.

I've travelled the length and breadth of this country, but the time spent in this pocket of Italy I will hold close to my heart forever. It's a land of ski trails, mountain scenery and forest bounty, nestled in Italy's Dolomites.

A large swathe of the Dolomites is UNESCO Heritage protected – this designation extends over regional borders into Veneto and Friuli Venezia Giulia. In Trentino-South Tyrol, these mountains are the main attraction. Travellers visiting them can take part in wellness activities, nature walks, skiing and après-ski, all while enjoying Italian hospitality with a Central European touch; here, Renaissance and Baroque monuments are replaced by castles, Romanesque architecture by alpine timber, 'buongiorno' by 'guten Morgen'.

It's a place to escape the chaos of city life, reconnect with the natural world and be utterly awed by the beauty of our planet: a wonderful chance to heal with fresh mountain air, while also experiencing cultural heritage and a wide

array of Michelin-starred restaurants that showcase everything from traditional alpine fare to cutting-edge cuisine.

The chic hotels in the Dolomites juxtapose soft white pillows with hair-raising mountain edges (the drive through this bizarre rock formation isn't for the faint-hearted). It's quintessentially Italian, in that it's a panoramic show-off. I like to describe it as another type of Italy: one that's ever changing in its landscape. It's in constant flux, engendering wonder as the sun rises and sets, every angle offering a different shade, a different perspective. The Dolomites have a special ability to remind us of nature's vastness.

Within all that vastness, the cuisine is a hearty alpine fusion of Italian, Austrian and German influences. The area's rich history, cultural diversity and unique ecosystem are all reflected in its gastronomy.

In South Tyrol, dumplings are the most popular appetiser and come in many flavours, including spinach, cheese, speck, turnip and sweet versions filled with

ricotta, chocolate or apricots. Homemade-pasta lovers can enjoy typical dishes like *schlutzkrapfen* (ravioli) and spinach spätzle (page 98), while potatoes are a staple for soups and main courses, served with grilled trout or as *geröstl* (a potato fry up). And of course, the classic *cotoletta alla viennese* (wiener schnitzel) is served with cranberry jam.

Around the more 'Italian' Trento area, the cuisine is not all that dissimilar, although you will find smoked würstel sausages sitting alongside cured meats like speck. Another must-try is *carne salada* (thinly sliced cooked or raw beef).

And when it comes to dairy, the area around Trento has some of the best pastures anywhere in Italy. The entire region is rich in grazing land though, with large expanses of wild grasses, herbs and flowers which livestock happily graze on. This is reflected in the quality of the region's meat and dairy. Cheese connoisseurs will find much to love across Trentino-South Tyrol, as the region is home to over 200 different types of cheeses.

Many are unique to the northerly province – specialties include the soft and briny Stilfser, fruity Vinschger and Alta Badia, the last of which resembles nutty Swiss cheeses like Gruyere.

As opposed to other parts of Italy, pasta is not usually the star of the first course in Trentino-South Tyrol: that honour is reserved for the area's substantial soups. While dumplings and stuffed pasta dishes like casunziei are popular, the comfort food of choice in this region is probably polenta. It's served in various forms: most commonly with a creamy consistency. It's the perfect accompaniment to Trento's second course meat dishes, such as pork, lamb, venison, boar and even tripe; in line with alpine cuisine, these meats are most often served in hearty stews or braised alongside locally grown vegetables.

Street food is also popular, with stalls in Trento serving up a variety of local delicacies, such as *schüttelbrot* (a crispy rye bread). All over the city and its surrounds, you'll find more traditional Austrian desserts, like *apfelküchel* (apple cake), strudel and *sachertorte* (chocolate cake with apricot jam), which are much the same as their counterparts north of the border.

Conveniently, no matter what season you'd like to come try any of these dishes in, Trentino-South Tyrol is an all-year-round destination with unparalleled hospitality and a cuisine far removed from what you'd expect to find in Italy. So, whether you decide to trek, ski or spa, rest assured you'll eat and drink exceptionally well, with the soulful and ever-present Dolomites as a perfect backdrop for an exploration of the region's eclectic history and culture.

Trentino-Alto Adige

NORTHERN ITALY

Strudel reigns supreme here. Yes, strudel.

Just one of the many traditional specialties of this region that proves Italy isn't simply pizza and pasta territory.

MARIA'S TOP 10 DISHES OF TRENTINO-ALTO ADIGE

1 CANÉDERLI

Also known as *knödel*, *canéderli* are a favourite during the cold Trentino winters. Large dumplings made with stale white bread, chopped speck, onion and chives, they are usually cooked in meat broth and served piping hot.

2 GULASCH ALLA TIROLESE CON POLENTA

Following the standard flavours of goulash, this local version generally has less sauce than the Hungarian original. This stew of beef with onions, cumin, marjoram, garlic, red wine and plenty of paprika is usually served with polenta for a warming winter dish.

3 KAISERSCHMARRN

This is one of the best ways to warm up in the mountains. It's a plate of shredded sweet pancakes flavoured with rum and vanilla and served sprinkled with icing (confectioners') sugar, with a side of red currant jam and sometimes custard for extra luxury.

4 KRAPFEN

With a history that dates to the 17th century, *krapfen* were made for Carnevale celebrations in the Austrian city of Graz. Today, they are also a specialty of Trentino. These yeasted, sweet doughnuts are fried, filled with jam, cream custard or Nutella, then rolled in sugar.

5 POLENTA E CAPUS

Polenta, cabbage and sausage unite in this hearty secondo. The cabbage is thinly sliced and cooked slowly with onions and luganega pork sausages for at least two hours, then served on a bed of polenta.

6 PRETZEL

South Tyrol's ties with Austria are evident in its love affair with the *pretzel*, also known as *bretzel* in dialect. A dough of flour, yeast, water and malt is rolled and formed into the instantly recognisable knotted shapes. They are boiled before being baked to achieve their glossy, dark brown colour.

7 RACLETTE

Although of Swiss origin, *raclette* is also found in many mountain areas of the Dolomites. Similar to fondue, the cheese is melted by the fire or with a special heat lamp, then scraped directly onto a plate with bread, potatoes, vegetables, cured meats and pickles.

8 SPÄTZLE

Spätzle (also called *gnocchetti tirolese* in dialect) are made from a dough of flour, water and egg, with some spinach. The dough is pushed through a perforated, stainless-steel tool which drops little dollops directly into a pan of boiling water. When they rise to the surface, the spätzle are scooped out and added to a sauce of speck, cream and butter.

9 STRUDEL DI MELE

Perfect with a glass of *vin brulé* (mulled wine), *strudel* has Turkish origins but is now a symbol of Trentino-South Tyrol. This treat is made with a roll of delicate, flaky pastry baked around a filling of apples, raisins and cinnamon.

10 TORTA FORESTA NERA / SCHWARZWÄLDER KIRSCHTORTE

Although famously from Germany, Black Forest cake is also found across Austria and in the northern part of Trentino. Multiple layers of chocolate sponge, cherries and whipped cream form this towering and decadent dessert.

Other dishes to look out for

The cuisine of Trentino-South Tyrol is a rich tapestry of indulgent comfort dishes, where fried potato, chunks of meat and melted cheese are all on offer. Add to that a good German-inspired pastry, and you'll be in food heaven.

Antipasti

Smacafam

With a name translating to 'smash hunger', *smacafam* is a savoury cake that crushes the appetite. It is made during the Carnevale period with a dough combined with luganega sausage and pancetta or lardo. It is best eaten straight out of the oven.

Tortei di patate

Despite requiring just three ingredients, *tortei di patate* are a delicious fried potato snack served alongside antipasti of meats and cheeses. To make them, grated potato is mixed with a little flour and a pinch of salt before frying in oil until crispy.

Primi

Minestra da orz

This rustic barley soup comes from the farmers of the Non Valley area. Carrots, potatoes, celery, onions and pancetta are all finely diced and put into a cold pan with barley, water and salt. The soup is cooked slowly on a gentle heat so the flavours have time to blend and the consistency can thicken.

Risotto ai finferli

The woodlands of the region are home to many different varieties of mushrooms that are frequently foraged by locals in late summer and early autumn. Chanterelles are especially popular and, in this dish, they are cooked in a silky, saffron-flavoured risotto.

Schlutzkrapfen

These semicircular pasta shapes from South Tyrol are most commonly filled with spinach and ricotta and are served with butter, chives and parmigiano. Sometimes rye or buckwheat flour is added to the pasta dough for extra bite.

Strangolapreti alla trentina

Literally translated as 'priest strangler', *strangolapreti* are dumplings made with old bread soaked in milk and then mixed with egg, flour and spinach. They are usually served in melted butter and sage or other local herbs.

Tagliatelle con ragù di cervo / capriolo

In Trentino, fresh tagliatelle and pappardelle are commonly matched with a rich tomato ragù, usually made with local *cervo* or *capriolo* (venison) and flavoured with cloves, cinnamon and juniper: perfect for the alpine climate.

Trentino-Alto Adige

NORTHERN ITALY

Secondi

Stinco di maiale affumicato

In this dish, smoked pork shin is roasted or simmered until the meat falls from the bone. It's often cooked with beer or wine along with vegetables, which are then used to make a sauce. Potatoes or polenta and a side of cabbage may also be served.

Stracotto

Known as *tonca de pontesel* in dialect, this stew is a slow-cooked mix of fresh meats, including beef and pork, with pancetta, lardo, wine, and stock thickened with flour. Towards the end of cooking, pieces of luganega sausage are added. The stew is served with polenta.

Uova, patate e speck

This Tirolese specialty is also known as *spiegeleier* (skier's plate) due to its warming and energising qualities. Chunks of potato are boiled and fried in butter with onions, while eggs are fried with strips of smoky speck. It's all plated with chives on top.

Contorni

Crauti alla tirolese

Thinly sliced cabbage is cooked with strips of smoked pancetta and juniper berries until aromatic. Onion is cooked separately in butter, coated in flour then fried until golden. It is then stirred through the cabbage and served with würstel sausages or canéderli.

Insalata di cavolo cappuccio con cumino

This fresh dish balances well with the region's rich flavours. White cabbage is thinly sliced and dressed with olive oil, apple cider vinegar and cumin seeds. It's left for a few hours to allow the flavours to develop before it's served with meats or polenta.

Dolci

Heisse Liebe

Translated as 'hot love', this dessert is indeed a match made in heaven. Cold vanilla gelato is topped with a hot sauce of raspberries, creating a contrast not only between temperatures but also between the sweet cream of the gelato and the acidic kick of the raspberries.

Strauben / Frittelle tirolesi

Eggs, flour, milk, sugar and a dash of grappa form the batter for these fried treats. The batter is poured through a special funnel straight into boiling oil, forming a spiral. The strauben are served coated in icing (confectioners') sugar with cranberry jam on the side.

Torta de fregoloti

This easy almond cake is a simple mix of flour, sugar, butter, almonds, egg yolk and grappa. The result is beautifully light and crumbly.

Torta di grano saraceno

Evidence of Trentino's strong ties with Austria, this cake is found on both sides of the border. It is made from buckwheat flour, grated apple and almond flour or hazelnuts. The slightly bitter, nutty flavour of the sponge is tempered by a middle layer of sweet, sharp berry jam.

Zelten

A rich, jewelled fruitcake made for Christmas, *zelten* gets its name from the German word for 'seldom': a reference to the fact it is only prepared once a year. Dried and candied fruit, nuts, orange zest, rum, nutmeg, cloves and cinnamon are packed into the cake. Traditionally, it is intricately decorated with almonds and candied fruit that form flowers or hearts.

... and to drink

Trentino-South Tyrol's terroir, including its mountainous terrain and diverse microclimates, offers ideal conditions for grape cultivation. It has a cool to moderate overall climate, influenced by the Dolomites, which is especially ideal for sparkling wines: particularly those produced using the *metodo classico* (traditional method).

Despite being in an alpine region, the valley floors here tend to warm up rapidly on summer mornings, sending warm air up to the vineyard-covered slopes. This, along with the bright alpine sunshine, produces rich and ripe wine styles that you wouldn't expect from such a cool and fresh area. The region shares this climate with Ticino in Switzerland, just 160 km (100 miles) to the west and known for its Merlot. The region also sits at the same latitude as central Burgundy in France (which you could say knows its way around good wine!).

Some of the key wine-producing areas in Trentino-South Tyrol are the Adige Valley, the Isarco Valley and the hills around Lake Garda; beyond these areas, the terrain is generally too mountainous for viticulture.

Like much of this corner of Northern Italy, Trentino-South Tyrol is mostly known for its crisp white wines. In the past, the indigenous lagrein and schiava red grape varieties reigned supreme, but nowadays, white wines have taken over in terms of volume, crafted using grapes like pinot grigio, chardonnay and gewürztraminer. These are grown alongside lesser-known names like nosiola; this native variety produces dry and sweet wine and is a key

ingredient in the rare Trentino Vino Santo. Other popular grapes include müller-thurgau and sylvaner, and many winemakers in the region are now experimenting with grape varieties like the indigenous teroldego.

Wine enthusiasts will also want to try the well-regarded Trentodoc. This crisp and refreshing sparkling is produced with the metodo classico between the Alps and Lake Garda. It's pretty perfect for any occasion, with offerings that include blanc de blancs for spring, brut for summer, rose for autumn, and riserva for winter.

Beyond the region's vineyards, local alpine flavours are made into liqueurs and amari like Pasubio, made with mugo pine needles, herbs and wild blueberries. *Latschenschnaps* is made with young, freshly picked pinecones macerated in grappa.

Parampampoli is a mix of wine, coffee, honey, grappa and a top-secret blend of spices that is usually heated and flambeed before serving. Especially popular in winter, this drink is often enjoyed in alpine huts and at the region's famed Christmas markets.

And last but not least, South Tyrol is home to my favourite cocktail – the Hugo, a spritz made with Prosecco, elderflower liqueur and fresh mint.

For those seeking a non-alcoholic beverage, the abundant local apples and grapes are pressed into delicious juices, using only fully ripe, local fruits. To ensure quality, the juices must be produced according to organic fruit-growing guidelines.

Culinary experiences

From a forest spa to a street food tour, you'll find the perfect intersection of nature and luxury in this alpine region's rich experiences.

Fly over the Dolomites and stop off for a mountain barbecue

Luxury tour provider Your Private Italy offers this truly unique mountain adventure that takes you to the skies! Your experience begins with a panoramic helicopter ride to San Cassiano, the heart of the Dolomites, where you'll meet your private guide and take a cable car up the mountain range. Enjoy a scenic hike through the green mountain valley before arriving at your private hut on the top of the Piz plateau for a traditional barbecue lunch. Afterwards, take in the breathtaking view one last time before a helicopter transfer back to your starting point. This really is a once-in-a-lifetime experience.

YOURPRIVATEITALY.COM

Forest cuisine and a spa hideaway at Forestis

Set above the clouds at 1,800 m (6,000 ft) above sea level, Forestis is a stylish and sophisticated adults-only spa hotel. Its idyllic setting in a densely wooded forest in the majestic Dolomites makes for a breathtaking panorama. Enjoy the spectacular views from the expansive restaurant, spa and opulent suites or the two penthouses, each with private pool and spruce wood sauna. You can take advantage of the location and ski in and out of the retreat, breathing in the purest mountain air (at the turn of the 19th century, Austrians built a tuberculosis sanatorium on the site because of the unmatched air quality!). Lock yourself away in this luxurious alpine world of wonder with healing spa treatments, foraging experiences and sustainable forest cuisine that combines ancient techniques and prized mountain produce with modern flair. Then wind down in the evenings at one of the world's highest bars with forest-infused cocktails.

FORESTIS.IT

Take a street food tour in Bolzano

Let experts guide you through Bolzano, a quaint town where you'll discover businesses that are a living testimony to local history. You'll get to savour at least five delicacies along the way, from the best sausage in town to the local breads and sweets. Finally, finish up with wine or craft beer. All the while, you'll see monuments and learn about this multicultural region's fascinating and complex history. Tours at Christmastime mix food with light shows and decorations, creating a magical atmosphere. The team also runs wine tastings, cooking classes and cheese workshops.

BOLZANOSTREETFOODTOUR.COM

Visit an apple orchard in Merano

Explore the story behind the South Tyrolean apple on a tour led by CAFA, Merano's local fruit cooperative. After a short introductory film, specialists take you through facilities where you learn about storage, sorting, packaging and transportation. They'll reveal some of the secrets behind the local apple's quality, its varieties and how to store them at home. At the end, you get to taste plenty of apples! Combine the tour with a stay high above Merano at Miramonti Boutique Hotel, with its striking infinity pool and classic Stube restaurant, where you must give in to a luscious raclette dinner.

MERANO-SUEDTIROL.IT, HOTEL-MIRAMONTI.COM

Food- and wine-filled days around Trento

Trento is a great base for your adventures across the region. Visit local markets like the one at Piazza delle Erbe to find fresh produce, cheese and meats. When all the food makes you thirsty, book into a wine tasting tour. Trento is especially renowned for its sparkling varietals, and you won't be short of wine bars for an aperitivo. Download the TrentoDoc app for more than 200 labels to try at over 60 local winemakers. To wind down, premier hotel spa brand Lefay has a Dolomites property just an hour northwest of Trento. Their state-of-the-art wellness facilities come with the perfect mountain backdrop.

TRENTODOC.COM, DOLOMITI.LEFAYRESORTS.COM

SAGRE

JANUARY

Maratona dei Canéderli, Marathon race and canéderli festival, Val di Casies

MARCH

FarmFood Festival, Local products festival, Merano

Festival del Formaggio, Cheese festival, Campo Tures

JULY

Giornate dello Yogurt, Festival of yoghurt, Vipiteno

AUGUST

Note di Birra, Beer festival, Arco

SEPTEMBER

Festa dello Speck, Speck festival, Bolzano

Knödelfest-Festa del Canederlo, Festival of canéderli, Imer

OCTOBER

Pomaria, Apple festival, Cles

Dolo-Vini-Miti, Wine festival, Val di Cembra

Törggelen, Open farmhouses wine and food evenings, Valle Isarco

Culinarium Urtijëi, Culinary festival of tastings and dinners, Ortisei

NOVEMBER

Merano WineFestival, Wine event, Merano

Strudel di mele

Apple strudel

Few desserts are as comforting as the humble apple strudel. Despite the recipe now spanning the world with numerous interpretations, for the definitive version it's always good to head to the source. I spent an unforgettable time at Lefay Resort & SPA in the Dolomites. Yes, the place is stunning and, yes, the massages were divine, but to me the strudel, being one of my all-time favourite desserts, was the true taste of the region. This version, from Chef Matteo Maenza, wraps up all that strudel signifies in a recipe that encapsulates family Sunday lunches, passed from generation to generation.

SERVES 6

40 g (¼ cup) pine nuts

700 g (1 lb 9 oz) apples, (preferably rennet or golden delicious variety) peeled, cored and cut into small pieces (about 1 cm/½ in)

60 g (2 oz) granulated sugar

50 g (1¾ oz) raisins

zest of 1 lemon

50 ml (1¾ fl oz) rum

1 tablespoon ground cinnamon

25 g (1 oz) butter, melted

50 g (1¾ oz) dried breadcrumbs

beaten egg, to glaze the pastry

icing (confectioners') sugar, for dusting

Pastry

160 g (5½ oz) plain (all-purpose) flour, plus extra for dusting

1 tablespoon sunflower oil

1 egg

To make the pastry, put the flour and a pinch of salt in a large bowl, make a well in the centre and add 50 ml (1¾ fl oz) of water, along with the oil and egg. Use a fork to mix everything together, then knead the dough on a lightly floured work surface for 1–2 minutes to form a smooth ball. Cover with plastic wrap and leave to rest for 30 minutes.

Preheat the oven to 180°C (350°F) fan-forced.

Toast the pine nuts in a small frying pan over medium heat for 2–3 minutes, until golden.

Place the apple, toasted pine nuts, sugar, raisins, lemon zest, rum and cinnamon in a large bowl and gently mix to combine.

To assemble the strudel, place a large sheet of baking paper on a clean work surface and dust with a little flour. Roll out the pastry, adding a sprinkle of flour to stop the dough from sticking, to form a 35 cm × 45 cm (13¾ in × 17¾ in) rectangle, about 2 mm (¹⁄₁₆ in) thick. If the pastry becomes too elastic and springs back as you roll it, allow it to rest for a minute or two.

Brush the pastry lightly with the melted butter and sprinkle over the breadcrumbs. Now spread the apple filling over the top, leaving a 2 cm (¾ in) border on three sides and taking the filling to the edge on the long side closest to you. Fold the short sides of the pastry over the filling, then, starting from the long edge, carefully roll up the strudel, using the baking paper to help you, until you have a log with the seam underneath. Carefully transfer the strudel on the baking paper to a large baking tray, then brush all over with the beaten egg.

Transfer the strudel on the tray to the oven and bake for 30 minutes, then reduce the temperature to 170°C (340°F) and continue to cook for another 25–30 minutes, until the pastry is crisp and lightly golden.

Remove the strudel from the oven and allow to cool to room temperature. Dust with icing sugar, then cut into slices and serve.

Valle
d'Aosta

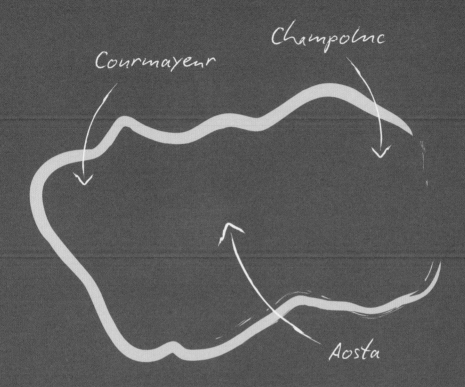

Courmayeur

Champoluc

Aosta

Regional produce

It was historically difficult to supply fresh products to Aosta Valley – an isolated, mountainous area – which created a dependency on locally grown and reared produce. Though now easier to reach, Italy's smallest region still has limited flat space for farming, concentrating on cattle, orchard fruits and wild game. The alpine climate calls for heavy, winter dishes of meat, cheese and polenta or potatoes in place of the South's pasta and tomatoes.

- Apples
- Boudin blood sausage
- Brossa cream
- Chamois meat
- Fontina cheese
- Fromadzo cheese
- Honey
- Jambon de Bosses ham
- Lard D'Arnad lardo
- Mocetta
- Porcini mushrooms
- Reblec cheese
- Séras ricotta
- Toma di Gressoney cheese
- Trout

Breuil-Cervinia

A osta Valley is the last of Italy's 20 regions that I ticked off my list. Before visiting this far north alpine treasure, I imagined green hills, castles, fondue and a lot of yodelling, and that's precisely what I found – that and a whole lot more.

Aosta Valley is the smallest and least populated region in the country. It's wedged right between Piedmont, France and Switzerland, and it's bursting with natural treasures beyond mountaineering and ski resorts, from valleys to lakes and waterfalls.

Thanks to its location, it boasts an eclectic blend of French and Italian influences, creating the unique hybrid culture known as Valdostan. You can see and feel these influences in the region's charming alpine architecture, hearty mountain cuisine and preservation of the fascinating local language, Franco-Provençal, or Valdôtain.

The legacy of the Romans who conquered the region in 25 BCE lives on, captivating visitors with ruins that are a tangible connection to the past. The valley became part of Italy in 1821, but its ties to the former royal House of Savoy endure, infusing the region's way of life with Savoyard traditions. The locals effortlessly navigate between French and Italian, enriching the Valdostani cultural fabric.

The capital, Aosta, exudes charm with its captivating blend of Roman ruins and medieval architecture. On my visit, I loved exploring the well-preserved Roman walls and picturesque old town with its narrow cobblestone streets. The city and its landmarks, such as the Roman Theatre and the Arch of Augustus, are framed by snow-capped mountains, the stunning surrounds offering ample opportunities for outdoor adventures.

Towering above the capital and the wider region are some of Europe's iconic peaks, including the awe-inspiring Mont Blanc,

the legendary Matterhorn, the majestic Monte Rosa and dizzying Gran Paradiso. The region offers unparalleled snow experiences: here, you can descend daringly into France and Switzerland via glaciers or soar through the skies in cable cars, including those of the Skyway Monte Bianco, a marvel of engineering.

While Aosta Valley is a coveted destination for savvy skiers during the winter, it's a perfect summer destination too, with small villages to wander, trails for hikers and culinary traditions that have started to attract food connoisseurs all year round.

At an elevation of 1,224 m (4,000 ft), Courmayeur stands proudly as the region's crown jewel and one of its most popular destinations. Here, I ate my weight in cheese! The illustrious resort town is renowned for its breathtaking scenery and has rightfully earned a reputation for luxury. Its offerings span access to world-class slopes, après-ski entertainment and lavish hotels. With its proximity to Milan, Courmayeur is a favoured destination among skiers, not least because it boasts an impressive array of over 100 km (60 miles) of ski runs and a staggering 14 peaks reaching extreme altitudes. Visitors have easy access to the legendary Vallée Blanche, the world's longest lift-served run, and adventurers can also effortlessly reach the lofty heights of the Punta Helbronner viewpoint, at a staggering 3,462 m (11,400 ft) high.

This adventuring is sure to stir appetites, and Courmayeur provides a cuisine designed to give you energy and keep you warm. You can't help but feel grateful for life here, enjoying the ultimate in comfort food with the imposing beauty of Mont Blanc in view from any angle. With the peak as the perfect, snow-white backdrop to my visit, I ate incredible dishes like alpine foraged porcini mushroom, crumbed and fried golden, and *zuppa alla valdostana* (a delectable cheese and bread soup). I dipped wholegrain

*You can't help but feel
    grateful for life here,
enjoying the ultimate
in comfort food with
the imposing beauty of
    Mont Blanc in view
from any angle.*

croutons and slow-cooked polenta into *fonduta* (Fontina cheese fondue; page 112), and I sampled the creamiest and most unforgettable alpine milk–flavoured ice cream.

The region's agricultural economy relies on mountain cattle, which provide dairy and meat. The milk and butter from these cows are high quality, and cheese – particularly the prized Fontina – plays a vital role in the local diet. This alpine cheese is the star of the region and features in many of the iconic local dishes, including fonduta, risotto and polenta. Together with prosciutto, it also helps fill the local version of a cordon bleu, the *costolette alla valdostana* (page 112).

Polenta is the staple carbohydrate, often served alongside rich stews. In this region, it's enhanced by Fontina – this preparation is known as *polenta concia* (page 112). Polenta is also used for *chnolle* (page 112), a local variety of gnocchi or dumpling. Then

there's the symbol of Gressoney-Saint-Jean, *chnéffléne* (page 112); these are similar to spätzle (page 98), and are served topped with Toma, a luscious mix of local butter and cheese.

Beef stews and soups and salted beef are common dishes, while local game and pork also feature on the menu. Aosta Valley's preservation traditions are evident in its protected charcuterie specialties, including Speck, a local variety of the smoky cured ham; Jambon de Bosses, another dry-cured ham; and Lard d'Arnad, a local variation of lardo.

The region's limited farmland means there's not a big focus on vegetables, although onions and cabbages are used in stews, and local herbs add freshness to dishes. In the far north, the mountain areas are historically known for dishes like *seupa à la vapelenentse* (page 112) – a layered soup made with day-old bread, butter and Fontina

Gressoney-Saint-Jean

(of course) – and the popular, hearty stew *soça* (page 112). And from the French House of Savoy's repertoire comes the decadent bake *tartiflette*, a mix of potatoes, lardons and onions traditionally topped with a round of Reblochon (or sometimes Fontina around here).

Apples, pears, walnuts and chestnuts thrive in the alpine climate, and they feature widely in pies, pastries, preserves and salumi boards. Then there is the traditional bread, known as *pan ner*, made with rye and wheat flour, again reflecting the hearty and fibre-filled diet in the mountainous region.

For dessert, *tegole valdostane* (tile-shaped hazelnut-flavoured cookies) are a popular treat, accompanied by coffee, cream or chocolate. And speaking of chocolate, the locals in Cogne, a town in the centre of the region, are quite protective of their version of chocolate mousse. The velvety *crema di Cogne* has a hint of rum and is topped with

crushed nuts. There's also *flantze* (page 112), a cookie-type treat, and – at Christmastime – *mécoulin* (page 114), a raisin-filled sweet bread that resembles the classic panettone (page 68).

The region is a bit like these desserts: a small, unexpected delight. Aosta Valley is a haven of natural wonders and heart-warming dishes. In fact, you'll probably come for the skiing or the scenery, the castles or the glaciers, but you're guaranteed to leave impressed by the food and cultural fusion.

MARIA'S TOP 10 DISHES OF VALLE D'AOSTA

1 CHNÉFFLÉNE

Similar to Tyrolean spätzle (page 98), these tiny dumplings from the Gressoney Valley are made by pressing a dough of flour, egg and milk through a perforated gadget straight into boiling water. They're then drained and served with onion softened in butter and topped with a dash of black pepper or Toma.

2 CHNOLLE

An alpine take on gnocchi, *chnolle* use polenta or cornmeal in place of potato. They are usually boiled in water or meat broth, but can also be baked in the oven with cooked rice and Fontina for the much-loved *riso e chnolle*.

3 COSTOLETTE ALLA VALDOSTANA

To prepare this dish, a boneless veal cutlet is slit open, filled with prosciutto and Fontina, and then coated with egg and breadcrumbs. The *costolette* are rigorously fried in plenty of butter until beautifully golden with an oozy cheese filling.

4 FLANTZE

Bread in this region used to be baked in communal ovens just a few times a year and distributed to all the locals. Bakers would turn any left-over bread into *flantze*, a sweet creation of rye flour dough enriched with dried fruit, nuts and butter. Even though it's now sold in bakeries, it's still inextricably linked to the history of the region.

5 FONDUTA VALDOSTANA

Perhaps the region's most famous dish, *fonduta* is a culinary demonstration of Aosta Valley's proximity to Switzerland. It uses the ever-present Fontina, this time melted and mixed with eggs, milk and butter. It's served at the table in a fondue pot, surrounded by bread and potatoes to dip in the silky, cheesy blend.

6 INVOLTINI DI FÉNIS

A slightly different version of the classic Italian *involtino* (meat roll), this dish comes from the town of Fénis. Thin veal escalopes are filled with Fontina and a local cured meat called *mocetta*, which is made from lean cuts of meat, usually beef. The involtini are fried in butter then flambeed in brandy, with a drizzle of cream added to the sauce before serving.

7 POLENTA CONCIA

This recipe is a luscious amalgamation of polenta, butter and melted cubes of Fontina. It's eaten either by itself or served as a side with stews or roasted meats: the perfect warming dish to stave off the cold mountain temperatures.

8 SEUPA À LA VAPELENENTSE

Prepared in the cold mountains in the region's north, this casserole is made from layers of day-old bread and slices of Fontina. A meat broth with savoy cabbage is poured over the layers, followed by a drizzle of cinnamon-infused butter, before the whole thing is baked in the oven.

9 SOÇA

Hailing from Cogne, *soça* sees the Valdostana staples of beef, savoy cabbage, potatoes and Fontina come together in one inviting dish. The meat, which is first marinated in salt and herbs, is cooked with the vegetables on the stove before being baking in the oven with slices of the cheese and melted butter.

10 TEGOLE

Invented in the 1930s, *tegole* were inspired by a recipe from Normandy. One of Aosta Valley's best-loved sweets, these thin, moreish cookies are made with almond and hazelnut, and also come in a chocolate-coated variety. One is never enough!

Other dishes to look out for

Enjoyed against a scenic alpine backdrop, the cuisine of this compact region is warming and cheese-loaded. Cosy fondues, hearty soups, exquisite sweets ... hit the slopes and ski straight into these irresistible dishes!

Primi

Favò e puarò

Favò e puarò are the two most common soups of the region. *Favò*, from the town of Aymavilles, uses broad (fava) beans, which are boiled with a small pasta shape, then mixed with cubes of local rye bread, Fontina, butter and herbs. *Puarò* uses leeks and potato instead, stirred together with meat stock.

Gnocchi alla bava

This dish's name captures how enticing it is: *bava* literally translates to 'drool'. In true Valdostana style, this first course matches classic potato gnocchi with the requisite Fontina, which is mixed with milk or cream to create a hot, cheesy sauce.

Secondi

Carbonade valdostana

Not just any beef stew, the Aosta Valley *carbonade* is characterised by its dark, almost black colour, which gives it its name (*carbone* means 'coal'). The distinctive shade comes from marinating the meat and then cooking it low and slow in red wine, seasoned with warming cloves, cinnamon and bay leaves.

Civet di camoscio

The chamois goats of the region provide the gamey flavour for this local stew. Chunks of meat are slowly cooked with a base of carrot, celery, onion, herbs and lashings of red wine for an inviting dish served with polenta.

Milza ripiena

The Aosta Valley recipe for *milza* (veal spleen) sees it sliced down one side and hollowed to form a pocket. The scooped-out spleen is then combined with left-over meat, which is chopped, along with garlic, parsley and parmigiano, with egg used to bind the mixture. This is stuffed into the spleen's pocket, which is secured and boiled for two hours.

Dolci

Crema di Cogne

This dessert is perfect served with Aosta Valley's great cookies. Cogne's *crema* is a thick chocolate cream made with egg yolks, cream, sugar and rum. It's served warm with grated chocolate, chopped hazelnuts or flaked almonds on top, and eaten with a spoon or, even better, scooped up with tegole.

Valle d'Aosta

NORTHERN ITALY

Mécoulin

The first snowfall used to indicate it was
time to start preparing this sweet bread,
which is the local version of panettone.
Now made throughout the year, although
principally at Easter and Christmas,
mécoulin is a light, fluffy cake flavoured
with lemon zest and rum-soaked raisins.

Torcetti di Saint Vincent

Saint Vincent's famous *torcetti* cookies
are ideal for dipping in tea, coffee or sweet
wine. They're made with a butter-infused,
leavened dough which is rolled into strips,
each of which is then pinched together at
the end to form a ring-shaped cookie. Once
baked, they're dusted with a sugar coating.

... and to drink

Nestled in the Alps, Italy's smallest region boasts a rich, alpine winemaking tradition influenced by both Italy and France. Aosta Valley's viticultural heart sits in the narrow mountain valley stretching from the heights of Mont Blanc to the Piedmont border. This strip of land offers a unique blend of vines and terroir, with a number of designated DOC areas.

Most of the region's vineyards are situated on the steep, south-facing slopes above the Dora Baltea river, with the best vineyards found on the lower slopes; these ascend to altitudes of around 1,300 m (0.8 miles). The climate where they grow is unique, with warm and dry summer days followed by significantly cooler nights. To mitigate this temperature variation, vignerons train vines into pergolas, ensuring even distribution of ground heat during cold nights. Terracing is also common in the fragmented vineyards, aiding accessibility during harvest and preventing erosion. The conditions and thin, rocky soils are demanding, but they result in exceptional grapes that yield fascinating, complex wines.

You'll find red and white wines from a diverse selection of native and introduced grape varieties. Given the region's proximity to France, there are French names like chardonnay and gamay, alongside Italian specialties like dolcetto and the most popular: picotendro, the local variant of nebbiolo.

Several grapes native to the region are well suited for varietal wines, while others are used exclusively in blends. Notable examples include petit rouge, fumin and vien de nus, which contribute to the creation of taut, spicy red wines. Fruity white wines

Valle d'Aosta

are also produced in both dry and sweet styles using grapes like prie blanc, moscato bianco and pinot grigio.

And around these parts, you'll find digestif liqueurs including amari distilled with varieties of alpine shrubs. Grappa is also very popular: the perfect way to end rich, hearty meals. Look out too for *génépy* (or *genepì*) – a herbal liqueur made from local mountain ingredients like wormwood. While it originated over the border in France, it has become a regional favourite. Enjoyed on its own, it's also mixed together with cognac and grappa to spice up coffee: this creation is called *caffè alla valdostana*, and is more of a ritual than a drink. Traditionally, the ingredients are infused together in a purpose-made, hand-carved wooden 'friendship cup' used for communal drinking.

Culinary experiences

Blend a glam ski trip with a culinary adventure, get up close to heritage winemaking traditions or take a deep dive into the regional cheese scene – it's all here in this luxurious pocket of Italy.

Escape to nature with a gourmet eco stay in the picturesque Champoluc

At Au Charmant Petit Lac Ecohotel Spa & Parc, nature lovers can take scenic hikes around the Blue Lake, explore lush forests and swoon at the breathtaking views. Fishing enthusiasts can throw a line and snag a trout or other freshwater fish in the crystal-clear waters. For those seeking relaxation and rejuvenation, there's a spa as well as outdoor yoga and meditation. From wellbeing to fine dining, this is a perfect, immersive escape amid nature's splendour. Here in Champoluc, you'll also find the Hotellerie de Mascognaz, where you can feast on local food while taking in the peace of a stone village overlooking Monte Rosa (at an altitude of 2,000 m/6,600 ft!).

CHARMANTPETITLAC.COM
HOTELLERIEDEMASCOGNAZ.COM

Wellness, skiing and dining in Courmayeur

In recent years, Courmayeur has joined the prestigious Best of the Alps group, alongside 12 other renowned ski resorts like Chamonix and St Moritz. Beyond its magnificent slopes, the area is known for its alpine identity, commitment to the environment and luxury hospitality, with the option to book into cosy boutique hotels like the Auberge de la Maison. A stay here perfectly combines a town and mountain experience. Take in the chalet-style decor, soak away stress with alpine herb–infused spa treatments or feast on local dishes inspired by Mont Blanc flavours. Cadran Solaire, the hotel's off-site restaurant in the heart of the town, serves up heritage Aosta Valley cuisine and has some hidden, private dining rooms and a garden terrace.

AUBERGEMAISON.IT

Try wines at the region's largest private winery

The renowned Les Crêtes winery was established in 1989 and is known for crafting exceptional wines from indigenous grape varieties. Its vineyards, situated on steep slopes, benefit from a high altitude and a cool climate. With a focus on quality and sustainability, Les Crêtes produces wines that reflect the unique terroir of the valley region. You can experience its winemaking heritage firsthand with tastings and guided tours. In the winery's tasting room, you'll get to sample the wines and learn about production, with an option to try local cheeses.

LESCRETES.IT

Lose yourself in the world of Fontina

Fontina, made from unpasteurised milk and aged for 90 days, embodies this region's rich traditions. A visit to the Fontina Cooperative is an immersive, educational experience and cheese lover's dream. Established in 1957 with 46 partners, the cooperative now encompasses 200 members producing over 200,000 wheels of Fontina annually. Step into the ageing grotto, where walls adorned with wheels stretch endlessly, showcasing the dedication to quality. At the cooperative, a tasting journey awaits, with the chance to enjoy variations, from the classic to smoked, alongside the sublime Fontina Alpeggio, made with milk from cows grazing at over 600 m (2,000 ft).

FONTINA-VALLEDAOSTA.IT

Visit the home of this region's ham of excellence

Located just 20 minutes out of Aosta, the Prosciuttificio de Bosses is the home of the famed DOP Vallée d'Aoste Jambon de Bosses. This unique, high-quality product dates to the 14th century and is the pride of the region. Take a guided tour to learn about the intricate production process behind jambon, which is distinct from traditional Italian prosciutto. The latter is dried, but jambon is hung in an ageing room to catch the air currents, infusing it with its distinct flavour. Meticulously prepared, the meat maintains its succulence. If you didn't appreciate the artistry of ham curing before your visit, you certainly will after.

DEBOSSES.IT

SAGRE

JANUARY

Polenta e Peperonata, Polenta festival, Pont-Saint-Martin

FEBRUARY

Fagiolata della Verna, Bean festival, Pont-Saint-Martin

JUNE

Prosciut Tiamo, Prosciutto festival, Saint-Marcel

Bierfest, Beer festival, Gressoney-Saint-Jean

JULY

Festa del Jambon de Bosses DOP, Prosciutto festival, Saint-Rhémy-en-Bosses

Sagra della Seupa à la Vapelenentse, Bread and cheese soup festival, Valpelline

AUGUST

Festa del Lardo di Arnad, Arnad lardo festival, Arnad

Festa di Trifolle, Potato festival, Allein

CHOCOLAThuile, Chocolate festival, La Thuile

OCTOBER

Festa delle Mele, Apple festival, Gressan

BY NICOLA RICCIARDI, CADRAN SOLAIRE
AT AUBERGE DE LA MAISON

La fonduta del cadran

Cadran's fondue

As cliched as it sounds, the first time I tasted this dish in
Courmayeur I felt I'd died and gone to cheese heaven! If there was
one dish that could iconically represent this region, this would be
it. It warms the heart and soul, and is pure comfort food at its best.
Cadran Solaire is the off-site restaurant of the Mont Blanc boutique
hotel haven that is Auberge de la Maison. Owned by the Garin
family, the restaurant showcases heritage recipes of the region,
and I promise that recreating this fonduta at home will transport
you to the Italian Alps at first bite.

Valle d'Aosta

NORTHERN ITALY

SERVES 4

250 g (9 oz) rindless Fontina
DOP, cut into 1 cm (½ in) cubes

200 ml (7 fl oz) full-cream
(whole) milk

2 tablespoons cream

3 tablespoons rice flour

To serve

boiled potatoes

polenta chips

toasted rye bread (see Note)

Note: In Aosta Valley, fonduta
is typically served with toasted
rye bread known locally as
pane nero (black bread).
You can also use any close-
crumbed or other rustic bread.

Place the Fontina, milk, cream and rice flour in a bowl
and stir to combine. Cover with plastic wrap, then set
aside in the fridge overnight.

The next day, set a heatproof bowl over a saucepan
of barely simmering water. Add the cheese mixture and
cook, whisking occasionally, for 20 minutes or until the
cheese has melted into a smooth sauce.

Strain the fonduta through a fine-mesh sieve into
a serving bowl and serve with boiled potatoes, polenta
chips and toasted rye bread for dipping into the
cheese sauce.

Veneto

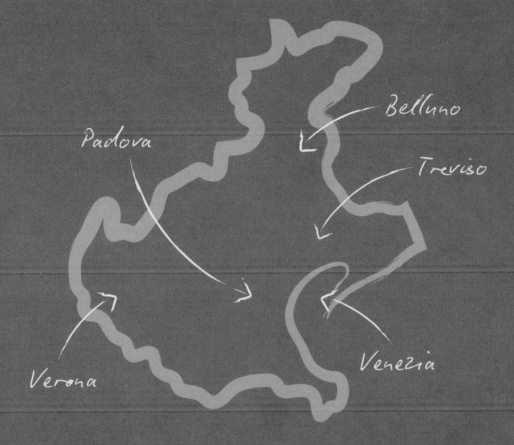

Padova

Belluno

Treviso

Verona

Venezia

Regional produce

While Veneto is known for seafood from
the Venetian lagoon and its coast and
ports, the region's inland and mountain
areas also produce quality meats and
renowned cheeses. Rice, legumes and
corn abound, contributing to the wide
range of recipes utilising risotto, beans
and polenta, while leafy lettuces, white
asparagus and bitter radicchio are the
region's signature vegetable elements.

- Asiago cheese
- Baccalà
- Bassano's white asparagus
- Biancoperla corn
- Cotechino
- Horse meat
- Lamon beans
- Lusia's lettuce
- Montasio cheese
- Polenta
- Soft-shell crab
- Soprèssa Vicentina
- Taleggio
- Treviso's radicchio
- Vialone Nano rice

Venice

In pictures from one of my first visits to Veneto, my parents and I are feeding the pigeons of St Mark's Square in our finest 1980s fashions. At that age, I'm pretty sure a gelato was on my mind. As luck would have it, I've had the chance to enjoy the dessert in Venice since then, though in more up-to-date fashion.

Venice, that shimmering, fairytale-like city on the water, attracts millions of tourists every year – either to Carnevale, the Biennale, the film festival or simply to cruise the Grand Canal. It's a cinematic city of winding canals, gondoliers and ornate bridges, with a fascinating cuisine that I've had the pleasure to slowly discover on my many visits.

But discovering that cuisine can be a challenge: roaming Venice is a tight squeeze, as it's one of Italy's most visited cities, and the tourist-heavy St Mark's and Rialto areas are full of mediocre restaurants. You've got to work to find good food – not because it's rare, but because large swathes of the city are now commercial tourist havens and locals are protective of their traditions.

When you manage to escape the tourist areas, though, the cuisine reflects both the city's unique location on the Venetian lagoon (which comprises a staggering 118 islands) and its rich cultural history as a major maritime force during the Middle Ages and Renaissance. Venice's strategic location on the Adriatic Sea allowed it to establish a powerful merchant fleet and trading posts throughout the Mediterranean, Black Sea and the Middle East, making the city a hub for luxury goods, spices and exotic ingredients.

As a city on water, Venice, along with the surrounding islands, naturally has a fishing heritage. This is especially palpable on Burano, where fishermen painted their houses in bright colours to make them more visible from the sea, and to distinguish them from each other. The vibrant colours are iconic, as is the food you can find on the island. I often crave Burano's specialties, like *risotto di gò* (page 126), made with goby fish typical to the lagoon, and *moeche* (page 126), a fried dish of baby crabs that are found only in the lagoon, and only during spring and autumn – a reflection of the area's unique eco-climate, which allows for so many dishes that can only be found here.

The same can be said of the wider Veneto region, with its unique blend of mountains, fertile valley plains and proximity to the Adriatic Sea. Belluno, in the Dolomites on the Austrian border, has an alpine repertoire of cheese, venison and filled casunziei pasta (page 127). Further south, Treviso is said to be where tiramisù (page 126) – the world's favourite Italian dessert – was created. And we can thank Vicenza for Asiago and Padua for Aperol, one of the world's most popular aperitifs.

The province of Verona, which is separated from Lombardy to the east by Lake Garda, is home to the Bardolino winemaking area, and it's also where you'll find many variations of risotto on offer. The city of Verona was made famous by Shakespeare's famous star-crossed lovers, Romeo and Juliet, and is also known for its star-shaped *pandoro*: a sweet brioche-style cake dusted with icing (confectioners') sugar to evoke the snowy peaks of the Dolomites. At Christmastime it rivals the Milanese panettone (page 68), and Italians usually place their loyalty with one or the other. I am generally team pandoro because it's made without candied fruit, which I'm not a huge fan of. Its recipe is similar to that of another Christmas cake: *nadalin*, a flatter, less-commercialised version that traces its roots to the 1200s. Many Veronese prefer this cake due to its long link to the city.

Beyond the region's cakes, Veneto's choice of carbohydrate isn't the typical pasta. Here, that role is played by the double act of polenta and rice.

The Veneti have been eating polenta since Roman times, and it's served in a variety of ways, from soft and creamy to crispy and fried. One popular preparation is *polenta e osei*, a dish that combines creamy polenta with small game birds, such as quail and pigeon. The dish is a symbol of the region's rural heritage and is typically served around Christmas. Then you have *risi e bisi* (rice and peas; page 127), which is a much-loved local treat.

There *is* one pasta that you'll find throughout the region, though, and that's *bigoli* (page 126). While locals debate its origins, they agree that it dates to the 15th-century Venetian–Turkish wars. Most theories suggest that after losing a lot of durum to the Turks, the Venetians began stretching their pasta dough with common wheat flour, and so bigoli was born.

With the region's proximity to the coast, seafood is a big part of Venetian cuisine. Classics like sarde in saor (page 126),

baccalà mantecato (page 126), baccalà alla vicentina (page 128), and risotto di mare feature the region's abundant offerings, from sardines and anchovies to mussels and prawns (shrimp).

Veneto boasts decent cheese production too, with varieties like the cow's milk Asiago (fresh and aged) and Grana Padano. In terms of salumi, you'll find soprèssa, made with roughly ground meat and a hint of garlic.

And, of course, these are all complemented by wine, Prosecco or a spritz. Yes, the spritz: whether prepared with Aperol or Select, the cocktail is seen on bar tables from Treviso to Padua to Venice.

In Venice, the canals are lined with *bàcari* (bars) serving up drinks during the city's version of aperitivo: *ombre e cicchetti* (wine and bar snacks). *Ombre* means 'shadow' in Italian, and is the Venetian term for a glass of wine. Why? No one can say. There's a number of stories that locals can't agree on (some relating to drinking wine under the shadow of St Mark's bell tower).

Etymology aside, cicchetti culture is deeply rooted in the social fabric of Venice, with locals gathering after work to chat with friends and enjoy a few casual drinks and snacks. I love how you can walk into any bar and there will be a spread of tiny delights for you to sample, like meatballs, fried calamari, mini sandwiches and little crostini topped with all sorts of local, seasonal produce. Unlike aperitivo across the rest of the country, here it feels like it's always ready and waiting for you. On average, each piece will set you back just a couple of euros.

The city's famous markets, such as the Rialto and its Pescheria, have long been sources of fresh produce and seafood, while the influence of nearby regions like Friuli Venezia Giulia, Lombardy and Emilia-Romagna can be seen in dishes like *pasta e fagioli* (pasta with beans). Venetian cuisine has also been influenced

Palazzo del Capitaniato, Vicenza

... Veneto's cuisine has a centuries-long history that combines produce from the sea, lagoon, plains and mountains.

by the city's Jewish community, which dates to the 16th century. Dishes like risi e bisi and *fegato alla veneziana* (Venetian-style liver) are rooted in Jewish cooking traditions. Today, the city's cuisine continues to evolve and adapt to modern tastes while still honouring its rich history and cultural heritage.

From cicchetti to risotto, pandoro to tiramisù, Veneto's cuisine has a centuries-long history that combines produce from the sea, lagoon, plains and mountains. This dynamism makes for a fascinating menu that leaves me wanting to learn more every time I visit. Add to that the homestyle dishes you find in small, cosy bars, trattorie and osterie, and Veneto has you feeling more and more like a local with each visit.

MARIA'S TOP 10 DISHES OF VENETO

1 BACCALÀ MANTECATO

Baccalà mantecato is used extensively for Venetian cicchetti and can also be eaten as an antipasto. Rehydrated and boiled stockfish is whisked with a gradual addition of oil to create a dense, mayonnaise-like sauce that is usually spooned onto bread or polenta before serving.

2 BIGOLI IN SALSA

Veneto's beloved *bigoli* are a thick spaghetti with a rough exterior, which catches the accompanying sauce. Originally made with buckwheat flour, they are now more commonly prepared with white or wholemeal (whole-wheat) flour. In Venice, bigoli are usually served with *salsa*, a mixture of salted anchovies or sardines and onions, but the pasta can also be partnered with a thick, meat-based ragù.

3 CICCHETTI DI VENEZIA

Found on every bar counter in Venice, *cicchetti* are a type of Venetian tapas which are served throughout the day with an *ombre* (glass of wine). They usually consist of crostini or blocks of polenta topped with local cheese, vegetables, cured meat or seafood, but can also be small fried snacks, meatballs or fried fish.

4 GRATIN POLESANO

This comforting dish comes from the town of Rovigo, southwest of Venice. Slices of potato are layered with pancetta and fontina and covered in vegetable stock, then baked in the oven until the liquid is absorbed and the top is bubbling.

5 MOECHE FRITTE

A delicacy from the depths of the Venetian lagoon, *moeche* are small, baby crabs that are caught during the few hours when they are without their hard outer shell and still soft and tender. They are doused in a batter of flour and egg, then fried.

6 POLENTA

A staple of Veneto, both the yellow and pearly white *biancoperla* varieties of polenta are used as a side for fish and meat dishes. While other regions serve the polenta 'wet', here it is often grilled in blocks that can be used for cicchetti.

7 RISOTTO DI GÒ

Known as Burano's risotto, this dish uses the bony goby found in the lagoon waters. The fish is used to make a rich stock, which is slowly added to locally grown rice until a thick, velvety risotto is achieved. Butter, parmigiano and parsley are stirred through before serving.

8 SARDE IN SAOR

This dish of fried sardines, dressed in a sweet and sour blend of onions, raisins, pine nuts and vinegar, was once a way for Venetian sailors to preserve fish while aboard. It is best eaten after a day or two when the flavours have melded and mellowed.

9 TIRAMISÙ

Though somewhat contested, the general consensus is that the roots of tiramisù lie in Veneto, and more specifically in Treviso. Now Italy's most famous pick-me-up, the layered pudding of savoiardi (ladyfingers), espresso and mascarpone cream is subject to countless interpretations.

10 TRAMEZZINI

With a name that means 'in between meals', these beloved sandwiches are found all over Italy as a much-loved snack, with Veneto providing one of the most famous versions. Here, soft, white, crustless bread is packed with fillings to form a little parcel. You can find *tramezzini* filled with cured meat, cheese, vegetables, fish and, traditionally, shredded horse meat.

Other dishes to look out for

From luxurious risottos and seafood dishes to snacks enjoyed with a glass of local wine, Veneto's food scene is worth a trip.

Primi

Bisato in tecia

The region's locally caught *anguilla* (eel) is called *bisato* is dialect. Used in a host of recipes, it's cooked here in tomato sauce for a tasty stew served with white polenta.

Bollito / Lesso

Bollito and *lesso* refer to a selection of boiled meats. Bollito means the meat is cooked in boiling stock, while lesso means it's added to cold water and brought to the boil. There are two main versions: the Verona version, which is served with the famous pearà bread sauce made with bone marrow, and the Padova version, which includes poultry and a selection of accompaniments.

Casunziei all'ampezzana

These half-moon ravioli are from the snowy peaks of Cortina d'Ampezzo. They're made from wafer-thin sheets of pasta stuffed with pureed root vegetables, including beetroot (beets), turnip and potato. Tossed in butter, they're topped with parmigiano and poppy seeds.

Gnocchi con la fioretta

Fioretta is a type of liquid ricotta from Vicenza. Shepherds would combine it with flour and then drop spoonfuls of the mixture into boiling water to form light gnocchi. Today, they're served with melted butter and sage or grated smoked ricotta.

Pasta e fasoi

The region's celebrated Lamon beans create a creamy consistency in this classic comfort dish in which egg pasta is added to a stew of blended beans, vegetables and stock.

Risi e bisi

The humble pea is the star of this dish, literally named 'rice and peas'. Historically prepared in Venice for the Feast of San Marco on 25 April, it's closer to a thick soup than a risotto. The pea pods are traditionally cooked down for a thick liquid, which adds extra flavour, along with butter, parmigiano and occasionally pancetta.

Risotto al nero di seppia

Squid ink gives this iconic Venetian dish its earthy, sweet flavour and striking black colour. Small squid are cooked in their ink until tender, then incorporated into a rich risotto. Other seafood may also be added.

Risotto al radicchio di Treviso

Autumn brings Treviso's famed radicchio. Its tangy, deep purple leaves give this earthy risotto a rosy hue. Parmigiano and butter are added to balance the radicchio's bitter notes.

Veneto

NORTHERN ITALY

Risotto all'Amarone

Typical to Verona, this risotto combines Vialone Nano rice with the celebrated Amarone wine from the nearby Valpolicella region, which turns the dish a deep red. It is enriched with butter, meat stock, parmigiano and sometimes bone marrow.

Risotto con bruscandoli

Another of Veneto's many rice dishes, this recipe uses the locally foraged *bruscandoli* (wild hop buds), which can be found between March and May. They are added to a basic risotto with parmigiano for a taste of springtime.

Risotto tastasal

Tastasal is the dialect term for the minced (ground) pork sausage meat that is cooked into this simple risotto. The dish hails from the Veronese countryside and is dusted with cinnamon or nutmeg before serving.

Sopa coàda

This dish from Treviso layers fried bread and pigeon meat. The pigeon is boiled and deboned, with the stock reserved and then poured over the layers of bread and meat. The top layer is covered with parmigiano and the dish is baked and served with extra stock on the side to pour over like gravy.

Tortellini di Valeggio

Verona's meat-filled tortellini come with a 14th-century legend. The local story goes that a captain of the duke of Milan's troops, who were camped on the banks of the Mincio, fell in love with a nymph named Silvia. Jumping into the river's depths to escape guards trying to capture them, the couple left a knotted handkerchief as a symbol of their love – the same shape as the pasta.

Secondi

Baccalà alla vicentina

Vicenza's signature dish is made with stockfish, which is soaked and then cooked with onions, salted anchovies or sardines, milk and parmigiano. The dense, flavourful stew is served with golden, grilled polenta.

Brodetto

Fishermen in Caorle and Chioggia would sell their most valuable catch at market and make this stew with the leftovers. It is cooked with *passata* (pureed tomatoes) and a dash of vinegar, to give the dish a longer shelf life.

Fegato alla veneziana

This classic has roots in ancient times when pig liver was cooked with figs to balance its strong flavour. Today, sweet onions are paired with calf liver for a dish whose decadent taste belies its economical ingredients.

Musét col cren

Musét (or *musetto*) is an aged sausage made with meat from the head, shin and rind of a pig. The sausage is boiled, sliced and served with a sharp horseradish sauce which cuts through the fattiness of the meat.

Dolci

Macafame

Vicenza's apple cake uses old bread soaked in milk as a base. The softened bread is combined with eggs, butter, raisins and chunks of apple, then baked and coated with icing (confectioners') sugar.

Pinza

Made for the eve of the Feast of Epiphany on 6 January, this rustic cake uses white flour and yellow cornflour (corn starch) as a base, to which nuts, dried figs, raisins, apple, fennel seeds and aniseed are added.

... and to drink

Veneto is among Europe's oldest winemaking areas, the local tradition dating to the Bronze Age. Villages here produced wine for consumption until the Romans arrived (around the 2nd century BCE), transforming the landscape with larger scale farms that laid the foundation for a growing economy. This led to the emergence of central villages like Verona and Venice, which eventually became wealthy, influential cities.

Veneto boasts a diverse variety of grapes across the region, from the shores of Lake Garda to the foothills of the Dolomites and the hills of Mantua. Colli Berici in the Vicenza area is known for its tai varieties and carménère, a grape which is popular in France but a rarity in Italy. The area is worth a visit, both for its wines and for the stunning Palladian Villas.

The region's indigenous whites include soave, garganega, chardonnay and pinot grigio, while its indigenous reds include amarone, valpolicella, corvina, raboso, cabernet and merlot. Rose lovers will rejoice here – Veneto is Italy's main producer, thanks to Chiaretto, produced from Lake Garda's bardolino grapes.

And, not least, we have Prosecco: one of Italy's most popular sparkling wines, which can only be produced in Veneto and Friuli Venezia Giulia. It has become an international obsession. In 2008, annual production sat at around 150 million bottles. In 2021, it hit 700 million, and Prosecco's worldwide unit sales now exceed Champagne's. The wine has three categories: brut, extra dry and dry.

It's not all wine here, however. The locals are not impartial to a cocktail: this is the region where some of Italy's most famous libations were born, like the Bellini (one of my favourites). Made with white peach puree and Champagne or sparkling wine, it was created by the founder of Harry's Bar, Giuseppe Cipriani, in 1948. The region is also home to the Aperol spritz; that said, locals prefer swapping out the aperitif for the more botanical blend Select.

There is plenty of amaro and liqueur to go around too, including the herbaceous Vaca Mora Poli, the strawberry-infused *fragolino*, and *cremovo*, a Marsala and eggnog creation. Grappa is produced with many local grapes, from amarone to moscato. Veneto is home to the town that created the Italian spirit: Bassano del Grappa. The town has several distillers which visitors can tour to learn about the production process and do a tasting (one of the area's most popular picks is the Poli1898 Grappa Museum).

For those looking to ward off hangovers, some winemakers have begun producing alcohol-free sparkling wines and aperitifs. And for those looking for a pick-me-up after a long night, the region takes coffee seriously – especially the capital. Venice is home to many *torrefazione* (coffee roasting houses) and cafes. Caffè Padovano, which is said to have originated in a Padova cafe in the mid-1800s, is a favourite. Locals here love the combination of an espresso shot, mint cream or syrup, chocolate and whipped cream – a coffee meets after-dinner mint, if you like.

Culinary experiences

Learn the secrets to the perfect risotto or get lost in the hidden culinary enclaves of Venice – any foodie experience in this scenic region will be truly memorable.

Veneto

Take a food and market tour in Venice

Have a local guide show you the food secrets of this city and the little places you just might miss. Experience cicchetti and wine at a local bacaro, try a real deal spritz and sample typical lagoon seafood. Walks of Italy run culinary activities in Venice for all tastes and budgets, including a sunset cicchetti and wine tour where, with a drink or gelato in hand, you'll see stunning views of Giudecca Island across the water as the sun goes down. The company also runs a market and food tour where you visit the famous Rialto Market to meet the fishmongers and then hop on a gondola for a short trip across the Grand Canal.

WALKSOFITALY.COM

Immerse yourself in the land of Prosecco

Spend a few days in Prosecco territory, an area that comprises 50,000 acres of vineyards that are heritage protected by UNESCO. Base yourself in either Conegliano or Valdobbiadene: the two towns are connected by a road called Strada del Prosecco (literally 'Prosecco Road'). Book in with luxury operator Imago Artis for a guided trip of the area. This way, you'll learn all about the production, from DOC to DOCG and the highest quality varietals, including Cartizze – considered to be the Grand Cru of Prosecco. The whole zone is full of luxury and boutique hotels, Michelin-starred restaurants, agriturismi and, of course, wineries. For a truly unique experience, La Vigna di Sarah offers Prosecco picnics on its estate and night harvest events guided by the full moon.

IATRAVEL.COM, LAVIGNADISARAH.IT

Learn how to make risotto in Verona

Nothing says Verona quite like risotto! So why not take a cooking class here with a local chef and learn how to perfect this age-old dish? Ways Tours run cooking classes daily, where you'll get your hands messy with a few local specialties, including tiramisù, then sit down to eat all you've created. The beauty of these experiences is that they are run in small groups, but you can also request to have a more private affair. Oh, and after all your hard work in the kitchen, you get to take your apron home!

WAYSTOURS.COM

Visit a castle in Soave wine territory

Soave Castle is a restored medieval fortress with stunning vineyard views, located in the Verona wine region. Visitors can take guided tours year round that end on the roof with panoramic views of the surrounding villages. The castle doesn't have a wine cellar, but nearby Cantina del Castello does. The historic winery and cellar are a short 20-minute walk away, and here you can taste the unique styles of Soave DOC wines, such as Ripasso, Amarone della Valpolicella, Soave Classico and Soave Brut.

CASTELLODISOAVE.IT, CANTINACASTELLO.IT

Eat your body weight in tiramisù in Treviso

Treviso is a great base for travellers, with all the charm of a small city and easy access to Venice (less than 40 minutes by car). Because of its beautiful architecture and canals, it's often referred to as the 'little Venice'. It's also known as the birthplace of tiramisù. Legend has it that the dessert was invented at a restaurant called Le Beccherie, which is still operating today. If you want to learn to make it, Le Cesarine are a network of Italians who welcome you into their homes for various culinary activities, and there are quite a few with offerings in this area.

CESARINE.COM, LEBECCHERIE.IT/EN

SAGRE

APRIL

Vinitaly, Wine event, Verona

Festa dei Bigoli a Torchio, Bigoli pasta festival, Limena

SEPTEMBER

Festa del Baccalà, Salt cod festival, Sandrigo

Made in Malga, Cheese festival, Asiago

Fiera del Riso, Rice event, Isola della Scala

OCTOBER

Festa dell'Uva e del Vino Bardolino, Bardolino wine festival, Bardolino

La Festa della Castagna di Colmaggiore di Tarzo, Chestnut festival, Tarzo

Tiramisù World Cup, Treviso

Gnoche n Festa, Gnocchi festival, Auronzo di Cadore

Risi e bisi

Rice and peas

Risi e bisi is the quintessential Venetian comfort food. This version was gifted
to me by Gio's Restaurant of the magnificent St. Regis Venice and, in line
with its dining motto of 'shake the tradition', it flirts with convention. Chef
Giuseppe Ricci crafted it in collaboration with Chef de Partie Zaccaria Fais,
who used his grandmother's recipe and Venetian roots to infuse it with a
sense of cherished family heritage. Available at the restaurant only on request,
this recipe elevates the classic with a contemporary twist by incorporating
hummus and pea tuilles. At the restaurant, the risi e bisi is served with a spray
of sea fennel aroma to further invigorate the senses. A unique experience that
pays homage to tradition, while keeping an eye on the future.

Veneto

NORTHERN ITALY

SERVES 4

260 g (4½ oz) Acquerello rice
(or carnaroli)

200 ml (7 fl oz) Prosecco, plus
extra as needed

1.2 litres (41 fl oz) Parmesan
broth (see below), warmed,
plus extra if needed

2 tablespoons butter

large handful of freshly grated
parmesan

Parmesan broth (see Notes)

500 g (1 lb 2 oz) parmesan
rinds

Pea hummus

300 g (10½ oz) unpodded
peas, trimmed with strings
removed

20 g (¾ oz) tahini

Pea tuilles

15 g (½ oz) pea powder

50 g (1¾ oz) butter, melted

50 g (⅓ cup) gluten-free plain
(all-purpose) flour

50 g (1¾ oz) egg whites

Notes: Ask your local
cheesemonger for left-over
parmesan rinds.

This recipe makes more
parmesan broth than you
need for the risi e bisi. Store
the leftovers in an airtight
container in the freezer for
up to 3 months and add to
soups and stews.

To make the broth, place the rinds in a stockpot with
1.5 litres (51 fl oz) of water and bring to the boil. Reduce
the heat to low and simmer, partially covered, for 2 hours.
Strain and reserve the liquid. Return the rinds to the
stockpot and add 1 litre (4 cups) of water. Repeat and
combine both stocks in the stockpot. Bring to the boil and
cook for about 10 minutes, until the stock tastes cheesy and
slightly acidic, and has reduced slightly. Remove from the
heat and allow to cool, then transfer to an airtight container
and leave overnight in the fridge. The next day, remove and
discard the layer of fat that has formed on the surface.

For the hummus, pod the peas and set the pods aside. Boil
the peas in a small saucepan of water for about 5 minutes,
until soft. Drain and refresh in cold water, then drain again.
Blend the peas with the tahini, adding salt to taste and
gradually incorporating water, 1 tablespoon at a time, until
you have a smooth cream. Refrigerate until required.

To make the pea tuilles, preheat the oven to 60°C (140°F)
fan-forced.

Place the reserved pea pods in a saucepan, cover with
water and bring to the boil. Simmer for 5 minutes or until
tender, then drain and place on a baking tray in a single
layer. Cook for 4–5 hours, until completely dried out. Blend
in a high-speed blender to a fine powder.

Increase the oven temperature to 135°C (275°F) fan-
forced. Line a large baking tray with baking paper.

Combine 15 g (½ oz) of the pea powder with the rest
of the tuilles ingredients in a bowl and whisk until smooth.
Put 1 tablespoon of the mixture on the prepared tray and
use the back of a spoon to form a circle about 9 cm (3½ in)
in diameter. Repeat with the remaining mixture. Bake for
8 minutes or until dry and firm to touch. Let cool on a wire
rack and store leftovers in an airtight container in the pantry.

When all the separate components are ready, heat a
saucepan over medium heat, add the rice with a pinch
of salt and cook, stirring, for 2–3 minutes, until lightly
toasted. Add the Prosecco and cook for a couple of minutes
until the alcohol evaporates and the liquid has reduced.
Pour in the parmesan broth, reduce the heat to medium–
low and simmer, stirring occasionally, for 15–20 minutes,
until the rice is al dente. If the pan starts to dry out before
the rice is cooked, add a little more parmesan broth. Reduce
the heat to low and add the butter, parmesan and another
dash of Prosecco, if needed, stirring until you have a
creamy consistency.

Spread the hummus across the base of four plates and
cover with risotto. Garnish with pea tuilles and serve.

Abruzzo

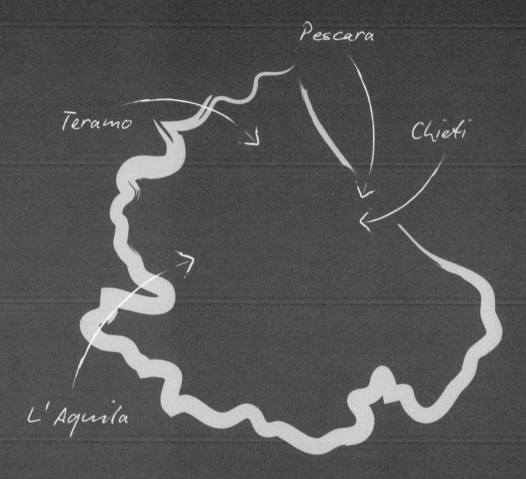

Pescara

Teramo

Chieti

L'Aquila

Regional produce

Abruzzo's wild, unspoiled terrain and
thick forests provide endless possibilities
for foraging and hunting truffles,
snails, wild boar and mushrooms,
while expanses of fields and farms offer
vegetables and legumes in abundance,
as well as celebrated cheeses, meats
and salumi. Olive groves and vineyards
dot the region, producing quality oil and
wine, as well as the olives and grapes
used in local recipes.

- Atri's liquorice
- Diavoletto d'Abruzzo red chilli
- Lamb
- Liver salami
- Mushrooms
- Pecorino
- Polenta
- Pork
- Saffron
- Sulmona's red garlic
- Altino's sweet red peppers
- Truffles
- Turchesa purple potatoes
- Ventricina Vastese and
  Ventricina Teramana (salami)
- Wild boar

Piazza Garibaldi, Sulmona

From valleys to lakes to the sea, Abruzzo's landscape has a bit of everything, but, in general, think mountains: lots of them. Even in summer, slightly snow-capped peaks of the Gran Sasso and the national parks of Abruzzo and Maiella can be seen from the Peligna Valley area, which is where my parents were born – Prezza, to be precise. It's a small, beautiful town etched into a mountain, and it's where my love affair with Italy began.

My very first memories of the country were made there, as a six-year-old. It was the 1980s, and my recollections of small Italian towns in summer are of religious festivals and fireworks, eating gelato at my uncle's bar, stealing sips of my nonno's homemade wine and rolling small gnocchi on a wooden board with my nonna. I've always cherished those memories. They were the beginning of my obsession with Italy and my special bond with Abruzzo.

The food memories continue: aperitivo on the banks of Lake Scanno, porchetta sandwiches at a beach club in Ortona and Easter lunches that went on for hours at relatives' homes. Tasting my first *sise delle monache* (a local cake; page 140) in Guardiagrele, seeing arrosticini (page 140) ordered by the hundreds at family gatherings and being completely captivated by the brightly coloured displays of floral *confetti* (sugared almonds; page 142) on the streets of Sulmona. I also cut my first spaghetti alla chitarra at a cooking class in Sulmona, tasted local wines in towns around Chieti, like Tollo, and ate my first ravioli teramani and *pallotte cacio e ova* (balls of bread and cheese; page 140) with friends in Pescara.

My family brought these Abruzzese tastes and traditions with us to Australia. My mum has made *pizzelle* (Abruzzo waffles; page 140) almost weekly for as long as I can remember, and I grew up eating my dad's pizze fritte and dishes made with *baccalà*

(salt-dried cod; page 141). Every winter, we would have polenta night at my Zia Luigina's, the polenta served just as my aunt's generation ate it as kids – topped with a rich pork ragù (page 140) and enjoyed communally at a long wooden table. For dessert, my zia made my favourite – fried doughnuts coated in sugar (we call them *le cioff* in our dialect).

More recently I experienced fine dining in my ancestral land, with the culinary prowess of chef Niko Romito. His work is now global thanks to a collaboration with Bulgari Hotels and Resorts, and his restaurant, Reale, has three Michelin stars. I am so proud to be tied to a region that is fairly untouched by mass tourism and remains true to its agricultural and farming traditions, yet has begun to innovate and look to the future when it comes to dining.

But, for now, let's look to Abruzzo's past. This was shaped by the region's geography, with its mountains and coastline, and defined by a long history of sheep farming. This all guided the local cuisine, as did many groups over the centuries, including the Romans, Lombards and Normans. They brought new ingredients and cooking techniques, which were adapted and incorporated into local dishes. For example, the Normans introduced olive oil in cooking, while the Romans are responsible for the *confetti* that Sulmona is famous for: the candied treats, which were created to celebrate weddings and births, are the foundation of the town's wealth to this day.

Sulmona's artisan confectionery makers have produced confetti since the late 1700s, and the main drag, Corso Ovidio, is lined with shop windows full of candied displays – sugared almonds fashioned into floral bouquets, beetles and butterflies. It's a feast for the eyes and tastebuds, with flavours that go beyond the traditional almond and into chocolate and pear or strawberry and cream. The town is also known for its *torrone* (nougat; page 140) made in all shapes and flavours (my favourite is the soft chocolate and hazelnut variety).

The region's harsh climate and rugged terrain mean the people of Abruzzo have had to rely on ingredients that are readily available, such as pork, lamb, bell peppers (capsicums), eggplants (aubergine) and tomatoes. As a result, Abruzzese cuisine is known for its hearty, rustic dishes, slow-cooked and full of flavour.

As mentioned, sheep farming has been a significant part of Abruzzese life for centuries, and the region is known today for its excellent sheep's milk cheese – namely, pecorino. Lamb is also a popular ingredient in Abruzzese cuisine, as is pork, which is used to make salumi and porchetta. In many of the mountainous areas, pork sausages team up with roasted scamorza as a popular combo. Caciocavallo, a cow's milk cheese, can also be found across the region.

In recent years, there has been a renewed interest in traditional Abruzzese cuisine in Italy, and this focus on local, seasonal ingredients and traditional cooking techniques has helped preserve and promote the rich and varied culinary heritage of Abruzzo: a heritage that changes across the region's provinces, given their varied locations, histories and climates.

For example, while Chieti and Teramo lie closer to the sea and Pescara is right on the water, L'Aquila is completely landlocked. Many dishes transcend these differences, but each part of Abruzzo has distinct produce and traditions. That includes the strong tradition of fish stews and dishes like stuffed calamari along the Adriatic coastline. The stretch from Ortona to Vasto, known as the Trabocchi Coast, is over 40 km (24 mile) lined with former fishing structures repurposed into seafood restaurants that are definitely not to be missed.

Arrosticini grilling

Abruzzese cuisine is known for its hearty, rustic dishes, slow-cooked and full of flavour.

Throughout the region, though, there is that one staple – pasta. Abruzzo is home to many quality producers that export globally (brands like Verrigni, Rustichella d'Abruzzo and De Cecco, to name a few) and make types ranging from spaghetti alla chittara to dry semolina pastas to sagne: all varieties that are eaten right across Abruzzo.

Ultimately, the food of this region is cucina povera. Literally 'poor food', these humble, traditional dishes use minimal ingredients and avoid waste. Abruzzo links pastoral, mountain and coastal cuisines, making for an abundance of variety served with a simplicity that allows the flavours of quality ingredients to shine through.

In the absence of a local focus on industry, this region's cuisine is marked by its focus on tradition. Many of the dishes that are popular in Abruzzo have been passed down through generations. Like my family, everyone has their own recipes or techniques for dishes like pizzelle, arrosticini and spaghetti alla chitarra, which are usually closely guarded secrets. This has helped to preserve Abruzzese cuisine and keep it authentic.

As the region is neither geographically north or south, there aren't too many local stereotypes or criticisms applied to Abruzzo, and so when I tell people that's where my parents were born, it's always received well. Most will respond with, '*Si mangia bene in Abruzzo!*' (You eat well in Abruzzo!). It's not a myth, and that's a promise.

MARIA'S TOP 10 DISHES OF ABRUZZO

1 ARROSTICINI

Also known as *arrustelle* in dialect, *arrosticini* are one of Abruzzo's most beloved dishes. Small cubes of mutton or lamb are threaded onto skewers and cooked over wood or coal until charred, then served sprinkled with salt. The *furnacella* (a long, gutter-shaped grill used specially for arrosticini) is an integral part of the Abruzzese household and a common feature at summertime barbecues.

2 BRODO COL CARDONE

An egg drop soup often eaten as part of Christmas lunch, this broth features local cardoons added to a rich meaty stock, along with small veal meatballs and stracciatella. An egg is whisked with grated cheese and scrambled in the broth at the last minute.

3 FIADONE / TORTA RUSTICA

Although technically an Easter recipe, *fiadone* is prepared all year round in Abruzzo's bakeries. A large parcel of dough is stuffed with a cheese-based filling made with either pecorino or ricotta, egg and spices. There's also a sweet version.

4 PALLOTTE CACIO E OVA

Using just three simple ingredients – bread, sheep's cheese and eggs – *pallotte* were created as a way to make meatballs that didn't require costly ingredients. They are usually served in a simple tomato and basil sauce, and are a great way to use up stale bread.

6 PIZZELLE

These sweet, thin waffles (also known as *ferratelle*) can be crunchy and crispy or soft and chewy. The dough of eggs, flour, sugar and butter or oil is often flavoured with vanilla or anise and is cooked using traditional irons, which are moulded with intricate designs and patterns.

5 POLENTA ALL'ABRUZZESE

The Abruzzese method of serving polenta is unique. Here, it is cooked until thick and creamy, then poured onto a *spianatoia* (a large wooden board) and spread flat. A hearty tomato sauce spiked with sausages, pork ribs and pancetta tops it, and grated pecorino covers the board. Everyone dives in together with forks.

7 SISE DELLE MONACHE

Also named *tre monti* after the three peaks of the nearby Maiella mountains, this symbol of Guardiagrele consists of three sponge cakes sandwiched with a lemon pastry cream. The slangier moniker of 'nun's breasts' is thought to reference the fact that local nuns once made the cakes, or the fact that many nuns, in an effort to seem more pure, sought to make their chests less prominent by creating a 'third breast' with fabric.

8 SPAGHETTI ALLA CHITARRA

Abruzzo's symbolic egg pasta is usually served with a rich meat sauce. The thin strands are traditionally made on a box with metal wires known as a *chitarra* (literally 'guitar'). The dough is placed on the wires and rolled with a rolling pin to create the square-cut spaghetti.

9 TIMBALLO TERAMANO

This baked pasta dish is similar to a lasagne but is made with thin crepes called *crespelle* (or *scripelle* in dialect). They're layered with a meat ragù, tiny beef meatballs and mozzarella or scamorza and then baked. Sometimes enriched with ingredients like peas or boiled eggs, this dish is eaten for Sunday lunch or on special occasions.

10 TORRONE

Christmas means *torrone*, and Abruzzo is famous for its nougat's quality. Offerings include the soft, chocolate and hazelnut version from L'Aquila and Sulmona, and the crunchy, almond- and candied fruit-studded variety from Guardiagrele.

Other dishes to look out for

From lamb and simple stews to rustic boards of meat-laden polenta, the food of Abruzzo may be humble in its ingredients, but its seasonality and traditions give it a poetry all of its own.

Primi

Cannelloni abruzzesi

This twist on cannelloni uses cornmeal for the dough instead of egg pasta. The filling mixes minced (ground) pork, beef and lamb, pecorino, cinnamon and sometimes nutmeg.

Pancotto

A cheap, quick way to feed farm workers and shepherds, this recipe uses up old bread by cooking it in stock or water flavoured with bay leaves to make a thick soup. It is served with olive oil and plenty of grated pecorino.

Pasta alla mugnaia

From the town of Elice, this thick, rustic fettuccine's dough is traditionally rolled into one thick strand and then cut. It is served with a rich tomato and meat sauce made from veal and pork.

Pizza e foglie

Quite literally 'pizza and leaves', this unleavened bread made of maize flour is broken into chunks and served with seasonal greens, as well as Sulmona's famous red garlic and sweet dried peppers from Altino.

Scrippelle 'mbusse

Legend states that, in the early 1800s, Chef Enrico Castorani was preparing crepes for French troops stationed in Abruzzo. He dropped them into a pan of broth by accident, and scripelle 'mbusse (drenched crepes) were born. Today's version features thin crepes sprinkled with black pepper and pecorino, rolled and cooked in chicken stock.

Virtù teramane

A thick soup, Teramo's 'virtue' is traditionally eaten on 1 May. It usually involves a mix of dried legumes, such as chickpeas (garbanzo beans) and lentils, combined with fresh peas, seasonal vegetables, pork and pasta, all cooked over the fire.

Secondi

Baccalà all'abruzzese

Baccalà (salt-dried cod) is sometimes referred to as 'poor man's meat'. In Abruzzo, it is cooked until soft and flaky, along with potatoes, garlic, onion, olives, chilli and parsley, in a tomato sauce. It commonly appears as part of the Christmas Eve fish supper, which is served across Italy.

Brodetto alla pescarese

Fish stew is popular all along the Abruzzo coast, and this version from Pescara is the best known. To make it, a mixture of local seafood, such as monkfish, scorpionfish and squid, is cooked with dried, sweet red bell peppers (capsicums) and broth.

Ciammariche al sugo

Ciammariche are Abruzzese land snails from the countryside. Once boiled, they are served in their shells, which are filled with a mixture of breadcrumbs, parsley, garlic and pecorino, everything covered with a herby tomato sauce.

Cif e ciaf

This recipe was historically prepared in celebration on the day of the pig's slaughter by the eldest family member, who gathered the pieces of jowl, belly, breast and ribs to create this hearty stew made with tomato, garlic, rosemary and bay.

Dolci

Bocconotti

Created when coffee and chocolate arrived in Abruzzo in the 18th century. The shortcrust (pie) pastry is shaped like a coffee cup, which is filled with a mix of chocolate, coffee and almond, and topped with a pastry lid.

Caggionetti

These sweet, fried ravioli are made during the Christmas period. The fillings change by area: around Teramo, a chestnut paste made with rum, dark chocolate, almonds and cinnamon is popular, while near Ortona and Chieti, jam made from wine grapes, nuts and cocoa is used. Around l'Aquila, a chickpea-based filling is more common.

Confetti

In Sulmona, these sugared almonds are often sold in flower-like bunches. There are endless variations, with flavours like strawberry or apple, tiramisù, cookies and cream, pear and chocolate, and coffee.

Mostaccioli

These soft, rich cookies appear across Italy. Abruzzo's most celebrated come from Scanno and are made with almond and vincotto. They are coated in chocolate and often decorated.

Parrozzo

Created in 1920, this dome-shaped cake is made from a dough of cornmeal, almond, citrus and amaretto. It is coated in melted dark chocolate to give the impression of the crust of *pane rozzo*, a rustic loaf of bread from which its name is derived.

Pizza di ricotta

Despite the name, this is a tart of shortcrust pastry with a light filling of sweetened sheep's milk ricotta and lemon, and sometimes candied fruit, rum and chocolate.

Pizza dogge / dolce abruzzese

Teramo's sweet 'pizza' is made with circles of sweet sponge soaked in liquor (often coffee or alchermes liqueur or rum). They're stacked with alternating layers of chocolate cream, creme patissiere and almond cream, iced and decorated with almonds and sugar sprinkles.

Sassi d'Abruzzo

To make these sweet 'stones of Abruzzo', almonds are toasted and tossed in sugar syrup flavoured with cocoa powder, which forms a crunchy coating.

Abruzzo

... and to drink

Abruzzo's winemaking history was driven, in part, by monasteries. They played a crucial role in the development of an industry here during the Middle Ages. Unfortunately, due to population decline, viticulture was sidelined for many centuries, but in the 20th century, the industry experienced a revival, producing exceptional wines like Montepulciano d'Abruzzo, Trebbiano d'Abruzzo and Pecorino.

Montepulciano d'Abruzzo is the most prominent red grape in the region. The wines it produces tend to be full-bodied, dark and fruity and are often aged in oak barrels. Thanks to their price point – generally less expensive than Italian wines of similar quality – they have enjoyed an increase in local and global popularity.

Trebbiano d'Abruzzo is the most widely planted white grape in the region. The wines it produces are light-bodied with a fresh acidity and flavours of citrus, apple, white peach and apricot. And although pecorino is a less well-known grape variety, it has gained some popularity in recent years. Its produces a full-bodied wine with a bright, golden colour and a complex profile that includes notes of tropical fruits, honey and hazelnut.

Montonico is a white wine with a delicate aroma and crisp acidity that pairs well with light seafood dishes or aperitifs. Passerina is known for its fruity and floral flavours, while Cococciola is a refreshing white, ideal for summer days and pairing with seafood. Finally, you have Cerasuolo d'Abruzzo, a beautiful and flavourful rose made from the montepulciano grape.

Beyond wine, the region also produces a host of liqueurs and distilled spirits made with herbs that grow locally in the Grand Sasso and the Majella National Parks. This includes the bitter and earthy *genziana*, which is made by soaking gentian roots in Pecorino wine.

Centerba, which translates to '100 herbs', is another pride of Abruzzese liquor: think orange and lemon leaves, chamomile, sage, juniper, cloves, cinnamon, toasted coffee beans, saffron, mint and marjoram. My dad told me that the creator left money to all but one of his children, to whom he left his recipe. I've never been able to verify this story, but it certainly makes a great tale at the dinner table. Then you have Punch Abruzzese, often consumed mixed with hot milk in the winter or as a simple amaro.

For something a bit more refreshing, San Pasquale may be just the thing: a bright green digestif made with a blend of herbs and roots in the Chieti area. The recipe for San Pasquale has been passed down for centuries, its name taken from a nearby monastery where monks have made the digestif since the 1400s.

For those with a sweet tooth like me, *ratafia* is a must-try. This liqueur is made from a blend of black cherries and red wine and has a rich, fruity flavour. Legend has it that the name comes from the Latin phrase *rata fiat* (to make an agreement) – hence why ratafia was traditionally served to toast the conclusion of important deals, making it a perfect choice for celebrations.

Abruzzo

CENTRAL ITALY

Culinary experiences

Between cheesemaking lessons and visits to historic villages, sample Abruzzo's Michelin star dining and finish the day with luxury glamping.

Culinary experiences curated by locals

Let Rosy, Annabella and the whole family welcome you into their Pescara home to cook up a traditional feast. Learn how to make pallotte cacio e ova and pasta from scratch, and then sit down to a family lunch with wine, sweets and stories. Rosy can also arrange a delicious seafood lunch at a *trabocco* (fishing structure turned restaurant) on the coast as well as aperitivo and wine tastings. She even offers a cheesemaking tour that includes a hands-on demonstration and a chance to sample local cheeses, followed by a lunch with seasonal specialties. For an elevated trabocco experience, head to Gli Ostinati for some catch of the day prepared with gourmet flair. And then let Australia-Abruzzo duo Katri and Marco of Italian Provincial Tours take you to organic wineries, breweries, agriturismi and farmers' markets on their group or private tours.

COOKINGWITHROSY.COM, GLIOSTINATIRESTAURANT.IT
ITALIANPROVINCIALTOURS.COM

See how confetti are made in Sulmona

A visit to the Confetti Pelino Museum and factory is a must. The family, who has been making confetti since 1783, is the most prestigious name in the industry, locally and internationally. They produce and export to the world and have employed generations of Sulmontini. The museum features well-preserved original equipment and photos, and you can taste and buy confetti during your visit.

PELINOSTORE.COM

Winemaking and glamping in a vineyard

Farm and winery Agricola Cirelli sits in the hills of Atri, between Teramo and Pescara, and offers a unique glamping experience that exemplifies slow travel at its best. The stylish tents provide a blend of luxury and nature with panoramic views of the local landscape. You can indulge in organic farm-to-table dining, savouring locally sourced ingredients prepared by skilled chefs. The on-site winery allows for tastings of the region's rich viticulture. After a hike or one of many farm activities, you can unwind in the spa. The seamless blend of luxury amenities, culinary delights and immersive nature experiences makes glamping at Agricola Cirelli a memorable and rejuvenating escape.

CIRELLIWINES.COM

Step back in time in a Middle Ages village

Book a stay at Sextantio in Santo Stefano di Sessanio. This tiny town is on the list of Italy's most beautiful *borghi* (hamlets). With around 100 inhabitants, it was in decline before Sextantio saved the day. Here, boutique hospitality and historic preservation are married through the *albergo diffuso* concept in which 'diffused hotels' fit themselves into nearly abandoned villages, honouring history while providing modern comfort. Try local specialties at the restaurant and book into cooking classes in town. You can also hike, ride horses or learn about ceramics and goldsmithing.

SEXTANTIO.IT

Stay in a monastery and enjoy fine dining

Niko Romito, who runs Reale with his sister Cristiana, is a self-taught chef who was awarded three Michelin stars in 2013, making Reale one of Italy's few restaurants with this distinction. Their menu offers a combination of haute cuisine and locally sourced ingredients from Abruzzo and Romito, with a vegetarian tasting menu rarely seen at this level of dining. Reale is housed in a 16th-century monastery turned boutique hotel, and so you can wake to a gourmet breakfast too! Word to the wise: a stay doesn't guarantee a dinner booking, so be sure to organise one well in advance.

NIKOROMITO.COM/CASADONNA

SAGRE

APRIL

Festival del Carciofo, Artichoke Festival, Cupello

Arrostiland, Arrosticini 'rave', held each Easter Monday, roving location

JULY

Sagra del Tartufo, Truffle festival, Campovalano di Campli

Sagra del Baccalà, Salt cod festival, Sant'Omero

AUGUST

Pecorino & Pecorini, Cheese and wine festival, Farindola

Sagra della Porchetta Italica, Porchetta festival, Campli

Festival del Peperone Dolce, Sweet pepper festival, Altino

SEPTEMBER

Regina di Miele, Honey festival, Tornareccio

Sagra delle Lenticchie, Lentils festival, Santo Stefano di Sessanio

OCTOBER

Festa della Castagna, Chestnut festival, Senarica

Le pizzelle di Lina

Lina's pizzelle

It wouldn't be a Sunday growing up in my house if you didn't wake up to the sweet scent of my mum making pizzelle. These typical waffle-style cookies vary in shape and texture (my aunt in Abruzzo makes the soft version, while Mum's are crunchy), but anyone that's eaten them will agree – they're absolutely addictive. When I was a child, Mum would make them one by one using a traditional waffle iron held over a gas flame, but nowadays she uses an electric one. And even though she makes a couple of hundred at a time, they really don't last long – between her gifting them to family and friends and everyone just snacking on them at all hours, they're gone before you know it. You'll need a waffle maker or a pizzelle iron to make these. Invest in one and I promise it will be worth it.

Abruzzo

MAKES 80–100

6 eggs

165 g (¾ cup) granulated sugar

180 ml (6 fl oz) extra virgin olive oil, plus extra for brushing

squeeze of lemon juice

dash of liqueur (preferably Frangelico)

500 g (3⅓ cups) plain (all-purpose) flour, approximately, as needed

Beat the eggs with a wooden spoon, then add the sugar and olive oil, followed by the lemon juice and liqueur. Gradually add the flour and stir until the consistency is that of a thick batter, which should fall off the spoon in dollops.

Preheat a waffle or pizzelle iron over a low flame on the stovetop or turn on an electric waffle/pizzelle maker and allow it to warm up. Brush the metal grid lightly with olive oil, ready for the first pizzelle. Add a heaped tablespoon of the batter to the centre of the pizzelle iron or waffle maker and close. Cook, turning the pizzella iron frequently over the flame if that's what you're using, for 45–60 seconds, until golden. Remove and leave to cool on a wire rack. Repeat with the remaining batter.

The pizzelle will keep for several weeks stacked in an airtight container in the pantry.

Lazio

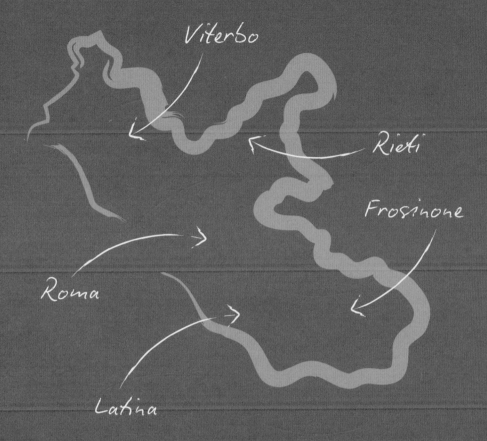

Viterbo

Rieti

Frosinone

Roma

Latina

Regional produce

Lazio combines rich, fertile land and a mild climate, making it the ideal spot for crops and livestock. The heavily wooded Tuscia area to the north is famous for its chestnuts and hazelnuts, while across the countryside, products from sheep such as guanciale and pecorino form the basis of some of Lazio's most famous dishes. Fish is plentiful along the Tyrrhenian coast, as well as in the region's many rivers and volcanic lakes.

- Atina's cannellini beans
- Bassiano's prosciutto
- Chicory
- Coppiette
- Gaeta's olives
- Guanciale
- Lamb
- Latina's kiwis
- Porchetta
- Pecorino Romano
- Puntarelle
- Ricotta romana
- Romanesco artichokes and broccoli
- Sperlonga's white celery

Colosseum, Rome

While Rome might be one of the world's most famous cities, the rest of Lazio shares little of the spotlight. But off tourist maps, the region is full of hidden gems that are worth the trip, even if just for a meal or two. You might not have heard of Ciociaria or Tuscia, Ponza or Ventotene, Lake Bracciano or Castelli Romani, but they are well worth discovering. Trust me!

Like many cuisines of the Centre and South, Lazio's is founded on the principles of cucina povera. Which brings me to the real Roman cuisine: offal, or its Roman name, *il quinto quarto*. 'The fifth quarter' is slang for what's left after animals are slaughtered and quartered. Traditionally, prime cuts went to the upper classes: a quarter each to the clergy, nobility, bourgeois and military. Workers at slaughterhouses in Rome's Testaccio neighbourhood were paid in offcuts – stomach, spleen, tongue, you name it.

These delicacies are eaten to this day, cooked in the traditional manner or given new life with a modern deconstruction. You'll find them listed on blackboard menus: dishes such as *trippa alla romana* (tripe in a tomato sauce; page 157), *coratella* (pan-fried lamb offal; page 156) and *la pajata* (pan-fried calf intestines; page 156). My favourite – although hardcore offal lovers will dispute that it's even offal – is *coda alla vaccinara* (page 154): slow-cooked or braised oxtail in a rich tomato sauce made with carrot, celery and cocoa.

Of course, some of Rome's dishes need no introduction. You can't talk about the city without mentioning the pasta quartet: four dishes tied together by the king of Roman cheeses, Pecorino Romano. There's *cacio e pepe* (page 156), with its loads of black pepper; *gricia* (page 156), which features guanciale; *amatriciana* (hailing not from Rome, but Amatrice), which features guanciale and tomato; and of course, *carbonara* (page 154), made with guanciale and eggs. Everyone in Rome has an opinion on carbonara: whether you can use pancetta, or what pasta it should be served with. One thing's for sure: it does *not* have onion, butter or cream, as you'll often find outside Italy.

Roman antipasto varies, but something fried is bound to hit the table, from *fiori di zucca* (stuffed zucchini/courgette flowers) and *filetti di baccalà* (salt-dried cod fillets; page 155) to the classic *supplì* (mozzarella-filled rice balls; page 155).

As for pizza, the Neapolitans may have invented it but, quite frankly, the Romans don't care and have their own version, which is paper thin with charred edges: *pizza romana*, also affectionately called *scrocchiarella* (crunchy). Then there's *pizza al taglio* (by the slice; page 155), *pizza alla pala* (*pala* is a wooden paddle used to pull slabs of bakery pizza from the oven) and *pinsa* (a thicker, oblong pizza).

And then the vegetable emblem of the city: the *carciofo* (artichoke). This is a side or starter that Romans will insist you can't live without. They prepare it two ways: *alla giudia* (double fried) or *alla romana* (page 157), braised until tender with calamint, a wild local mint.

The other classic Roman sides include *cicoria* (chicory, usually ripassata) blanched and then fried with chilli and a clove of garlic. In the winter months, *puntarelle* (page 154) hits menus, and this local endive isn't to be missed, nor is *broccolo romanesco*. This chartreuse beauty is like a cross between broccoli and cauliflower. In Rome and surrounds, you'll find it as a side or in the ancient classic *minestra di broccoli e arzilla* (broth with skate fish).

In Lazio, mains include flame-grilled or baked *abbacchio* (suckling lamb; page 154), *pollo ai peperoni* or *alla romana* (chicken with bell peppers/capsicum), *saltimbocca alla romana*

Church of San Pietro outside of Tuscania

(veal with prosciutto and sage; page 157) and porchetta (page 154), generally from the town of Ariccia in the Castelli Romani; here, the outskirts of Rome merge into rolling hills, and locals are known for their rolled pork artistry. Ariccia's porchetta is some of the best in the country, which you can eat as a course or in a panino with a glass of local Castelli wine.

It's not all livestock, though. Seafood is also a staple, given Rome's short distance from the Laziale coast, which takes us to perhaps Italy's most underrated coastlines. North of Rome, I've had many a seafood lunch at beachside towns like Santa Marinella, Santa Severa and Ladispoli. Then west of Rome is Fiumicino, where I love stopping off at the waterfront for a casual *cartoccio* (paper cone) of fried prawns (shrimp) and calamari or the gourmet offerings at one of the town's award-winning restaurants.

But, for me, the southern coast is the real gem. Here you have the Circeo National Park, which juts out into the sea, and the Gulf of Gaeta, which cradles the spectacular yet under-the-radar Pontine Islands. The former fortress and fishing town of Gaeta has a proud seafood tradition, as well as some great olive farms. I've eaten my heart out here, including one of the best *spaghetti alle vongole* (with clams) of my life! The town's pride, *la tiella di Gaeta* (page 154), is a savoury pie–like delicacy most commonly filled with octopus and is not to be missed. You won't be lucky like me and eat the best one in town at my beautiful friend Tina's house, but Gaeta's bakeries, bars and beach clubs also do a good job.

Off the coast, the Pontine Islands will delight and surprise. The first time I visited Ponza, I couldn't believe my eyes. The waters and grottoes transport you to the Caribbean or the Maldives. Ponza is an assemblage of colourful buildings filled with boutiques,

The area has modest dishes with lots of legumes and grains on offer, as well as wine.

In the mountains bordering Abruzzo, the province of Rieti offers simple yet unforgettable pasta dishes, such as *fregnacce alla reatina* (with a tomato, olive and mushroom sauce), and *stracci di Antrodoco*, in which *crespelle* (crepes) are baked and filled with meat and tomato sauces and cheese.

And of course, the Castelli Romani, which offers a tranquil escape from Rome. It's a collection of charming towns with green hills and lakes, which were formerly volcanoes. Romans flock here on summer weekends to enjoy highlights like Frascati's wine, Castel Gandolfo's hilltop views and the scenic Lake Albano. The area is famous for its *fraschette*: rustic restaurants where you go to socialise as much as to eat and drink, enjoying hearty comfort foods like polenta with pork ribs, washed down with wines from Frascati and surrounds.

And now, finally, dessert. The most common in Rome and nearby towns is the much-loved *maritozzo* (page 154), a fresh cream–filled bun and the pride of the region. Then there's *crostata* (a sweet tart or pie; page 158), usually of the ricotta and sour cherry variety. And of course *ciambelline al vino* (page 158), which are cookies eaten across the region, typically dipped in wine.

With the modern-day capital's ties to Ancient Rome evident not only in its glorious landmarks but in today's food culture, the Eternal City's culinary heritage is like a voyage through time. But the treasure trove doesn't end here. Prepare yourself for an extraordinary gastronomic trip through the rich and varied traditions of Lazio.

bars and restaurants whose chefs proudly make local specialties like *coniglio alla ponzese* (a rabbit stew; page 156).

Returning inland, you have a number of fascinating areas like Ciociaria, home to Lazio's Cesanese wine. At just an hour southeast of Rome and known for its agricultural abundance, the area makes for a perfect foodie break, showcasing cucina povera at its finest with lots of beans, meat, cheeses, mushrooms, olive oil and traditional sweets. Cannellini beans are particularly popular in simple pasta dishes like sagne e fagioli (page 154), and local meats, like lamb and chicken, are often grilled or baked.

Tuscia sits to the north with a picturesque landscape that includes lakes like Bolsena (which boasts some fascinating fish and eel). Tuscia was the homeland of the Etruscan civilisation, and the area's medieval towns later became popular destinations for Romans seeking an escape from the city.

MARIA'S TOP 10 DISHES OF LAZIO

1   ABBACCHIO

Abbacchio (the dialect term for suckling lamb) is popular in Lazio, particularly in springtime, when the tender meat is prepared roasted with potatoes and herbs. Another common dish is lamb *scottadito* (burnt fingers): small cutlets that are grilled and eaten with the hands. You can find them crumbed and fried too.

2   CODA ALLA VACCINARA

To make this dish, chunks of oxtail are slow-cooked in a rich tomato sauce with pine nuts and cocoa. Tradition dictates that it should be eaten with the hands, as the meat should fall off the bone, while the excess sauce is served with pasta or gnocchi as a primo.

3   MARITOZZO

Once the region's breakfast pastry of choice, the *maritozzo* has fallen out of favour in recent years, replaced by the *cornetto* (Italian croissant). However, for a decadent morning treat, it cannot be beaten. This yeasted brioche bun is packed with freshly whipped cream and was once gifted by a *marito* (betrothed man) to his beloved, often with a piece of jewellery hidden inside.

4   PIZZA E MORTAZZA

Pizza e mortazza is a dreamy creation of straight-from-the-oven *pizza bianca* (a light, chewy flatbread topped with olive oil and salt), stuffed with wafer-thin slices of mortadella that melt into the bread for one of the best-loved late-morning (or just about any time) snacks of the Eternal City.

5   PORCHETTA

Porchetta is found all over Central Italy, with the town of Ariccia claiming historical ownership. A large, deboned pork loin is seasoned, rolled with herbs and seasonings and slow-cooked in a wood-fired oven until the meat is tender inside and crunchy outside. Seasonings vary, but in Lazio, rosemary, garlic and salt are the most common.

6   PUNTARELLE

Trimmed from the inner, tender stems of catalogna chicory, strips of puntarelle are placed into cold water to curl and crisp up. They are served as a side dish, traditionally with a punchy vinaigrette of olive oil, vinegar, anchovies and garlic.

7   RIGATONI ALLA CARBONARA

Although the authentic Roman version uses just guanciale, eggs, pecorino and black pepper, this dish has been adapted around the world, making it one of Lazio's most famous exports. It's made from just a few simple ingredients, but an excellent carbonara still needs skill and experience to ensure a smooth, luscious sauce. It is often served with rigatoni, which provide the perfect hiding place for the chunks of salty guanciale.

8   SAGNE E FAGIOLI

From the Ciociaria area, which is known for agriculture, this take on pasta and beans uses *sagne* – a pasta made with flour and water that's cut into a small, angular shapes. The pasta is cooked in a sauce of cannellini beans with tomato, onion and sometimes guanciale and/or chilli.

9   SPAGHETTI CON LE TELLINE

The Lazio coastline rewards its diners with plenty of fresh seafood, and one of the best local dishes is this simple mix of spaghetti and tiny, sweet telline clams. Cooked with just olive oil, garlic and a touch of chilli, this recipe lets the flavour of the sea shine through.

10   TIELLA DI GAETA

This savoury pie from the southern, coastal town of Gaeta is available with various fillings, but the most common are octopus, tomatoes, garlic and the area's famed Gaeta olives.

Other dishes to look out for

Lazio's cuisine offers enough fried treats, traditional offal dishes and plates of cheesy pasta to keep you from ever going hungry.

Street food

Pizza al taglio

All over Lazio there are countless takeaway shops and bakeries selling *pizza al taglio* (by the slice), priced and sold by weight and topping. It is either rectangular, made *alla pala* (long and oblong, moved with a wooden paddle) or in a *teglia* (a wide metal baking tray).

Supplì

This fried rice ball reigns supreme as a Roman street food but is also found in pizzerias as an antipasto with many variations. In the classic version, a tomato sauce, sometimes with meat, is cooked with risotto rice, then cooled and rolled into an oblong with a piece of mozzarella hidden inside. It's then crumbed and deep-fried so the outside is toasty and the cheese inside is gooey. It is often called *supplì al telefono* in reference to the 'telephone wire' of stringy cheese.

Antipasti

Baccalà fritto

Baccalà (salt-dried cod) is a common ingredient in Roman cuisine. Here it is rehydrated and then dipped in batter and deep-fried until dark gold and crunchy. Fillets of fried baccalà are often served as an antipasto but may also be eaten as a street food.

Fregnacce

While different names are used across the Tuscia area, the most common one is *fregnacce* (as they are called in Viterbo). These thin savoury crepes are traditionally made for the Carnevale period. They are cooked in pork fat, sprinkled with grated pecorino and eaten hot or cold.

Primi

Acquacotta

From the area of Viterbo, this soup was made for farm workers after a long day out on the fields. Recipes vary, but it commonly features potatoes, onions, tomatoes and wild chicory boiled together and then poured over stale bread to serve. A piece of baccalà or poached egg may also be added for extra substance.

Bucatini all'amatriciana

From the town of Amatrice, this tomato-based sauce is made with the ubiquitous guanciale, Pecorino Romano and sometimes a hint of chilli. Adopted by Rome as part of its quartet of pastas, it is traditionally served with *bucatini*, a thick spaghetti with a hole running through the middle.

Farro al tartufo di Leonessa

Local spelt from the Tuscia town of Leonessa is the base of this dish. It is boiled and combined with a sauce of crumbled sausage and tomato, then topped with shavings of fresh truffle.

Lazio

CENTRAL ITALY

Fini fini

Thin strands of *fini fini*, a pasta from the Ciociaria area, are traditionally cooked in the city of Frosinone for Carnevale but can be found year round. They are usually served with a meat or tomato sauce.

Lombrichelli alla viterbese

Named for their similarity in appearance to *lombrichi* (earthworms), these eggless pasta strands are a typical shape of Viterbo. They're eaten with a tomato sauce made with crumbled sausage and red wine.

Pasta alla gricia

While it's the 'grandfather' of the four Roman pasta dishes, *gricia* is probably the least well known. The sauce features guanciale and Pecorino Romano – ingredients easily and cheaply found in the farming countryside – forming the basis of the other three pastas.

Rigatoni con la pajata

Pajata is the intestine of an unweaned calf, which is cleaned without removing the milk. The lengths of intestine are cut and tied into rings that are cooked, curdling the milk inside. They are served with rigatoni and a tomato sauce thickened with the ricotta-like milk squeezed from a few of the rings.

Stracciatella

Warming comfort food doesn't get better than this Roman egg drop soup. A mix of beaten egg, parmigiano and nutmeg is added to stock to form the *stracciatelle* (raggedy strips of egg).

Stringozzi alla reatina

A fresh pasta from Rieti, *stringozzi* (sometimes called fregnacce) are similar to the strangozzi of nearby Umbria (page 214). Made from flour and water, the pasta is rolled out and cut into thin strips, which are paired with a slightly spicy tomato sauce or a meat ragù.

Timballo alla Bonifacio VIII

A pasta pie created in honour of Anagni's Pope Boniface VIII, Lazio's *timballo* sees fresh fettuccine added to a tomato sauce cooked with guanciale and small meatballs. The pasta and sauce are poured into a tin lined with prosciutto and baked until firm.

Tonnarelli cacio e pepe

A gricia without guanciale, *cacio e pepe* is a triumph of two ingredients: grated Pecorino Romano and a generous hit of cracked black pepper, which are combined with starchy pasta water to form a creamy, cheesy sauce. *Tonnarelli* is the traditional pasta accompaniment; this square-cut spaghetti is made with egg and has a porous texture perfect for the sauce to cling to.

Zuppa di ceci e castagne

Once prepared for a meat-free Christmas Eve dinner, this soup pairs chestnuts, which grow all over northern Lazio, with chickpeas (garbanzo beans). A simple yet warming blend of autumn and winter produce, it's best when made with the local chestnuts of Monti Cimini.

Secondi

Baccalà con i ceci

Chickpeas pop up often in Lazio's cuisine, sometimes simply served with pasta, olive oil and a touch of rosemary. However, on Fridays they are usually found on sale with pearly white fillets of baccalà, the legumes and fish both pre-soaked and ready to cook together to form this historic dish.

Coniglio alla ponzese

From the island of Ponza, this dish is made in honour of the island's patron saint, Silverius, on 20 June. The rabbit is cooked with cherry tomatoes, garlic, onion and white wine, with a touch of bay leaf and chilli.

Coratella

The interiors of a lamb, including windpipe, heart, lungs and liver, are chopped and cooked in stages to ensure each part is tender. Sometimes served with onions, *coratella* is prepared with artichokes in spring.

Saltimbocca alla romana

Literally translating to 'jumping in the mouth', *saltimbocca* are slices of veal wrapped in prosciutto and a sage leaf. Each is dusted in flour and cooked in butter, with white wine added to create a thick sauce.

Sbroscia

Fish from Lake Bolsena are used for this traditional fisherman's dish once prepared straight off the boat, using water from the lake. A mix of fish, such as tench, eel and perch, is cooked with tomato, onion, wild mint and potatoes, then poured over a base of stale bread and eaten with the hands.

Seppie e piselli

Perfectly tender strips of squid, sweet peas and a tomato sauce are married in this Lazio classic which just begs to be served with plenty of toasted crostini to soak up the beautiful flavours.

Trippa alla romana

The Romans prepare tripe using the *cuffia* (the cow's second, honeycomb-textured stomach). The tripe is cut into strips and boiled until tender, then cooked in a tomato sauce and served with grated Pecorino Romano and *mentuccia* (a wild local mint). *Trippa* is also often served as an antipasto.

Votapiatto di calamarelle

From the coastal town of Gaeta, these small, tender baby squid are dusted in flour and pan-fried. They are served simply with a sprinkle of chopped parsley.

Contorni

Carciofo alla giudia

The Roman Jewish recipe for artichokes sees them trimmed and beaten to open up the leaves. They are usually fried twice in oil, first at a lower temperature. Once cool, they are flash fried at a higher temperature so the leaves crisp up and fan out like a sunflower. They are sprinkled with salt and served hot.

Carciofo alla romana

Shiny, round, globe artichokes are perfect for the Roman-style *carciofi*, particularly the local mammole variety, which lack a spiky choke. The artichokes are stuffed with a mix of calamint, garlic and parsley, and are braised with olive oil, white wine and water until beautifully tender.

Vignarola

A harmonious celebration of spring, *vignarola* is prepared when broad (fava) beans, peas, artichokes, romana lettuce and spring onions (scallions) are all sold at the market at the same time. They're cooked gently into a stew, sometimes with a little pancetta and garlic.

Dolci

Ceciaroli

Sweet ravioli from Tuscia that use chickpeas as the base of their filling. After soaking and boiling, the chickpeas are chopped and mixed with chocolate, honey, vanilla, cinnamon and sweet liqueur to form a stuffing. The ravioli are fried or baked and coated in icing (confectioners') sugar before serving.

Ciambelline al vino

Small, sweet cookie rings flavoured with red or white wine and consumed at the end of a meal. Made without eggs or butter, they have a hard texture so they're dipped in wine to soften them.

Crostata ricotta e visciole

This sweet ricotta and sour cherry tart hails from Rome's Jewish Ghetto but is now found all across the city. The tart originally had a pastry top to hide the filling, because Jews were forbidden from trading dairy products and therefore hid the ricotta inside the pie.

Frappe

Rome's number one Carnevale treat is known by multiple names across the country. Whether called *frappe*, *chiacchiere* or *bugie*, these strips of fried dough coated in icing sugar never fail to bring a smile at any age.

Grattachecca

When temperatures rise in Rome, there is nothing like the cooling hit of *grattachecca*. Sold in an ever-dwindling number of kiosks around town, this shaved ice is doused with a sweet, usually fruit-flavoured syrup.

Pangiallo

With its roots tracing back to ancient times, *pangiallo* is now a Christmas cake, but it was once prepared for the winter solstice, in anticipation of the return of the sun – hence the round shape and yellow hue. This dense cake of nuts, raisins, chocolate and orange and lemon zest is covered with a mixture of flour and water coloured with saffron to create its distinctive yellow coating.

Pizza ebraica

Also known as *pizza di beridde*, this recipe comes from the Roman Jewish Ghetto. It is a slab of unleavened, eggless dough studded with dried and candied fruits and nuts, with a crunchy exterior around a soft, fluffy centre.

Pizza di Pasqua

Tuscia's *pizza di Pasqua* is actually a sweet sponge cake eaten on Easter Sunday morning, along with the traditional savoury breakfast of meat, cheese and eggs. Similar in shape to a panettone (page 68), the cake is flavoured with aniseed or cinnamon and citrus.

... and to drink

I daresay no one dining outside of Italy has ever enquired with a restaurant about its wines from Lazio. Not that this region doesn't produce a good drop; it's just not *known* for wine. Its reputation more commonly conjures images of Roman trattorie and tumbler glasses filled with Frascati white or house red. However, nowadays you're bound to find a wine list or some Lazio DOC labels at even the most casual of trattorie.

Like most Italian wine regions, Lazio's vine heritage is ancient. Its first inhabitants were the Etruscans, though it was the Latins (or Latians) who gave the area its original name – Latium. The Ancient Romans brought the region into another era by improving trade and agriculture, though after the collapse of their empire, the land was neglected. Only in the 1870s, when Rome became the capital of Italy, did Lazio flourish once again as a wine region.

Lazio's volcanic hills provide an excellent base for viticulture, thanks to the fertile and well-drained land, with its lava and tufa soils which are rich in potassium. This type of soil is particularly suited to white grapes, as it ensures a good balance of acidity. Meanwhile, the region's proximity to the Tyrrhenian Sea tempers coastal heat with sea breezes, and the Apennines protect from cold, northerly winds.

All of this makes Lazio perfect territory for whites, although some quality reds are starting to gain popularity. When it comes to white wines, they are primarily made from trebbiano, malvasia di candia and malvasia puntinata grapes. Lazio whites are meant to be consumed young and pair well with local dishes like porchetta and abbacchio. The most well-known DOC varieties of the region are Frascati and Est! Est!! Est!!! di Montefiascone. Other notable appellations include Orvieto, Marino and Aleatico di Gradoli. Frascati Superiore and Cannellino di Frascati are prestigious DOCGs for dry and sweet wines, respectively.

Meanwhile, the Cesanese del Piglio DOCG and Velletri are noteworthy for red wines. A rare find also comes from around Lake Bolsena in the form of Aleatico di Gradoli: a sweet red which can also be transformed into a liquoroso or fortified wine.

Additionally, *vino da tavola* (table wine) made from cabernet sauvignon, merlot, aglianico, cecubo and abbuoto grapes is widely produced in the region.

Lazio doesn't produce any internationally renowned liqueurs or spirits, but prized local produce, such as artichokes and cherries, are distilled in some bottles. Rome, Viterbo and towns across the Ciociaria have their own sambuca, and *genziana* (gentian herbal liqueur) is also quite common.

Culinary experiences

Live like an Italian aristocrat in a 17th-century villa, take a tailored food tour, chill out in therapeutic waters, and do some forest bathing – life is good in Lazio.

Dive deep into Roman food culture

Get under the skin of this ancient yet modern capital with the local experts. In addition to private walking food tours, companies like Casa Mia Food Tours, Devour Tours and Local Aromas offer wine, craft beer and amaro tastings, aperitivo experiences and a wine and cheese pairing. Walking tours take place in neighbourhoods like the charming Trastevere or the historic Jewish Ghetto and can be customised by theme or foodie preference – think food and Vespa or cinema, pizza and gelato, or even *just* gelato. Explore stores and markets, and meet the people who make Rome the thriving food city that is.

CASAMIATOURS.COM, DEVOURTOURS.COM, LOCALAROMAS.COM

Dine at the Vatican and the Pope's residence

For the religious and the non, the Vatican is one of the most visited sites in the world, and with two experiences offered by Walks of Italy, you can combine your visit with food! Start the day with breakfast in a peaceful courtyard before exploring the Vatican Museums without the crowds. You'll be among the first to enter the Sistine Chapel to admire Michelangelo's masterpiece in tranquillity. The experience ends with special access to Saint Peter's Basilica. On a separate tour, in addition to the impressive art collection of the Vatican Museums, you can visit the Vatican Gardens (only accessible through a guided tour like this) and the Vatican Rail Station for a glimpse of the Pope's train. From here you journey to Castel Gandolfo, the scenic hill town located by Lake Albano that houses the Papal Palace, the Pope's summer residence. You'll enjoy a buffet lunch with local produce (including from the Pope's own farm) before touring the Papal Palace and exploring the charming town.

WALKSOFITALY.COM

Sustainable luxury tourism and Michelin stars

Nestled within the Labico National Park, the Colonna Resort is a retreat surrounded by nature. Contemporary design blends with lush surroundings, the rooms designed with wellness in mind. The resort boasts an expansive vegetable garden with produce that's transformed into gourmet dishes by owner and renowned chef, Antonello Colonna, at the in-house Michelin-starred restaurant. Dip in the thermal pool or indulge at the spa. The culinary program includes wine tastings and guided visits to the vibrant Zagarolo market to savour local produce. Ariccia, with its porchetta and museums, and Frascati, with its villas and wine, are nearby.

ANTONELLOCOLONNA.IT/RESORT-SPA

Detox and recharge in an ancient land

Only in Italy would a chef with three Michelin stars head up the kitchen at a wellness hotel! Palazzo Fiuggi stands as a testament to a bygone era: the beautiful palazzo has been transformed into a state-of-the-art medi spa that still exudes glamour. Here, Chef Heinz Beck of Rome's La Pergola created over 1,500 recipes, customisable for guests' needs. The hotel's Fiuggi Method is guided by medical, nutrition and holistic wellness experts, and is designed to be tailored to individuals. Therapeutic waters, cryotherapy, yoga and forest bathing – this is where you come to recharge. Beyond plush stays, tour operators like Imago Artis and Access Italy can arrange any details for your luxury Italian holiday and food adventure.

PALAZZOFIUGGI.COM, IATRAVEL.COM, ACCESSITALY.COM

Stay, eat and play at a noble seafront villa

Immerse yourself in the splendour of a noble villa that dates to 1640 at La Posta Vecchia in Ladispoli. Expect nothing less than impeccable service from the hospitality family behind the Tuscan institution that is Il Pellicano. Beyond the property, explore Lazio's coast or uncover nearby Etruscan ruins followed by a picnic by waterfalls. On site, delight in the culinary mastery of Executive Chef Antonio Magliulo. He'll take you through the gardens and into his vegetable patch, and you can even cook with him. This villa is more than just a place to stay: it embraces you like an old friend.

POSTAVECCHIAHOTEL.COM

SAGRE

APRIL

Sagra del Carciofo,
Artichoke festival, Ladispoli

JUNE

Sagra delle Fragole di Nemi,
Strawberry festival, Nemi

AUGUST

Sagra degli Stringozzi,
Stringozzi pasta festival,
Casperia

Sagra della Nocciola,
Hazelnut festival, Caprarola

SEPTEMBER

Roma Baccalà,
Salt cod festival, Rome

Sagra della Porchetta,
Porchetta festival, Ariccia

OCTOBER

Sagra delle Castagne,
Chestnut festival,
Soriano nel Cimino

Sagra dell'Uva,
Wine festival, Marino

Sagra della Patata,
Potato festival, Leonessa

Sagra del Tartufo,
Truffle festival, Canterano

Carbonara

In Rome, not much is debated more than the humble carbonara. Traditionalists insist on its unwavering authenticity and are horrified by any variations that stray from the classic. This beloved dish is strictly defined by its three ingredients: crispy guanciale, Pecorino Romano and eggs – notably, no cream. And the art of crafting the perfect carbonara hinges on precision, as a mere few seconds can mean the difference between a velvety masterpiece and scrambled eggs. Still my favourite in Rome, this recipe from Da Enzo al 29 is taken from my book *The Eternal City*. It's consistently satisfying with just the right balance of saltiness and decadent silkiness.

Lazio

CENTRAL ITALY

SERVES 6

700 g (1 lb 9 oz) rigatoni

350 g (12½ oz) guanciale, rind removed, cut into 1 cm (½ in) thick strips

4 whole eggs

2 egg yolks

300 g (10½ oz) freshly grated Pecorino Romano, plus extra to serve

Note: In Italy, carbonara is usually prepared with 'pasta gialla' eggs, which give the dish its yellow hue. Regular eggs will create a paler carbonara, but the flavour will still be the same.

Bring a large saucepan of salted water to the boil, add the rigatoni and cook until al dente.

Meanwhile, place a very large dry frying pan over high heat, add the guanciale and fry for 4–5 minutes, until the fat melts and the meat becomes crisp.

In a bowl, beat the whole eggs and egg yolks until well combined, then mix in the pecorino and season with a generous grind of black pepper.

Drain the rigatoni, reserving 125 ml (½ cup) of the pasta cooking water, and add the pasta to the pan with the guanciale, stirring well to coat the pasta in the fat. (If your pan isn't large enough to hold all the pasta, you may need to remove half the guanciale and fat and do this in two batches.) Turn off the heat and, if you are feeling confident, add the egg mixture to the pan, tossing the ingredients together rapidly to avoid the egg scrambling. If needed, add some of the pasta cooking water to help loosen the sauce. Alternatively, the foolproof method is to add the pasta and guanciale to the bowl with the egg mixture and stir well, along with some of the pasta cooking water. The heat from the pasta will cook the egg and the sauce will remain silky smooth.

Serve with a sprinkling of extra pecorino and a good grind of black pepper.

Marche

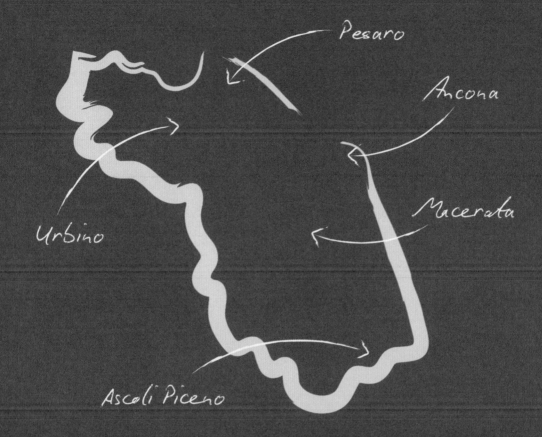

Pesaro

Ancona

Macerata

Urbino

Ascoli Piceno

Regional produce

Despite the region's amazing coastline and verdant hills bursting with top-quality produce, the cuisine of Marche is widely unknown. Inland, the menu is heavily meat-based, prepared with truffles and cheeses, while the port towns dotted along the Adriatic introduce fresh seafood into the mix. Many dishes play with sweet and savoury flavours, using fruit or spices, such as aniseed and wild fennel.

- Artichokes
- Casciotta d'Urbino cheese
- Castignano's green anise
- Ciauscolo sausage
- Figs
- Moscioli mussels
- Mushrooms
- Olives
- Peaches
- Prosciutto di Carpegna
- Rabbit
- Sapa
- Sibillini's pink apples
- Slattato cheese
- Truffles

Fratte Rosa

On my first holiday to Italy, in 1985, we stopped in Ascoli Piceno to visit my dad's friend Peppe. While living in Rome, I've stayed in touch with him and he, together with a couple of friends, makes up my small community of Marchigiani. They don't all know each other, but there are two things that unite them: a love and pride of Marche and the fact that, when they head back to their hometowns, they never return hungry from this region of sea, mountains and ancient villages that's still defined by a rich rural tradition.

Located along the Adriatic coast and nestled between Tuscany, Umbria, Emilia-Romagna, Lazio and Abruzzo, Marche is a hidden gem that is relatively uncrowded and still mostly tourist free. The region is made up of green, rolling hills and sprawling vineyards, medieval towns and the dramatic peaks of the Sibillini Mountains. Here, you'll find the eerily beautiful Frasassi Caves and breathtaking beaches along the Conero Riviera, with its crystal-clear waters and white cliffs, and the sandy beachesof Senigallia (which,

despite its small size, boasts an up-and-coming culinary scene, with five Michelin stars). The region's geography is particularly distinctive, as you can go from an altitude of over 2,000 m (6,500 ft) to sea level in just over an hour. This special dialogue between mountain and sea is evident in many local characteristics – not least Marche's cuisine, where meat and seafood often come together in mouth-watering dishes.

Among its towns and cities with a rich cultural heritage, some of the most famous are Macerata, Ascoli Piceno, Fermo, Ancona and, of course, Urbino. Florence might be the birthplace of the Italian Renaissance, but the small, stunning town of Urbino is where some of the greatest minds of the time lived and created (Raffaello, for one).

The region has long been a haven for small businesses and artisans, including cheesemakers, farmers, beekeepers and craft shops, which have all contributed to Marche's history. The locals' collective memory ensures that ancient customs and traditions endure, like the beloved practice of homemade pasta. You'll find an assortment of pasta interpretations here, from the rich egg varieties to the simpler types made with water and semolina.

At the very heart of Marche's cuisine are three ingredients: mushrooms, olives and truffles. These ingredients are essential to the rustic, flavourful cuisine of the region.

Marche is particularly known for its truffles, which are used in many pasta dishes and snacks. The region boasts both black and white varieties, with the Acqualagna truffle being one of the most prized.

Marche's delicious olives are also famous, enjoyed in dishes like *olive all'ascolana* (page 170). These fried and stuffed olives are extremely difficult and delicate to make, as the olives that grow here are softer than average.

Truffle hunting outside Mercatello sul Metauro

At the very heart of Marche's
cuisine are three ingredients:
mushrooms, olives and truffles.

As for edible mushrooms, Marche boasts a wide variety, including porcini, San Giorgio's mushrooms, ovoli, morels and chanterelles. These are used in a range of dishes, including soups, risotto and pasta.

Pasta is deeply ingrained in local culture, almost to the point of obsession. From town to town, you're spoiled for choice. You have the *lumachelle* of Urbino, a small, shell-shaped pasta that resembles a snail's shell. *Torcelli* is a ridged, tube-shaped pasta that is slightly curved and tapered at the ends, resembling a small trumpet, and *stroncatelli* is a short, twisted pasta with a spiral shape.

One of the most iconic pasta dishes in Marche is *vincisgrassi* (page 170), which is similar to lasagne bolognese (page 24),

but with some notable differences. It typically has more layers than lasagne (at least seven, but usually around 12) and instead of using a ragù made with beef and pork, here a rich tomato sauce enriched with chicken livers, sweetbreads or other offal is layered with a nutmeg-spiced bechamel. The origin of vincisgrassi is a source of local debate. The most famous variation comes from Macerata and includes meat sauce, giblets and bechamel. Another popular version is prepared with *maccheroncini di Campofilone*, a thin egg pasta similar to tagliolini – this variation is more like a *pasta al forno* (baked pasta).

Then there is the *frascarelli* (page 172), a traditional dish made with flour, rice and a variety of seasonings. Originally, it was made by using *frasca* (twigs) to mix the water and polenta. Sometimes referred to as 'polenta rice', it is considered one of the poorest dishes in local culinary traditions, but it's far from plain, typically topped with a range of additions from sausage and pecorino to vegetables and the prized white truffle of Acqualagna.

Every region has its flatbread, and here it's the *crescia* (page 170). Like focaccia, it's prepared in different ways depending on where you find yourself in the region. *Crescia sfogliata* is made with flour, water, eggs and lard, and is best eaten warm with sausage and cheese. Similar in appearance is the *crostolo di Urbania*, which is made with cornflour (corn starch). Other variations include greasing the bread with lard and olive oil, enhancing it with scraps of polenta and pork crackling, and stuffing it with other fillings, as is the case with the *chichì ripieno* of Ascoli. Further north, it's more of a savoury cheese pie typically prepared at Easter.

Ciavarro (page 171) is a soup of cereals and legumes typical of Ripatrasone, in the province of Ascoli Piceno. It is a simple dish of cucina povera that was once prepared on the first day of May, the symbolic day of passage between the new and old legume supplies. In the local dialect, *lu chavarre* (the remnants) were grains such as lentils, barley and *cicerchie* (the local legume), stored during the winter and finally used as the new season approached.

In the inland towns like those in and around Urbino, beef, lamb and rabbit are commonly on the menu, while on the coast, you have dishes like *brodetto all'anconetana* (page 172) from the seaside port Ancona: a decadent tomato and fish soup made with 13 different types of fish and shellfish. It's just one of many local brodetto variations.

With a long history of farming livestock, particularly in the hinterland areas, the region also has a long tradition of producing salumi and dairy products. And so, whether they're on the home table or served during aperitivo at a wine bar, salumi and cheese are always present.

The region's most famous salami is *ciauscolo* from the Macerata region, known for its spreadability. Made by mixing different parts of the pig with crushed garlic, pepper and wine, this traditional rustic sausage is also eaten at the end of meals. The *salame lardellato* is also emblematic of the region's charcuterie prowess; this typical salami from the Apennine hill towns is made with pork raised in the area and is flavoured with cubes of cured lard. And cheese lovers can indulge in – among many other types – the *pecorino conciato di Fossa*, which is wrapped in walnut leaves and aged in terracotta amphorae.

Those with a sweet tooth will want to try the indulgent *crema fritta* (page 170). This cooked cream delicacy is set in the fridge overnight, coated in egg and breadcrumbs, and deep-fried on skewers. The result is a blend of sweet and savoury, and you might even see it in the antipasto section of a menu, served with fried anchovies, or eaten as street food along with olive all'ascolana.

Because Marche remains relatively unspoilt by tourism, its culinary tradition, like many others, has been passed down through generations, so you can still easily find and enjoy it authentically in this region of cultured ease and rural seclusion. It's a place of great natural beauty, art and breathtaking landscapes. This is a secret slice of Italy just waiting to be uncovered.

MARIA'S TOP 10 DISHES OF MARCHE

1 CALCIONI

A perfect balance of sweet and savoury, these baked Easter ravioli are served as an antipasto and a dolce. They're made with a sweet dough filled with cheese (usually pecorino), lemon zest and sugar or cinnamon.

2 CONIGLIO IN PORCHETTA

In porchetta or *porchettato* means 'making porchetta' with different meats or fish. In Marche, porchetta-style rabbit is a common Sunday lunch or celebration dish. The rabbit is deboned and filled with herbs, including wild fennel. It is rolled up with sausage and pancetta, tied with string and roasted in the oven.

3 CREMA FRITTA / CREMINI

An unusual spin on sweet-meets-savoury, these crunchy cubes filled with sweet pastry cream are a fried favourite from Ascoli Piceno. The cream is flavoured with lemon or aniseed, left to set, then cut and rolled in breadcrumbs before frying.

4 CRESCIA

Found in Marche and Umbria, *crescia* is a version of a piadina (page 24): a thin flatbread cooked in a pan and served filled with local meats or cheese, or as an accompaniment to secondi. Recipes vary, some adding lard to the dough of flour and water.

5 FOGLIE DI SALVIA FRITTA

These fresh sage leaves are dipped in a light batter and flash fried. Served hot with a glass of sparkling wine, they're an aromatic appetiser.

6 OLIVE ALL'ASCOLANA

Named for the town of Ascoli Piceno, these delectable stuffed green olives are now found all across the region and, indeed, Italy. Plump and tender, they're stuffed with meat and then crumbed and fried. Often found as part of a meal or aperitivo, they can also be served in a paper cone and eaten as street food.

7 PASSATELLI

These short, stubby pasta strands are made from breadcrumbs, egg and parmigiano and are passed through a special tool called a *schiaccia passatelli* (or a potato ricer nowadays) to form their shape. They are standard in Marche, Umbria and Emilia-Romagna and are served swimming in a meat broth.

8 PESCHE DOLCI

Another traditional cake of Carnevale season, Marche's 'sweet peaches' are made from two halves of a light, sweet dough that are baked and then sandwiched together with chocolate or vanilla cream to form balls. They are then soaked in alchermes liqueur and rolled in sugar to give them their pink hue and peach-like appearance.

9 RAGÙ ALLA MARCHIGIANA

Using a mix of meats, including beef, pork and veal, as well as chicken livers and other offal, Marche's *ragù* is a kind of chunky bolognese. It is enjoyed with local pasta like maccheroncini, and is an integral part of vincisgrassi.

10 VINCISGRASSI

Similar to Emilia-Romagna's lasagne (page 24), *vincisgrassi* comprises layers of pasta and a chunky meat sauce. *Ragù marchigiano*, which can include sweetbreads and chicken livers or, in some cases, mushrooms or truffle, is layered with bechamel and sheets of pasta which can be flavoured with Marsala or wine must. Tradition requires at least seven layers, while most recipes ask for ten.

Other dishes to look out for

A region of meat roasts and fresh seafood, where dishes tango with sweet and savoury flavours: in Marche, you're in for a gourmet time.

Antipasti

Moscioli

Similar to mussels, *moscioli* are a wild mollusc found only along the Conero Riviera, where they are caught by just a handful of fishermen, as opposed to being farmed and harvested. They are in season between April and October and are usually served simply with a drizzle of oil and a squeeze of lemon.

Omelette al tartufo

Truffles shaved on top of a rich buttery omelette: this is one of the best ways to sample the earthy flavours of this delicacy.

Pizza al formaggio

An Easter recipe made all over Central Italy (particularly in Umbria and Marche). Despite its name, *pizza al formaggio* is actually cheese bread baked to serve with salami and cured meats on Easter morning. The bread is usually made with parmigiano and chunks of pecorino that melt as it bakes.

Primi

Ciavarro

Traditionally prepared on May Day to celebrate the produce of spring, *ciavarro* is a nourishing soup of vegetables, cereals and legumes. Ingredients may include beans, peas, corn, barley and chickpeas (garbanzo beans), with a little pancetta sometimes added for extra flavour.

Lumachelle all'urbinate

The history of this soup dates back to the 15th century, when it was apparently inspired by, and made for, Beatrice Sforza, the duchess of Urbino. Lumachelle are served in a *minestra* (thick soup) of cabbage, chicken livers, sausage and turnip cooked in meat stock and topped with parmigiano.

Lumachine di mare in porchetta

In the port of Ancona, these sea snails are sold by kiosks on the street. They are prepared *in porchetta* with a soffritto of carrot, celery and onion, garlic and wild fennel, and served with a toothpick to pull the tender snails out of their shells.

Maccheroncini di Campofilone

This pasta dates to the 15th century, when the farming families of Campofilone needed to use up excess eggs laid by their chickens. They would make these long, thin strands of pasta and dry them to use over the winter.

Marche

CENTRAL ITALY

Secondi

Brodetto marchigiano

Each port of Marche adds its own twist to this stew, all using local seafood from the Adriatic. Ancona's version adds plenty of tomato, while Porto Recanati skips the tomato and adds saffron. San Benedetto uses green tomatoes, bell peppers (capsicums) and lots of vinegar, while Porto San Giorgio uses at least 13 types of fish and no molluscs. Fano adds a dash of tomato concentrate and vinegar.

Frascarelli / Riso corco

Frascarelli was historically a poor dish in which flour and water were mixed into an intentionally lumpy texture to make the dish more satisfying. Nowadays, porridge-like rice is added to create the lumps. It's usually served with a sauce of sausage or pork.

Stoccafisso all'anconitana

Stockfish or baccalà (salt-dried cod) is the star of this recipe from Ancona. The fish is soaked to soften it and then cooked for two hours with potatoes, tomatoes, olives, capers and anchovies, along with local white wine, rosemary and parsley.

Dolci

Anicetti

Like biscotti, these aniseed-flavoured biscuits are formed, baked and then sliced and returned to the oven to dry and harden. They're often served at the end of a meal with a sweet wine or digestivo.

Cavallucci marchigiani

These half-moon cookies have been prepared since medieval times. They're filled with dried fruit and nuts, which are combined with a cooked wine must known locally as sapa. They are sometimes dipped in alchermes and sprinkled with sugar.

Cicerchiata

This Carnevale sweet is a variation on Naples' struffoli (page 262). Small, fried dough balls are tossed in warm honey, then formed into a circle with a hole in the centre. For decoration, colourful sprinkles or chopped nuts are added.

Frustingo

This festive cake of dried fruit and nuts traces its roots back to ancient times. It is dark and dense, enriched with dark chocolate, sapa, coffee, spices and olive oil.

Lonzino di fico

For hundreds of years, the Vallesina area produced large amounts of the dottati and brogiotti varieties of fig. To avoid waste after harvests, the figs were dried and combined with walnuts, almonds, star anise and vincotto or liqueur. The mixture is rolled into cylinders and wrapped in fig leaves.

Scroccafusi

Made for periods of celebration, scroccafusi are irregularly shaped sweet doughnut balls which are boiled before being baked or deep-fried. They're drizzled with rum or alchermes, dusted with icing (confectioners') sugar and served warm.

... and to drink

Marche's wines are influenced by the region's varied terroirs, which include soils that are calcareous, or rich in clay or limestone. As the region is flanked by the Apennine Mountains to the west and the Adriatic Sea to the east, varied climatic conditions mean local wine producers work in both warm and cool zones.

The Celts, Etruscans and later the Romans all had a hand in shaping the region's winemaking history over thousands of years, setting the foundation for Marche's current riches of vineyards – over 40,000 acres. The region certainly doesn't have the production numbers or reputation of nearby Tuscany, but what it does, it does well.

Although Marche's wine is largely sold as local or table wine, the region has around 20 DOC and DOCG titles – in particular verdicchio, which has been grown here for more than 600 years. The finest expressions of the grape can be found in the DOCGs Verdicchio dei Castelli di Jesi and Verdicchio di Matelica. Other white grape varieties grown in the area include bianchello, trebbiano, pinot bianco, malvasia tuscana and pecorino.

The region also produces high-quality reds, mainly made from montepulciano and sangiovese grapes. The best red wines include Rosso Conero Riserva, which is intensely fragrant and dominated by montepulciano and sangiovese, and Vernaccia di Serrapetrona, a sparkling DOCG wine made from vernaccia nera grapes. Other notable red grape varieties grown in the region include ciliegiolo, pinot nero and lacrima di morro.

Organic produce from vineyards, forests and natural reserves gives life to many distilled liquors, including grappa, and infusions, such as mandarin, sour cherry (look out for acquavite di visciole) and fennel.

Culinary experiences

From farming workshops to learning the arts of butchery and stuffing olives, there's no shortage of magical culinary adventures awaiting you in Marche.

Cook and stay in a 500-year-old farmhouse

Ashley and Jason Bartner are two Americans living the Italian rural dream with La Tavola Marche, their organic farm, inn and cooking school in Piobbico. Jason is a chef, Ashley is a food and travel writer slash filmmaker turned farmer, and together they host groups of curious travellers on the hunt for local culture, food and tradition. In a 500-year-old farmhouse agriturismo, they offer a unique culinary experience with a range of seasonal activities, from cooking classes to farming workshops that expose you to local artisans, farmers and winemakers.

LATAVOLAMARCHE.COM

Become an Italian butcher

If learning the art of butchery and actually getting your hands dirty sounds fun, then the Whole Hog Butchery Workshop offered by La Tavola Marche might just be for you. The team here run two-day workshops that cover different cuts of meat, how to properly break down a whole hog and how to prepare various dishes using the different parts of the animal. You'll also have the opportunity to taste the dishes that you've prepared, along with other traditional recipes. This workshop isn't for the faint of heart because, as you'd expect, it involves handling a lot of raw meat and using incredibly sharp knives (under the guidance of trained professionals).

LATAVOLAMARCHE.COM

Experience three Michelin stars on the beach

Hidden among the beach clubs on the magnificent Conero Riviera sits Uliassi. Unlike at other beach clubs, you'll have to plan your visit to this restaurant (and make your reservation) way in advance. Uliassi started life in 1990 as a simple beach cafe but has since evolved into a restaurant with three Michelin stars. Like so many of Italy's great restaurants, Uliassi is family-run, with Head Chef Mauro Uliassi and his maitre d' sister Catia working in tandem to create a truly memorable dining experience. Uliassi's cuisine is both inventive and authentic, and the restaurant is environmentally conscious too, banning the use of plastic and persuading its suppliers to avoid polystyrene when transporting their fish.

ULIASSI.COM

Deep dive into a complete olive experience

Local olive producer and exporter Agorà runs a bistro and store in the centre of Ascoli Piceno, as well as an olive mill and vineyard. Learn about the ancient art of olive oil-making with an olive oil course or enjoy a wine tasting. And of course you can't leave Ascoli Piceno without learning how to make the town's namesake: the meat-stuffed, crumbed and fried *olive all'ascolana*. Experiences are organised through a stay at the intimate Palazzo Ciotti hotel, with suites overlooking the beautiful Piazza Arringo.

AGORAASCOLIPICENO.COM, PALAZZOCIOTTI.IT

Go fruit picking outside a medieval town

Located near the small medieval town of Montelparo, La Golosa is a family-run business that produces fruit preserves, jams and juice. They use ancient methods and predominantly make things by hand, so their farm tour offers a fascinating insight into their industry. Walk through groves and savour the sweetness of seasonal fruits, such as peaches, cherries, figs and persimmon. Learn about their cultivation, harvesting and preparation from local experts and try your hand at fruit picking in the beautiful countryside.

WONDERFULMARCHE.COM

SAGRE

APRIL

Fritto Misto all'Italiana,
Fried food festival,
Ascoli Piceno

MAY

Sagra del Carciofo,
Artichoke festival,
Montelupone

JUNE

BrodettoFest,
Fish stew festival, Fano

AUGUST

Ascoliva,
Olive all'ascolana festival,
Ascoli Piceno

Sagra del Vino Cotto,
Cooked wine festival,
Loro Piceno

SEPTEMBER

Festa del Ciauscolo,
Ciauscolo festival, Sarnano

OCTOBER

Sagra dell'Uva,
Wine festival,
Cupramontana

*Fiera Nazionale
del Tartufo Bianco*,
White truffle festival,
Acqualagna

NOVEMBER

Diamanti a Tavola,
Truffle festival, Amandola

Il brodetto

Seafood stew

Uliassi is a beach shack turned Italian dining institution.
Opened in 1990 by siblings Mauro and Catia Uliassi, the Senigallia
beachfront locale was awarded its first Michelin star after ten years.
It now boasts three (one of only 11 restaurants in Italy, currently)
and has made the cut on the World's 50 Best Restaurants list.
Despite the accolades, it's still a relaxed family affair, and while
Mauro's menus and dishes are sophisticated, they're clean and
simple at the same time. Beach dining experiences don't get much
better than this. Recreate the feel at home with this brodetto, a
rich seafood stew based on local tradition, which has won awards
and acclaim for its flavourful decadence. Uliassi's full recipe is
supplied here, but at home you can substitute any of the Italian
seafood varieties with what you can source locally. Your fishmonger
should be able to guide you.

Marche

CENTRAL ITALY

SERVES 4

20 mussels, scrubbed and debearded

400 g (14 oz) datterini, grape or cherry tomatoes

extra virgin olive oil

½ small onion, finely chopped

4 garlic cloves, peeled

1 tablespoon red wine vinegar

250 ml (1 cup) fish fumet (see below)

150 ml (5 fl oz) crab stock (see below)

150 ml (5 fl oz) prawn (shrimp) stock (see below)

80 g (2¾ oz) turbot, cut into four even fillets

80 g (2¾ oz) sea bass, cut into 4 even fillets

80 g (2¾ oz) monkfish, cut into 4 even fillets

80 g (2¾ oz) skate, cut into 4 even fillets

80 g (2¾ oz) dogfish, cut into 4 even fillets

8 cuttlefish, cleaned

4 large prawns (shrimp) (60 g/2 oz each), split lengthways

4 tiger prawns (jumbo shrimp)

4 grancelle crabs

¼ teaspoon cuttlefish ink

70 ml (2½ fl oz) cuttlefish stock (see below)

8 cooked mantis shrimp, peeled

12 pencil squid or young squid, cleaned, tentacles removed

When purchasing the ingredients, ask your fishmonger for left-over offcuts and bones of fish, crab, prawns and cuttlefish to be used for the stocks.

To make the crab, prawn and cuttlefish stocks, place the heads, shells and offcuts in three separate small saucepans. Add one-quarter of the onion, carrot and celery to each pan, along with three black peppercorns and a pinch of salt, then cover with 500 ml (2 cups) of cold water. Bring to the boil, then reduce the heat to low and simmer, uncovered and stirring occasionally, for 1 hour, to release the flavours. Strain each saucepan and set aside.

For the fish fumet, heat the olive oil in a saucepan over medium heat, add the remaining vegetables and cook for 5 minutes or until starting to soften. Stir in the fish offcuts, followed by the white wine, then bring to the boil, reduce the heat to a simmer and cook for 4–5 minutes, until the alcohol has evaporated. Add enough water (about 750 ml/3 cups) to just cover the fish and add the remaining peppercorns and a pinch of salt. Bring to the boil again, then reduce the heat to low and simmer, uncovered, stirring occasionally and skimming any scum that rises to the surface, for 1 hour. Strain the fumet and set aside.

For the clam water, place the clams in a saucepan and add 200 ml (7 fl oz) of cold water. Cover with a lid, place over high heat and bring to the boil. Shake the pan and cook the clams for 1–2 minutes, until they open, then strain and reserve the water. Discard any unopened clams and set the rest aside.

Place the mussels in a large saucepan and add 200 ml (7 fl oz) of cold water. Cover with a lid, place over high heat and bring to the boil. Shake the pan and cook the mussels for 2–3 minutes, until they open. Discard any unopened mussels and set the rest aside.

Score a cross in the base of the tomatoes, place in a large heatproof bowl and cover with boiling water. Drain after 1 minute or when the skins loosen around the base. Refresh in cold water, then peel.

Heat a drizzle of olive oil in a large saucepan over medium heat, add half the onion and two of the garlic cloves and cook for 1 minute. Add half of the tomatoes and cook for 2 minutes, until softened. Add the red wine vinegar to deglaze the pan, then add 100 ml (3½ fl oz) of the fish fumet, along with the crab stock, prawn stock and 100 ml (3½ fl oz) of the reserved clam water.

chopped flat-leaf parsley,
to serve

toasted rustic bread, to serve

Crab, prawn and cuttlefish stocks, plus fish fumet

150–200 g (5½–7 oz) each of heads, shells and offcuts from crab, prawns (shrimp) and cuttlefish (ask your fishmonger for these)

4 onions, chopped

4 carrots, chopped

4 celery stalks, chopped

12 black peppercorns

50 ml (1¾ fl oz) extra virgin olive oil

350 g (12½ oz) fish bones, skin and offcuts (ask your fishmonger for these)

175 ml (6 fl oz) white wine

Clam water

16 clams, purged

Cook for 10 minutes over medium–low heat, then add all of the fish, the cuttlefish, prawns and crab. Cook for 2–3 minutes, until the seafood is half cooked, then use a slotted spoon to remove the seafood and set aside. Strain the remaining liquid in the pan into a clean saucepan, bring to the boil and cook for 10 minutes or until reduced by half. Pour into a heatproof jug.

Heat a drizzle of olive oil in the saucepan over medium heat, add the remaining onion and garlic and cook for 1 minute. Add the remaining tomatoes, the reduced cooking liquid, cuttlefish ink, another 100 ml (3½ fl oz) of the clam water and the cuttlefish stock. Simmer for 2 minutes, then strain and transfer the liquid to a large saucepan, add the half-cooked seafood, along with the mantis shrimp, and set over medium heat.

Meanwhile, heat a frying pan or griddle pan over high heat until very hot, then sear the squid on one side for a few seconds. Remove from the heat and add the squid to the fish stew. Increase the heat, add the cooked mussels and clams and cook for another minute until heated through.

Spoon the fish stew in a large serving dish or divide among shallow bowls. Sprinkle with parsley and freshly cracked black pepper and drizzle with olive oil. Serve with slices of toasted rustic bread to mop up the juices.

Molise

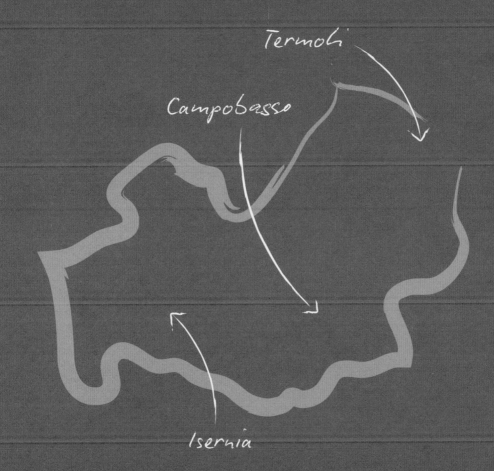

Termoli

Campobasso

Isernia

Regional produce

Italy's youngest region often flies under the culinary radar, but Molise's quality produce has much to offer. Featuring few swathes of development, the small region's unspoiled terrain provides abundant legumes, vegetables and fruits, which are paired with offal, lamb and fish to create rustic yet satisfying dishes.

- Baccalà
- Beans
- Caciocavallo di Agnone cheese
- Centofoglie endive
- Farro dicocco
- Isernia's onions
- Lamb and mutton
- Limoncella and zitella apples
- Liver sausage
- Mushrooms
- Polenta
- San Biase's long potatoes
- Truffles
- Ventricina spicy salami
- Yellow winter tomatoes

Molise

Mural in Portocannone

Until recently, I was just one Italian region short of visiting all 20. Italians who learned this presumed it was Molise that was missing from my list; in popular culture, Molise is touted as the region that doesn't exist because it's so small and undiscovered. The national joke has escalated to Molisn't merchandise and even a book entitled *Il Molise Non Esiste* (Molise Doesn't Exist). However, I can verify it does: I visited for the first time as a kid in the 1980s.

From Abruzzo, trips to Molise aren't uncommon, as the two regions used to be one: gli Abruzzi, a plural form that combined the two geographic areas. That region split in 1970, introducing Molise as Italy's newest region. Sadly, because of poor economic and labour stability, the region has experienced a steady decline in population since the late 19th century, which has contributed to its sense of isolation. This tiny and underrated area lives in the shadow of its neighbours – not just Abruzzo, but Apulia too.

You could say that mountains and hills, rather than people, crowd the interior, while Molise's short 35 km (21 mile) stretch of the Adriatic coast is guarded by flatter plains. Campobasso is the region's largest city and its capital, but the most appealing tourist destinations are Termoli, a charming coastal town known for its *trabocchi* (fishing platforms turned casual seafood restaurants), and Isernia and Saepinum, which offer glimpses of Molise's Palaeolithic and Roman history. Various tribes and kingdoms – from the Saracens and Goths to the Lombards and Romans – all vied for control of the fertile land through its history. Outside of the region's few developed areas, natural beauty is abundant, with lakes, mountains, waterfalls and coastline to visit.

Few people do visit, however. On my trips to Campobasso as an adult, it has always felt like one of the last authentic places left in Italy, uncontaminated by international tourism. The towns around the capital are

sleepy under the midday sun, their streets coming alive in the late afternoon with locals running errands and popping into bars for an aperitivo. Amid this bustle, I sampled the quality cheeses and salumi Molise is known for on my visits. At any given bar, they will serve a *tagliere* (board) almost bigger than the table with – among many other local delicacies – *caciocavallo di Agnone*, a delicate cow's milk cheese and local favourite, and ventricina salami, seasoned with paprika and hot red peppers. As Molise shares not only a border with Abruzzo, but also so many cultural and gastronomic similarities, I felt right at home.

The further away from Campobasso I went, the quieter the towns became. In fact, around 100 of Molise's villages have fewer than 2,000 residents. To save these underpopulated areas from further decline, the local municipal governments have joined those from other disadvantaged areas in Italy by inviting people from around the world to set up shop, giving away homes for less than the price of an espresso! Under the scheme, anyone willing to move to one of these villages will receive 700 euros per month for three years to help them settle in; all newcomers have to do is commit to residing there for at least five years and contributing to their village by starting a business. Any business. A restaurant, a bar, a bakery, a shop – basically anything that will provide an economic boost to the area.

Given these efforts, Molise may no longer be called 'sleepy' one day. At present, a handful of local entrepreneurs are working to jumpstart tourism, leaning into the 'Molise doesn't exist' phenomenon as a branding opportunity.

Of the offerings the area has to entice tourists, food and wine top the list.

Molise is still very much an agricultural region with a simple cuisine based on locally grown produce. Most farms here raise sheep, though pigs and cows also appear in pastures – the latter are mostly raised for dairy.

Molise's most sought-after products include extra virgin olive oil, black and white truffles, several types of salami and cheeses made from cow's, sheep's and goat's milk. One notable offering is *treccia di Santa* Croce *di Magliano*, a semi-spun cheese made with cow's milk, which is braided and carried on people's shoulders during festivities to bring good luck with harvests.

The region's cold winters mean polenta, comforting soups and hearty lamb dishes are on high rotation. *Agnello cacio e ova* is a lamb stew cooked slowly with cheese and eggs and, like in Abruzzo, *arrosticini* (grilled mutton or lamb skewers) are one of the most popular street food snacks. With a small but fruitful stretch of Adriatic coast, seafood is also an essential part of the diet, used in dishes like *spaghetti alle vongole* (with clams) and *u'bredette* (fish stew).

Notably, the region is undeniably one of Italy's pasta capitals, with cavatelli and fusilli in its wheelhouse. This is prime durum wheat territory, and one of the country's best-known pasta brands, La Molisana, originates in Campobasso, exporting to more than 50 countries.

It might be a small region, but its pasta shapes are unusual and never ending.

It's not just cavatelli and fusilli that call Molise home, though. There are a whole bunch that are unique to the area. The most popular include *sagne* (page 186), which are made by cutting strips of dough, and *agnoli*, which are stuffed. The latter are similar to tortellini in shape but much larger. Another local favourite is the *timballo*, a baked pasta dish featuring ziti pasta (as opposed to the Abruzzo version, made with crepes) and a filling of meat, vegetables and cheese.

Molise also has its own version of *maccheroni alla chitarra*, a long, flat pasta that is usually made by pressing the dough through a *chitarra* ('guitar': a box with metal wires). It seems all the regions of the Centre and South have their own name for this pasta shape. In Apulia, they are *troccoli*; in Abruzzo, they call them *spaghetti alla chitarra*; and in Molise, they're known as *creoli* or *crioli* (page 187). They are easily mistaken for regular spaghetti, but their profile is square rather than round, with each piece cut by hand.

The pasta doesn't end there, however. Molise also has laianelle and tagliolini and millefanti: the list goes on. It might be a small region, but its pasta shapes are unusual and never ending.

To finish meals, Molise has sweets on offer like the *bocconotto* – a delightful small pastry filled with chocolate and almonds – and *mostaccioli*, which are cookies made with a blend of honey, cinnamon and cocoa.

With family-owned restaurants and food markets and a commitment to producing high-quality products, Molise is an ideal destination for food lovers. Add to that its beautiful landscape and the fact that it's quite a way off the tourist track, and this region could just be one of Italy's last hidden gems for those seeking gastronomic exploration.

MARIA'S TOP 10 DISHES OF MOLISE

1 BACCALÀ AMMULLECATE O ARRACANATE

The folk of Molise prepare their *baccalà* (salt-dried cod) as a gratin, baked covered in crunchy breadcrumbs. Each family adds their own spin to the topping, mixing in different combinations of raisins, figs, walnuts, pine nuts, oregano, parsley and garlic.

2 CAVATELLI

Now adopted by the rest of Italy, and indeed the world, *cavatelli* were, according to some, born in Molise. These small pasta shapes are made with flour and water and shaped by hand to create a curve to hold sauce. Cavatelli are served in many ways, the most popular choices being with broccoli rabe or a meat-based ragù.

3 CONFETTI RICCI

Crunchy and sweet, Agnone's signature *confetto riccio* is easily spotted thanks to its bright white colour and distinctive, rugged surface. This treat consists of a whole almond coated in sugar.

4 FUSILLI ALLA MOLISANA

Another pasta shape born in Molise with worldwide fame. The name originates from a method of hand-making the pasta – the strips of semolina flour–based dough would be wound around a *fuso* (rod) to make a corkscrew before being left to dry. The spiral shape is perfect for capturing sauce, making it the ideal partner for a Molisana ragù of lamb, veal and pork sausage, each serve finished with a dusting of pecorino.

5 PEZZATA DI PECORA

A signature dish of the mountain town of Capracotta, *pezzata* is linked historically to the *transumanza* – the twice-yearly movement of sheep between the mountains and the lowlands. If a sheep was injured and unable to continue, it would be sacrificed, resulting in this slow-cooked mutton stew made with tomatoes and potatoes.

6 POLENTA

Polenta is a staple in Molise's mountainous areas. After boiling to give it a thick, doughy texture, the polenta is left to rest (usually on a round plate) before being sliced with a cotton thread. It is then served with a chosen accompaniment – local sausages cooked in a dense tomato sauce with onions is a popular choice.

7 SAGNE

Sagne are made in Molise, Abruzzo and Lazio from sheets of pasta dough that are torn to form flat, geometric pieces. They are used in a range of recipes, notably *sagne e cicerchie* with pork scratchings, prosciutto fat, tomato, basil and chilli. In the town of Roccavivara, they are served with a simple, fresh tomato sauce.

8 SALSICCIA DI FEGATO

An emblem of Molise's cured meat offerings, this salami is made from pork liver, lungs and heart, and seasoned with garlic, orange zest and bay. Depending on how long it is aged for, it can be soft or hard, and may even be stored in glass jars and covered in *sugna* (pork fat).

9 U' BREDETTE

Wherever there is a coastal town in Italy, there will be a local fish stew, and Molise (specifically Termoli), is no exception. This recipe traces back to fishermen who cooked unsold catch to make their evening meal. To this day, less commercially attractive seafood is added, such as small fish, razor clams, mussels and squid, all cooked in a tomato base with a hint of chilli.

10 ZUPPA ALLA SANTÈ

Traditionally prepared for special occasions, this 'holy soup to saints' was invented, some say, in Agnone in the 14th century in honour of Queen Giovanna II of Naples. The rich dish uses chicken broth as a base, with veal meatballs, chunks of toast and caciocavallo cheese added.

Other dishes to look out for

While Italy's youngest region often flies under the culinary radar, its abundance of quality produce conjures up some truly delicious dishes that are all its own.

Antipasti

Casciatelli

The saying goes that 'it wouldn't be Easter in Molise without *casciatelli* on the table'. These half-moon pastry parcels filled with grated cheese and egg can be eaten as part of a meal or devoured as a snack throughout the day.

Crostini con le cozze

Molise's stretch of Adriatic coast gifts the region plenty of seafood, including *le cozze* (mussels). In this dish, they are cooked with garlic, white wine and chilli, then removed from their shells and served on top of toasted bread with chopped parsley.

Centofoglie / Scarola venafrana

The fresh-flavoured *centofoglie* is a variety of escarole from the commune of Venafro. It's used in a range of Molisane dishes, one of the more popular produced by cooking it with beans in a traditional terracotta pot. It is often added as an extra element to zuppa alla santè.

Panonta di Miranda

This circular loaf of bread from the town of Miranda is sliced horizontally and layered with fillings, such as frittata, sausages, bell peppers (capsicums), onions and cheese. Best made a day in advance so the flavours can saturate the loaf, it is a popular picnic option and also used for aperitivo buffets.

Primi

Creoli / Maccheroni alla chitarra

Creoli or *crioli*, the local names for *maccheroni alla chitarra*, are a fresh homemade pasta similar to spaghetti, but with a square-cut shape usually made by hand using a chitarra. They are most often served with a meat ragù or *alla campuasciana* (with prosciutto) or with a sauce of baccalà and walnuts.

Frascatielli

Less known than some of Molise's more famous pasta shapes, *frascatielli* are nonetheless versatile and easy to prepare. Flour and water are combined into a dough, which is pushed through a sieve to form small grains of pasta, almost resembling rice or tiny gnocchi. They are usually prepared in a chicken or lamb broth or served with a tomato sauce. In Campobasso, frascatielli are traditionally served with a sauce of pork lardo, onion and fried parsley.

Laganelle con i fagioli

Made with just flour and water, *laganelle* look like small sheets of diamond-shaped lasagne and are the pasta of choice for this simple yet wholesome dish, which pairs them with white beans, garlic and a hint of red chilli. For extra crunch, it is topped with toasted breadcrumbs before serving.

Secondi

Scescille

Similar to the dumpling-like cacio e ova of neighbouring Abruzzo (page 140), *scescille* are made with cheese, egg and stale bread, formed into a ball or oblong. The Molise version, however, is cooked in the tomato sauce they're served in. While they can be eaten alone as a second course, they are also sometimes used to enrich local fish stews.

Pampanella

The tiny town of San Martino in Pensilis is famed for this vibrant contribution to Molise's cuisine. Cuts of pork are coated in a mix of spicy red chilli, sweet paprika and garlic and left to marinate. The pork is then covered with moistened parchment paper and baked, with a little white wine vinegar added at the end to make the red colour pop and the flavours sing. *Pampanella* can be eaten hot or cold and also makes for an amazing panino filling.

Dolci

Caragnoli

A delicious sugar fix made for Christmas and Carnevale, Molise's *caragnoli* require just eggs, flour and sugar to make a dough which is then twisted into knotted ovals. These are fried and doused in lashings of honey.

Ostie ripiene

Two paper-thin wafers are sandwiched together with a filling of chopped walnuts and almonds, honey, dark chocolate, cinnamon and orange zest in this typical Christmas treat that originated in the convent of Agnone.

Taccozze con fagioli e pomodoro

Another beloved pasta of the region, *taccozze* are similar in shape to laganelle but are made with semolina and flour. They are cooked with borlotti (cranberry) beans and tomato sauce for Molise's version of pasta with beans.

Zengarielle

A thick spaghetti made with spelt, *zengarielle* are an unusual, cereal-based pasta native to Molise with a wholemeal flavour and robust texture. They are usually prepared simply with olive oil and anchovies and are served heaped with toasted breadcrumbs.

Zuppa di farro

Cereals and grains are often used in Molise's cuisine. In this thick soup, spelt is soaked until softened, then cooked with tomato, guanciale, pork rind, onion and garlic. It is usually served with grated pecorino.

... and to drink

Molise has a rich history of winemaking dating to the Roman era. Today, the region's winemakers are committed to producing high-quality wines with great attention to detail, aided by the area's diverse range of terroirs and grape varieties. While relatively undiscovered, Molise has become a well-regarded region, producing wines under its own name.

The Biferno and Pentro di Isernia DOCs, granted in the 1980s and '90s respectively, helped to put Molise's wines on the map. For those curious to try them at their source, Molise's wineries are open to the public for tours and tastings; notable vineyards to visit include Di Majo Norante and Tenuta del Portale, known for their reds made from the montepulciano grape and the tintilia grape, respectively.

Montepulciano is the most widely planted grape variety in the region, renowned for its deep colour and rich, full-bodied flavour. Aglianico is also important, producing wines with a complex flavour profile and firm tannic structure. Tintilia is a lesser-known grape variety, but it has gained local popularity, thanks to its ability to produce wines with a distinctive flavour profile that has notes of ripe fruit and plum jam. The white wines of Molise are made from grape varieties, such as falanghina, trebbiano and malvasia, which produce fresh, crisp flavours and delicate floral aromas.

Molise is known for a few amaro varieties and liqueurs too, including Cynar: a versatile artichoke liqueur that balances sweet and bitter flavour with 13 botanicals. It can be used as an aperitivo, digestivo and cocktail ingredient, making it a favourite among modern bartenders.

Another standout is known as *poncio*; it had humble beginnings as a homemade concoction before making its way to the bars and pastry shops of the region. It is sweet and aromatic in flavour with a slightly bitter aftertaste, made from a blend of herbs and spices such as anise, fennel, cloves, cinnamon and orange peel. The exact origin of its name is a mystery, but it is speculated that it might be an Italianised version of 'punch'.

The sweet *liquore al latte* (milk liqueur) is traditionally produced in Campobasso, while many other liqueurs in the region are quite simply made with what grows locally. In Molise, this includes liquorice, used to make *liquirizia*; cherries, used to make *ratafia*; and grapes, which produce grappa.

Molise

CENTRAL ITALY

Culinary experiences

Soak up the hidden delights of this small region by trying cheesemaking, going grape picking and mastering one of Molise's signature pastas.

Go deep into the food heart of Molise

Escape the world for a week and fully immerse yourself in the food of one of Italy's most unexplored regions. Molise Cuisine are local experts who will take you on a guided tour to discover the local food traditions. Their tours include visits to olive oil mills, cheese factories and other food artisans. You'll spend your days enjoying tastings, cooking classes in a variety of unique settings and meals at traditional restaurants: an authentic experience of Molise's culture and gastronomy. If a week-long adventure isn't your thing, they offer customised shorter itineraries as well.

MOLISECUISINE.COM

Stay and eat farm to table in the Molise highlands

Near Agnone, the city of arts and crafts in the Apennine hills, Masseria Santa Lucia is an organic agriturismo run by Emma and her husband, Decio. They offer a variety of apartments that cater for all types, a pool, and homegrown dinners at long, convivial tables, served with the wine and peppery olive oil Emma and Decio produce. You can dine in the farmhouse or in the garden, enjoying Emma's traditional meals that never disappoint, featuring only ingredients sourced on site. If you prefer to stay in the centre of town, the couple has another property, Borgo San Pietro, and they can arrange tastings and hikes from either one.

SANTALUCIAAGNONE.COM

Taste the big wines of this tiny region

Enjoy grape picking at harvest, private tastings and vineyard tours with the wonderful team at Molise Cuisine. Embark on a journey through the countryside and visit some of the region's most renowned wine cellars. Meet the passionate owners and winemakers and stroll through vineyards where their prized tintilia grape thrives. The company offers both short tours and longer ones of up to a week, during which you'll drink (and eat too, of course!) while you discover the secrets behind this region's winemaking.

MOLISECUISINE.COM

Historic cheesemaking and cheese tasting

Agnone's Di Nucci family started working as shepherds in Molise's highlands in 1662 and have been making award-winning artisan cheese there ever since. Their factory, Caseificio di Nucci in Agnone, now offers an exciting tour for cheese lovers, during which you can learn about the history of cheesemaking and sample the different types the family produces: a chance to witness the entire production process and watch skilled artisans working their craft, using traditional techniques. Visiting is a must for anyone looking to experience authentic, high-quality Italian cheese.

CASEIFICIODINUCCI.IT

Become a cavatelli-making expert

Learn to make Molise's most famous pasta shape with Molise Cuisine. Under the guidance of experts, you'll learn the traditional way to craft cavatelli with the best regional ingredients, and you'll get to taste them too. The company offers a range of cooking experiences, which can be customised. Beyond the kitchen, their activities provide insights into Molise's culinary heritage, offering enriching experiences for food enthusiasts. Many nearby agriturismi also offer cooking lessons like La Ginestra, located just out of Campobasso. Along with sleeping and eating here, you can learn to make cavatelli among other local delights.

MOLISECUISINE.COM, LAGINESTRA.INFO

SAGRE

FEBRUARY

La Raviolata,
Ravioli festival, Scapoli

MAY

Sagra della Frittata,
Omelette festival,
Montaquila

JUNE

Fiera della Cipolla,
Onion festival, Isernia

AUGUST

Sagra del Pesce,
Fish festival, Termoli

Fiera del Tartufo Nero,
Black truffle festival,
San Pietro Avellana

Sagra della Pezzata,
Goat and mutton festival,
Capracotta

*Sagra del Baccalà e
Peperuol,* Cod and bell
pepper (capsicum) festival,
Frosolone

SEPTEMBER

Sagra dell'Uva,
Wine festival, Riccia

OCTOBER

*Mostra Mercato
del Tartufo Bianco,*
White truffle festival,
San Pietro Avellana

DECEMBER

Fagiolata di San Nicola,
Bean festival, Guardiaregia

Zuppa alla santè

Holy soup

There are restaurants, and then there are restaurants that are deeply tied to a place. Thanks to Chef Stefania di Pasquo, Locanda Mammì in Agnone is one of the latter. Her extensive experience drives her desire to gift diners unforgettable dishes that blend tradition with innovation. In Molise, *zuppa alla santè* is traditionally eaten at Christmas. It is said to have been created at the end of the 14th century in Agnone, to honour the queen of the kingdom of Naples, Giovanna II. A complete dish with meat, fried cheese and croutons, it truly warms the heart.

Molise

CENTRAL ITALY

SERVES 4

3 eggs

200 g (7 oz) stale rustic bread, cut into 5 mm (¼ in) thick slices

300 g (10½ oz) minced (ground) veal

3 tablespoons extra virgin olive oil

300 g (10½ oz) finely grated cheese (I use 100 g/3½ oz each of Pecorino, parmesan and caciotta)

peanut oil, for deep-frying

120 g (4½ oz) aged caciocavallo, sliced into thin triangles

1 litre (4 cups) chicken stock, heated

Parsley powder

60 g (2 oz) flat-leaf parsley leaves

To make the parsley powder, preheat the oven to 60°C (140°F) fan-forced. Place the parsley in a single layer on a large baking tray and cook for 3 hours or until dry. Allow to cool, then blend in a small blender to a fine powder. Alternatively, use a pestle and mortar to crush the parsley to a fine powder. Set aside. (Any leftovers can be stored in an airtight container in the pantry for up to 6 months.)

Increase the oven temperature to 170°C (340°F) fan-forced.

Beat two of the eggs in a shallow bowl, then coat the bread slices in the egg. Place the bread on a baking tray and cook for about 15 minutes, until golden. Remove from the oven, allow to cool slightly, then cut into cubes.

Meanwhile, combine the veal with the olive oil and season with salt and pepper. Roll teaspoon amounts of the mince into balls (about 7–8 g/⅓ oz each).

Combine the grated cheeses with the remaining egg and roll into small balls about the size of the meatballs.

Heat enough peanut oil for deep-frying in a large saucepan to 160°C (320°F). Working in 3–4 batches, deep-fry the meatballs for 2–3 minutes, until lightly browned. Use a slotted spoon to transfer the meatballs to paper towel to drain. Add the cheese balls to the oil and deep-fry for 2–3 minutes, until golden. Drain on paper towel.

Divide the bread among serving bowls. Roll the meatballs in the parsley powder and place atop the bread, then add the cheese balls and triangles of caciocavallo. Bring the stock to the boil, pour over each bowl, and serve.

Toscana

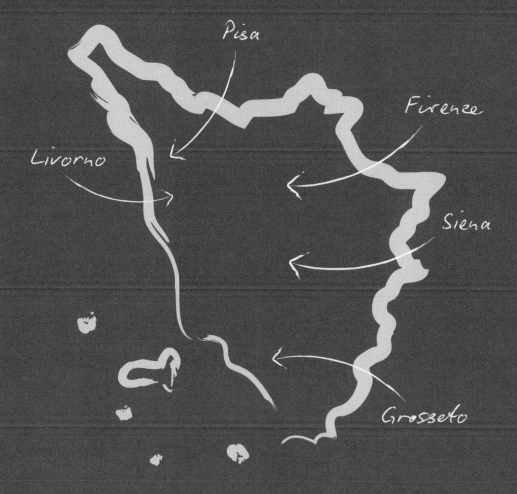

Pisa

Firenze

Livorno

Siena

Grosseto

Regional produce

Like much of Central Italy, Tuscany boasts the perfect climate and conditions for farming. Hilly terrain is covered with vineyards and olive groves, while cereals, vegetables and fruit are in plentiful supply. Known for its meat, Tuscany also has a long coastline, and you can find the treasures of the sea in the region's many port towns.

- Beans
- Cavolo nero
- Chestnuts
- Chianina beef
- Cinta Senese pork
- Eel
- Figs
- Finocchiona salami
- Lardo di Colonnata
- Lunigiana's honey
- Mushrooms
- Pecorino
- Prosciutto
- Truffles
- Wild boar

Florence Cathedral

One of the things I love most about Tuscany is the cliche versus the reality. The cliche is a stunning postcard of the Duomo of Florence, verdant rolling hills and days spent drinking Chianti Classico in the sun. And the thing is, it *is* like that. But that's not the whole picture. Tuscany is about so much more.

The capital, Florence, is a sparkling jewel and one of Italy's most important art cities. Rich with artistic and architectural wonders, it's always been a centre for artisans and tastemakers. It is home to some of Italy's most resplendent artworks, including Michelangelo's *David*. It was Italy's culture capital in the Middle Ages, and the cradle of the Renaissance – funded by that wealthy banking family, the Medicis. It's also where Gucci was born, as well as the signature steak *bistecca alla fiorentina* (page 200), which is grilled over an open flame and eaten *al sangue* (rare).

Italy's most enchanting city might be tied to its past, but the early 21st century has seen a modern-day revival, with irreverent art, edgy architecture and constant shifts in the food scene. The kitchens of the city are alive with young chefs flirting with the classics and new bars and restaurants popping up in historic buildings, keeping locals and visitors on their toes.

My Florentine memories are wonderfully food-filled! Dipping crunchy, almond-studded *cantucci* (page 200) into sweet Vin Santo on a rooftop overlooking the Duomo; catching the banter of stall holders in Sant'Ambrogio market while I burnt my lips on freshly fried *coccoli* (dough balls) stuffed with stracchino cheese; and my first ever *lampredotto* (page 200), at L' Trippaio di San Frediano, a historic stand that serves up this iconic Florentine sandwich, made with tripe from the cow's fourth stomach. Vans and kiosks selling lampredotto are dotted across the Tuscan capital, and it's the dish that those in the know associate with the city: a symbol of Florence's working-class roots and, for many locals, the comfort and nostalgia of their childhoods.

This city, revered by Leonardo Da Vinci, Michelangelo and Botticelli, is easy to fall for, and you'd be forgiven for starting and ending your Tuscan jaunt here. But that would be a mistake. Beyond the splendour of the capital, this region's countryside and towns will bewitch you with their beauty.

You have the medieval towers of San Gimignano, the old walled towns of Lucca and Volterra, the Leaning Tower of Pisa and the world-class wineries of Chianti, Montalcino, Montepulciano and Bolgheri.

Tuscany's coastline comprises the beaches of Maremma, the posh Forte dei Marmi, a lagoon in Orbetello, and an archipelago of islands which will turn your idea of Tuscany on its head. This long coastine means the region's cucina povera traditions sit in contrast with its luxurious seafood dishes.

Toscana

Beyond the splendour of the capital, this region's countryside and towns will bewitch you with their beauty.

CENTRAL ITALY

My first time eating *cacciucco alla livornese* (a fish stew; page 201) on the coast was a revelation. I knew the region wasn't landlocked, but somehow it still felt unexpected because of Tuscany's portrayal in popular culture. No other region has been so overrepresented in modern-day film: a romanticised vision of rustic farmhouses and elegantly crumbling villas being restored against a rolling green backdrop of undulating vines.

Of course, the dishes that are more commonly associated with Tuscany aren't myths. They exist and they each have a story to tell.

Tuscan cuisine has been shaped by various historical influences over the years. It dates to the Etruscans, who settled in the area around 800 BCE. They were highly skilled farmers and traders who introduced a variety of ingredients and culinary techniques, which influenced the region for centuries to come.

Renowned for their cultivation of grapes and olives – both of which are essential components of Tuscan dishes – the Etruscans also introduced herbs, such as rosemary, thyme and oregano. Additionally, they brought *pane sciocco*, a type of flatbread that is still popular; it's known for its absence of salt, which gives the bread a light crumb, chewy exterior and neutral taste. Salt was added later, but then omitted again – a decision which is explained by several theories, including high taxes on salt during the Middle Ages. Others attribute the absence to various conflicts between cities, including Pisa imposing a salt embargo on Florence. Despite these hazy origins, unsalted bread has become a defining characteristic of the region's cuisine and remains a staple for locals and tourists. Today, it is commonly made into toasted crostini, which are spread with creamy chicken liver pate.

Arezzo

After the Etruscans, the Roman Empire further shaped traditions, its influence felt in cooking techniques and inherited dishes from cooking over an open flame to prepare bistecca alla fiorentina to the use of truffles.

Throughout the Middle Ages, Tuscany played a vital role in European commerce, and trade exposed the region to new ingredients and culinary traditions, with Arab traders introducing spices such as cinnamon and saffron.

The Renaissance built upon these historic foundations: as artwork blossomed in Tuscany, so did the cuisine. Dishes began incorporating techniques such as roasting and braising, as well as the use of olive oil, which became a staple. The Renaissance also brought an increased emphasis on presentation, with dishes often designed to be visually appealing as well as delicious. Additionally, advancements in agriculture and ongoing trade allowed for a wider variety of ingredients to be cultivated and imported, further enriching the local cuisine. This period introduced many iconic dishes and marked the elevation of Tuscan gastronomy to a level of sophistication and artistry that continues to influence the region.

Nowadays, Tuscan cuisine starts and ends with its most popular and well-known dish, the famous bistecca alla fiorentina. Then you have *peposo* (page 200), a hearty, slow-cooked beef stew prepared with plenty of black pepper. There's also a bunch of dishes prepared with *cinghiale* (wild boar), from roasts and stews to a ragù for pasta. And of course, there's salumi, such as Prosciutto Toscano and Finocchiona, a salami infused with fennel seeds and spices produced since the Middle Ages. And for a perfect match with salumi and Tuscan wines, there's *pecorino di Pienza*, a sheep's milk cheese which is traditionally aged in wooden barriques.

Vegetarians are covered with Tuscan classics like *ribollita* (page 200), a filling soup of left-over bread, vegetables such as kale and beans, or *pappa al pomodoro* (page 200), a dense mix of stale bread and tomatoes.

These iconic dishes can be eaten across the region, but look out for dishes particular to each geographic area. Across the Maremma, which covers the provinces of Grosseto and Livorno, you'll find tortelli pasta filled with a wild boar ragù, *acquacotta* (a simple bread soup; page 201) and one of my favourites: *gnudi* (pillowy dumplings made with ricotta; page 200).

Further inland across Siena and Arezzo, where hunting is an age-old tradition, you'll find *pappardelle con la lepre* (served with hare), *bistecca con l'acciugata* (steak served with anchovy sauce) and *arista di Cinta Senese* (pork loin). Siena is also famous for its Christmas *panforte* (Italy's version of a fruitcake). Massa Carrara and Lucca are known for their *tordelli*, half-moon-shaped pasta stuffed with minced (ground) meat, cheese and herbs, and Prato for *crostini di fegatini* (pate spread on toasted bread). Closer to the sea, *bordatino alla pisana* or *alla livornese* is a dish made famous by sailors who cooked it on shipping vessels transporting corn. The dense soup is made with cornmeal, cavolo nero and cannellini beans, and is typical to Livorno and Pisa. And originating from the Prato and Florence areas, you have *schiacciata con l'uva* (page 201), a focaccia made with red grapes during wine harvest in September.

So you see, every town in Tuscany, every province, every dish, every wine has a story to tell. And every season too. Each ingredient, each dish has its own identity, its own history, from peasant roots to a glorious Renaissance past.

MARIA'S TOP 10 DISHES OF TOSCANA

1 BISTECCA ALLA FIORENTINA

Tuscany's iconic T-bone steak is a dream for meat lovers. The steak, which is cut three to four fingers thick, is cooked briefly on a wood-fired grill, without any extra condiments, until the outside is dark, charred and crunchy, but the inside is perfectly rare, tender and buttery. It is served with just a sprinkle of salt.

2 CANTUCCI

Known outside of Italy as biscotti, *cantucci* originated in Prato, a town northwest of Florence. The cookies are baked twice so they dry out and harden, allowing them to be stored for long periods. The traditional recipe uses almonds, but there are many variations. In Tuscany, it's customary to eat cantucci after a meal, dipping them in sweet Vin Santo.

3 GNUDI

Gnudi are light and pillowy gnocchi-like spinach and ricotta dumplings, prepared with a mixture that would usually be used to fill ravioli. Instead of covering them with pasta, however, the dumplings are left *nudi* (naked): hence their name. They're boiled and served tossed in butter and sage.

4 PANINO COL LAMPREDOTTO

Lampredotto is a dark-coloured tripe from the fourth (and final) stomach of the cow. This beloved ingredient is found in kiosks all over the city, where it is boiled in stock until soft and thrown into a panini with a herby salsa verde.

5 PANZANELLA

This tasty bread salad is found not only on menus across the region but in Tuscan households of all shapes and sizes! It's a classic favourite. Cubes of stale bread are soaked in water and white wine vinegar, then mixed with tomatoes, cucumber, onions and fresh basil to form a true taste of Tuscan summer.

6 PAPPA AL POMODORO

Stale bread never goes to waste in Italy. Instead, it often ends up as *pappa al pomodoro*. A tomato sauce is made with garlic and olive oil, then stale bread and water are added and the mixture is covered and cooked until the bread completely breaks down into a thick tomato soup. The dish can be served hot or cold, garnished with fresh basil leaves.

7 PAPPARDELLE AL RAGÙ DI CINGHIALE

Wide, flat ribbons of pappardelle are the ideal vehicle to carry Tuscany's rich, gamey boar ragù. The meat is left to marinate overnight in red wine and herbs, then cooked slowly with tomatoes until tender. The dish is topped with grated pecorino.

8 PEPOSO

This beef stew from Impruneta, a town south of Florence, is made with garlic, wine and lots and lots of black pepper. The meat is cooked slowly in Chianti for two or three hours until the wine reduces to a rich, dark sauce and the meat is so tender it falls apart.

9 PICI

Pici is an eggless, hand-rolled pasta like fat spaghetti. It is often coupled with a heavy meat ragù made with wild boar, duck or beef, or topped with *briciole* (breadcrumbs). The most iconic dish is *pici all'aglione*, in which pici is served with a sauce made of aglione garlic (a sweeter and less pungent variety) and tomato sauce.

10 RIBOLLITA

The name of this hearty, wholesome soup translates to 'boiled twice'. After vegetables, potatoes and beans are simmered in a tomato-based broth, the soup is cooled. Stale bread is laid out in a dish and the soup is poured over and left to be absorbed by the bread. When it's ready to serve, the soup is boiled again and stirred to break up the bread.

Other dishes to look out for

Tuscany's cuisine is all about getting maximum flavour out of a handful of quality ingredients, from standout steak and classic breads to humble but delicious soups.

Carcerato pistoiese

Pistoia's 'prisoner' soup dates to a time when the city's prison was surrounded by butchers who donated left-over offal to feed prisoners. The interiors are slowly cooked in water with vegetables, then set side. Stale bread is added for thickening, then the offal is added back in.

Garmugia

Lucca's springtime soup, *garmugia* is a perfect blend of seasonal vegetables, including asparagus, artichokes and fresh peas. They're cooked in stock with minced (ground) beef and pancetta for extra flavour.

Ginestrata

This egg yolk soup was made in the Middle Ages for the bride and groom at weddings. The yolks are stirred into wine, chicken stock, nutmeg, sugar and sometimes cinnamon.

Manafregoli della Garfagnana

A thick peasant soup from the Garfagnana area, made by stirring chestnut flour into salted water until smooth. It's served piping hot, with cold milk, cream or ricotta.

Testarolo artigianale pontremolese

Pontremoli is renowned for its *testaroli*: thin, circular crepes. They're traditionally cooked over a fire, then cut into diamonds and boiled. A pesto-style sauce of basil, olive oil and grated parmigiano is served with them.

Secondi

Scottiglia

This stew comes from a tradition of shared meals around a fire, with neighbours adding meat to the pot. The meat – any combination of pork, beef, chicken, lamb and game – is browned and cooked in a tomato and red wine.

Sedani alla pratese

Celery is the star of this dish from Prato. After boiling, the stalks are sandwiched around a filling of minced veal, mortadella and parmigiano, rolled in flour and egg and fried until golden. The celery is served in a rich sauce, traditionally made with duck.

Trippa alla fiorentina

While lampredotto uses the cow's fourth stomach, this dish calls for the first and second, which are recognisable by their honeycomb texture. They are boiled and cut into strips, then cooked with a tomato sauce and covered with grated parmigiano.

Dolci

Bomboloni

Airy, fried doughnuts rolled in sugar. Round or ring-shaped, they're typically served plain, or occasionally filled with cream or jam.

Castagnaccio

This rich, unleavened, chestnut flour cake is topped with pine nuts and sprigs of rosemary for a rich, autumnal flavour.

Ricciarelli

Made in Siena since the 14th century, these oval cookies were once reserved for nobility. Made with almond flour and sugar folded into egg whites, the dough is coated with icing (confectioners') sugar. They're baked until soft and chewy with a cracked surface.

Torta co' bischeri

Pontasserchio's tart was once offered to pilgrims. It's filled with a cream of rice, chocolate, raisins, candied fruit, pine nuts, liqueur and spices. *Bischeri* (violin pegs) are shaped along the edge of the pastry lattice top.

... and to drink

In this region synonymous with world-class wine, there is no shortage of varietals to discover. Tuscany is home to many household names, the most famous of which is undoubtedly Chianti Classico. It emerged as the region's best-selling wine during the Renaissance, and in 1716, it received legal protection, the region from which it takes its name becoming the world's first officially demarcated wine region. In the 1960s, Chianti Classico and Vernaccia became the first wines to receive a Designation of Origin, or DOC.

Tuscany is also home to the Super Tuscans, which blend traditional Tuscan grapes such as sangiovese with international varieties like merlot. These wines were created in the 1970s by winemakers who wanted to experiment with varietals and techniques outside of Italy's strict regulations, which dictated what grapes could be used. Today, Super Tuscans are highly sought after for their bold flavours and high quality, including elegant Bolgheri DOC wines, which have made best wine lists globally since the 1980s.

While the region is predominantly a red wine zone, it produces quality whites too. Among the many to sample, there's Vermentino di San Gimignano and the not-to-be-missed Vin Santo: perfect for dipping cantucci into.

While you're in Florence, keep an eye out for *buchette del vino* (wine windows once attached to shops). These small, unassuming arched windows emerge from the walls of palazzi. Over the course of three centuries, millions of bottles and glasses of local wine were sold through them. Today there around 150 left around the city centre (mostly in the Santo Spirito neighbourhood), but almost all have been closed up or converted into mailboxes or doorbells.

Spirits and liqueurs also play an important role in the local gastronomic culture, like the most popular *alchermes*: an ancient liqueur made with rose and orange blossom water, and the vanilla- and anise-flavoured Galliano. Biadina and Santoni are two of the more popular amari.

And of course, when it comes to mixology, Florence is the birthplace of one of Italy's most popular cocktails: the Negroni. Its origins trace back to the Caffè Casoni in Florence, where it is believed that, in 1919, Count Camillo Negroni replaced the soda in an Americano with gin. For those who like their gin, Tuscany is home to the famous dry Vallombrosa, which is made by Benedictine monks in an abbey.

Culinary experiences

Take a hot air balloon ride over vineyards, learn how to make a real deal Negroni or indulge on castle grounds – this is how to take your Tuscan adventure to the next level.

Dine under the stars in a Chianti vineyard

Nestled in the lush hills and vineyards of Chianti lies Querceto di Castellina, a 16th-century castle that offers a picturesque backdrop for indulging in the world-renowned Chianti Classico. Explore the estate's 15th-century grounds and organic winery on a guided tour, followed by a tasting of their exquisite offerings. For a more immersive experience, participate in a cooking class or attend one of their enchanting vineyard dinners. To fully unwind in one of the most stunning regions of Tuscany, consider a stay in one of the estate's apartments. As the owners like to say, 'Come for the wine, linger for everything else.'

QUERCETODICASTELLINA.COM

Deep dive into seasonal food and natural wine in hilltop San Miniato

Food and wine lovers will want to join award-winning Australian-Japanese food writer and author Emiko Davies and her Tuscan-born sommelier husband, Marco Lami, in the medieval town of San Miniato. Here at their Enoteca Marilu and Cooking School, they run weekly market and cooking classes, wine tastings and special events. You can also drink at the enoteca and buy organic, sustainable, low-intervention wines. Their five-day workshops (for a maximum of eight people) run throughout the year and will have you fully immersed in a world of seasonal, locally sourced produce and artisans such as beekeepers, winemakers, cheesemakers and grain growers.

ENOTECAMARILU.COM

Experience multi-day slow travel adventures

KM Zero Tours is a boutique slow travel company based in Chianti with tours that promote sustainable tourism and support local communities. Choose from a three-day or seven-day stay at a farmhouse, complete with a pool, and see Italy through local producers and artisans with cooking classes, bread- and pizza-making, wine tastings, olive oil farm visits and cheesemaking demonstrations. Untold Italy run multiple day tours in Tuscany and beyond for small groups. Their unique offering takes you to the heart of each destination with bespoke activities like food tours, tastings and feasts in unforgettable locations.

KMZEROTOURS.COM, UNTOLDITALY.COM

Learn mixology during a luxury stay in Florence

Luxury Italian hotel Relais Santa Croce by Baglioni Hotels and Resorts has teamed up with the lavish Locale cocktail bar in the historic Palazzo Concini to offer a Negroni masterclass and a tour of the palazzo's impressive halls and wine cellar. The hotel's Renaissance-era palazzo, complete with resplendent frescoes, houses the celebrated Enoteca Pinchiorri, the only restaurant in the city with three Michelin stars. Beyond cocktail lessons, the hotel staff can arrange helicopter or hot air balloon tours over vineyards.

FLORENCE.BAGLIONIHOTELS.COM

Combine design and food at a boutique hotel

There is no shortage of show-stopping vineyard stays in this region, but some, like Il Borro, will stick with you long after you leave. In 1993, Ferruccio Ferragamo (of the design family) purchased a medieval village and land between Florence and Arezzo. He created what the family describes as a combination resort, winery and organic farm, and so Il Borro was born. It embodies organic farm-to-table cuisine and boutique wine production and is the perfect mix of medieval Tuscan history, contemporary culture and luxury. You can book into a seasonal cooking class, sample wine at a tasting event or attend an artisan workshop to learn about leather work or how to make jewellery or shoes.

ILBORRO.IT

SAGRE

FEBRUARY

Festa del Cioccolato,
Chocolate festival, Florence

Pitti Taste,
Food and wine event,
Florence

AUGUST

Sagra del Cinghiale e del Tortello,
Wild boar and tortelli festival,
Montepescali

Sagra della Bistecca,
Steak festival, Cortona

Festa del Fagiolo,
Bean festival, Sorana

SEPTEMBER

Sagra della Porchetta,
Porchetta festival,
Monte San Savino

Festa dell'Uva,
Wine festival, Impruneta

Expo Chianti Classico,
Chianti wine event,
Greve in Chianti

OCTOBER

Sagra delle Castagne,
Chestnut festival, Marradi

NOVEMBER

Mostra Mercato Nazionale del Tartufo Bianco, White truffle fair, San Miniato

Tagliatelle ai grani antichi con ragù di cinghiale maremmano

Ancient grain tagliatelle with Maremma wild boar

Beyond the famed bistecca fiorentina, nothing screams Tuscan meat more than *cinghiale* (wild boar). Michelino Gioia, hailing from Tuscany's iconic Hotel Il Pellicano (Restaurant Il Pellicano – a Michelin-starred restaurant, no less), is a passionate culinary artist known for innovative creations that push the boundaries of traditional cooking. As you prepare his dish at home, let the flavours transport you to the seaside magic of Il Pellicano, undoubtedly one of Italy's most chic hotels. And as you eat, let your imagination wander and savour every bite!

Toscana.

CENTRAL ITALY

SERVES 4

700 g (1 lb 11 oz) minced (ground) Maremmano wild boar (see Notes)

150 ml (5½ fl oz) extra virgin olive oil

1 large onion, finely chopped

1 celery stalk, finely chopped

1 carrot, finely copped

300 ml (10½ fl oz) red wine

⅓ cup tomato paste (concentrated puree)

400 g (14 oz) tomato passata (pureed tomatoes)

30 g (1 oz) nutmeg

2 bay leaves

small handful of thyme sprigs

500 ml (2 cups) beef stock, plus extra if needed

Marinade

1 large onion, roughly chopped

1 celery stalk, roughly chopped

1 carrot, roughly copped

3 cloves

5 juniper berries

1 strip orange zest

1 strip lemon zest

300 ml (10½ fl oz) red wine

Ancient grain tagliatelle

550 g (1 lb 4 oz) ancient grain flour (see Notes)

125 g (1 cup) semolina

100 g (3½ oz) egg yolks (about 4 yolks)

250 g (9 oz) whole eggs (about 5 eggs)

To serve

50 g (1¾ oz) butter

40 g (1½ oz) grated De Magi's Pecorino 'Croccolo' (or similar)

Place the wild boar pulp and all of the marinade ingredients in a large non-reactive bowl, then cover and refrigerate for about 18 hours. The next day, remove the meat from the marinade (discard the marinade) and mince the wild boar pulp using a meat grinder. Alternatively, finely chop the meat by hand.

Heat a large heavy-based saucepan over medium heat, add the olive oil and cook the onion, celery and carrot for 6–8 minutes, until lightly browned. Add the minced boar meat and cook, stirring occasionally, for 10 minutes or until the meat is starting to stick to the base of the pan. Add the red wine and stir to deglaze the pan.

Once the wine has evaporated, add the tomato paste, passata, bay leaves and thyme, along with the beef stock, and season with salt and pepper. Reduce the heat to low and cook, stirring occasionally, for 2 hours or until the boar is cooked through. If the sauce starts to dry out, add a little more stock.

Meanwhile, to make the tagliatelle, place the flour and semolina on a clean work surface or in a bowl. Make a well in the centre, add the egg yolks and whole eggs and lightly whisk the eggs until smooth.

Use a fork or your fingertips to gradually incorporate the flour into the beaten egg, then switch to your hands and knead the dough for about 10 minutes, until smooth. Wrap the dough in plastic wrap and refrigerate for at least 30 minutes.

On a lightly floured work surface, roll out the pasta dough until it is 1–2 mm (¹⁄₁₆ in) thick. Cut the dough into long strips of tagliatelle, about 6 mm (¼ in) wide.

Once the meat is ready, bring a large saucepan of salted water to the boil, add the tagliatelle and cook for a few minutes, until al dente.

Add a splash of the pasta cooking water and the butter to the ragù and stir through, then whisk the ragù gently to give it a smooth consistency.

Drain the tagliatelle and add it to the ragù, gently stirring to coat the pasta in the meat sauce. Divide the pasta among plates and serve with the pecorino sprinkled over the top.

Notes: While boar is available at specialty butchers, minced (ground) beef or pork is a perfectly acceptable replacement.

Ancient grain flour can be purchased at specialty grocers, but plain (all-purpose) or type 0 flour is a good substitute.

Toscana

CENTRAL ITALY

Umbria

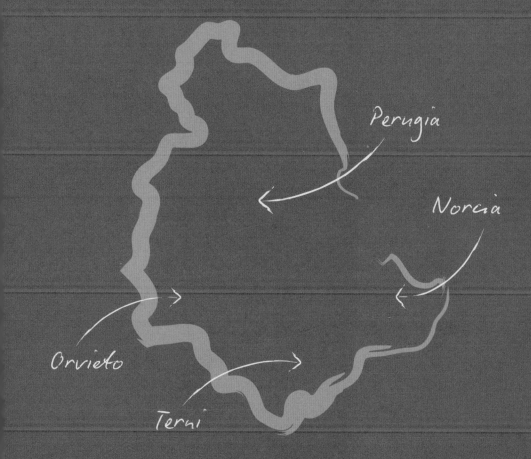

Perugia

Norcia

Orvieto

Terni

Regional produce

The forests, fields, hills and farmland of this green region provide an abundance of produce that earns Umbria its place on the culinary map. Wild game abounds, along with fish from Lake Trasimeno, while the cured meats and cheeses from Norcia are famed for their excellence. Legumes and unique vegetables grow across the region, balancing the rich, robust flavours of traditional Umbrian meat dishes.

- Black truffle
- Cannara's red onions
- Cardoons
- Castelluccio di Norcia's lentils
- Chestnuts
- Colfiorito's red potatoes
- Fagiolina del Trasimeno beans
- Freshwater fish
- Prosciutto di Norcia
- Roveja peas
- Saffron
- Trevi's black celery
- Venison
- Wild boar
- Wild pigeon

Basilica of Saint Francis of Assisi, Assisi

I f I was to describe Umbria in a nutshell, I'd say it was medieval towns, black truffles, chocolate and salumi.

My first visit to Perugia, the region's capital, was spent at the biannual Eurochocolate festival. It rained the whole time, but that didn't stop me eating chocolate in every shape and flavour at stand after stand under my umbrella.

Umbria has a long history of chocolate production, which includes the Perugina Chocolate Factory. Founded in 1907 by the Buitoni family, Perugina is famed for its dark chocolate and hazelnut Baci chocolates (with little love messages tucked inside the wrapping); adding these notes was the idea of famous Italian fashion designer Luisa Spagnoli, the wife of one Giovanni Buitoni. Today, the company, along with dozens of others, participates in Eurochocolate, which attracts visitors from around the world. If you're a chocolate lover like me, put it on your calendar!

On another, less chocolate-focused visit to Umbria, I headed to Norcia, a beautiful town famous for its incredible butchers and charcuterie. The Centro Storico was lined with food stores and displays of salumi – think wild boar sausages, prosciutto and ciauscolo.

Norcia's reputation for producing top-quality pork goes back all the way to the Ancient Roman era, when the town's expert butchers (each known as a *norcino*) were highly respected for their skills: so much so that they were sometimes called upon to perform basic operations on humans. But, by the Middle Ages, 'norcino' had taken on a negative connotation, referring to unscrupulous individuals doing cut-rate surgeries while travelling the countryside.

Despite the reputation that once plagued the term, today 'norcino' is a revered title for those who carry on Norcia's rich heritage of expert pork butchery. As you wander

through the town's charming streets and piazze, you'll notice that many of the family-owned shops are adorned with the word *norcineria* over the door, a testament to the town's enduring tradition. I was delighted to find these shops still filled with skilled artisans who take the finest cuts of pork and turn them into mouth-watering products, including the sausage used to make the creamy pasta alla norcina (page 214). Ever since I tried the dish, life really hasn't been the same.

Then there is Spoleto, another town I'll never forget, not least because of its beautiful and imposing cathedral and the trattoria tucked behind it, where I enjoyed a black truffle frittata. This region is black truffle heartland, and I also enjoyed it on the local *strangozzi* pasta (taken from the Italian verb *strangolare*, which means 'to strangle'; page 214). According to one legend, this pasta was served to parish priests when they visited parishioners for dinner. The idea was to serve them such large portions of strangozzi that it would 'strangle' their appetite and prevent them from indulging in any other foods, to prevent gluttony. However, there are different versions of this story: some say the pasta takes its name from *strenghe*, which refers to long shoelaces. The name's origin is varied and debated, but all I know is that the pasta is long and lush and, with pungent black truffle, delicious.

I could go on: this picturesque region's offerings are abundant. Bordered by Tuscany, Lazio and Marche, the region is landlocked with no coastline, but its mountains, hills, lakes, streams and rivers offer a special charm: a paradise for nature lovers. Touted as the country's green heart, Umbria is famous for its medieval hill towns, such as Perugia, Assisi and Spoleto. Here, dense forests provide an abundance of game and foraged mushrooms, which are both essential to Umbria's no-fuss cucina povera. Here, this tradition is characterised by the

Shop in Norcia

simple, traditional methods that produce the region's superior cured meats, wines, cheeses and olive oil.

Yes, one of the most popular ingredients in Umbria is olive oil: the region's olive groves yield some of Italy's finest. But while Umbria places strong emphasis on these prized products, it also focuses on local produce, such as grains, fresh herbs and some unique vegetables, including the black celery of Trevi and the prized red Cannara onion. And, of course, truffles, which play a significant role in many dishes. They are used in antipasti, pasta, risotto and even to season cured meats and cheeses.

Legumes, particularly lentils and chickpeas (garbanzo beans), are also staples, used to make hearty soups with seasonal vegetables, chestnuts and farro or spelt. They're also used in stews and pastas.

When it comes to pasta, beyond the creamy norcina, you have ciriole alla ternana (page 214), tagliatelle with truffles, meat-filled cappelletti in broth, and *fettucine alla norcina*: not to be confused with the norcina that changed my life, this dish is prepared with anchovies, black truffles and garlic.

Traditional Umbrian meats, such as lamb, pigeon, pork, frogs and goose, are often used in ragù. The region's abundance of meat dishes extends beyond sauces, though. Lamb, pork and game, in particular, are often grilled over a fire or cooked on a spit with plenty of herbs. The region is famous for roast suckling pig and, one of my favourite dishes, *porchetta* (page 214). The slow-roasted pork is a staple and is often served at festivals and celebrations.

From its freshwater sources (especially Lake Trasimeno), Umbria has abundant fish, including carp, trout, mullet, pike

and perch. These are transformed into the region's specialties, which include *regina in porchetta*: carp cooked in a wood oven in the same manner as the classic porchetta (rolled with plenty of herbs). *Tegamaccio* is also popular, this cross between a soup and a stew prepared with any of the fish found in the lake. And of course *umbricelli in salsa di Trasimeno*: pasta that's prepared with perch fillets.

When it comes to bread, Umbria is similar to Tuscany in that some of its bread doesn't have salt. This tradition's origins are debated, with some theorising high taxes in the Middle Ages led bakers to go without. However, a little salt has made its way back into some breads today, like *torta al testo*, which is a popular flatbread cooked on a *testo* (cast-iron disc) over the fire and filled with cured meats, sausages or sauteed greens; it is served by itself and as an

accompaniment to the region's meats and stews. Then there's the *pizza al formaggio*, a round bread made with a variety of cheeses (and salt), traditionally served at Easter.

Traditional Umbrian desserts are typically oven baked and made with ingredients like almonds, honey, spices and candied fruit. The two largest cities, Perugia and Foligno, are renowned for their pastry and sweets, boasting some of the region's oldest pasticcerie selling traditional sweets like the *torcolo di San Costanzo*, a rustic, sweetened yeast doughnut with pine nuts, raisins and anise that's prepared for the feast of Perugia's patron saint, Constantius, on 29 January. Other towns have their own sweets for patron saints including Itieli, a small town in the province of Terni. Its *ciammella di Itieli* are soft, aniseed-flavoured doughnuts, prepared for the festival of San Nicola on the third Saturday in May. Three families are nominated each year to prepare the ciammelle for the whole town.

In short, this green heart of the country knows boundless quality. From the unique richness of truffles unearthed in its forests to the golden hue and robust flavours of its renowned olive oil, Umbria spoils the senses with a tapestry of gastronomic delights. Each dish is a testament to the region's commitment to honest, unpretentious cooking, rooted in tradition and perfected over generations. Whether you're indulging in a velvety square of dark chocolate or savouring a rustic bowl of pasta, every bite embodies the essence of Italian home cooking at its finest. But amid this abundance, it is the simplicity and authenticity of Umbrian cuisine that truly captivate.

MARIA'S TOP 10 DISHES OF UMBRIA

1 BRUSTENGOLO

A simple mixture of polenta, sugar, apples, raisins and nuts, *brustengolo* is a dense, rustic cake that was once made at Christmas with cheap ingredients already found in the home. Now enjoyed all through the year, this nutritious cake lacks eggs and flour which means it's a vegan, gluten-free dessert for everyone to enjoy.

2 CICOTTO DI GRUTTI

Since the 16th century, porchetta has been prepared in the small town of Grutti with the addition of *cicotto* (the extra parts of the pig, including the ears, shin, tongue and trotters). These are placed underneath the main cut of loin so the excess fat and herbs can drip onto them. After a slow 12 hours of cooking, the cicotto is left to cool and then served in a panino as street food.

3 FRICCÒ ALL'EUGUBINA

Gubbio's signature stew is traditionally made with chicken, rabbit and lamb (or just one or two of these). The meat is cut into chunks on the bone and cooked slowly with tomatoes, garlic and rosemary until tender and juicy. It is served with the local crescia flatbread to mop up any left-over sauce.

4 PARMIGIANA DI GOBBI

From Perugia, this take on the classic eggplant (aubergine) parmigiana uses local wild cardoons in place of the eggplant. The cardoons are battered and fried, layered with a tomato and meat sauce, creamy bechamel and lots of grated cheese, then baked in the oven.

5 PAMPEPATO

This Christmas cake is found all over Umbria, particularly in Terni. The ingredients were traditionally preserved and then put aside through the year. Each family used different amounts of nuts, dried and candied fruits, spices, coffee and chocolate, so there are now hundreds of passed-down recipes.

6 PASTA ALLA NORCINA

Norcia's long history of pig butchery means it's no surprise that its eponymous pasta dish features crumbled local pork sausages. Once made with sheep's milk ricotta diluted with pasta water, it's now commonly made with fresh cream and sometimes topped with a grating of black truffle.

7 PIZZA DI PASQUA

A savoury cake made with pecorino and usually eaten on Easter Sunday, accompanied by a local Umbrian salami called *corallina*. There is also a sweet version made without cheese or salami, topped with icing and sugar sprinkles instead.

8 PORCHETTA

The origins of this rolled, slow-roasted pork dish are hotly contested, with Norcia, among other towns, laying claim. All agree that the authentic version should be cooked in a wood-fired oven to ensure a crispy skin (the crackling is often the most sought-after bit). The seasoning varies from region to region across Central Italy, with the subtle aniseed notes of wild fennel playing a signature role in the Umbrian recipe.

9 STRANGOZZI / UMBRICELLI / CIRIOLE

These long strands of pasta are known by several names, depending on the area – *strangozzi* in Foligno and Spoleto, *umbricelli* in Perugia and *ciriole* in Terni. However, all agree that they must be made by hand from wheat flour and water, rolled out and cut into thin strips. They're often served with local truffles or meat-based sauces.

10 ZUPPA DI CECI E CASTAGNE

Once made and eaten on Christmas Eve, this hearty soup uses local chestnuts that are combined with chickpeas (garbanzo beans), garlic and rosemary. The soup is served with toasted bread for dipping and a drizzle of Umbrian olive oil.

Other dishes to look out for

Umbria's small size means that its cuisine is sometimes overshadowed by its famous neighbour, Tuscany. However, the wilderness and farmland of this green region provide plenty of inspiration to put Umbria on the culinary map.

Antipasto

Arvoltolo

Also known as *tortuccia*, this dish is prepared with a dough of flour, water and oil which is formed into large rounds and then fried in lots of olive oil until crisp. It may then be dusted with salt and eaten with cured meat and cheese as an antipasto or coated with icing (confectioners') sugar and enjoyed at the end of a meal.

Bandiera

Meaning 'flag' in English, Umbria's patriotic *bandiera* vegetable dish gets its name from the colours of the ingredients – green peppers, white onions and red tomatoes. The vegetables are cooked slowly and gently in olive oil to bring out their natural sweetness and are often served at room temperature as the perfect accompaniment to the region's hearty, meaty dishes.

Brosega

Brosega is similar to Naples' *uova al purgatorio* (eggs in purgatory), which is a baked egg dish of sorts. In Umbria's version, whole eggs are cracked into a thick tomato and onion sauce and then baked – the onions are usually missing from Naples' recipe. Originally made in Umbria by the farmers of Paciano, this dish is eaten straight from the pan with a spoon and plenty of bread for dipping.

Lumache alla ternana

Snails are frequently collected and eaten in Umbria's countryside. In this recipe from Terni, they are cleaned and boiled, then cooked with local herbs and a tomato sauce.

Primi

Farrecchiata di roveja

Roveja is a small, greenish brown pea cultivated predominantly in Umbria and neighbouring Marche. Usually sold dried or semi-fresh, roveja can be ground into a flour and used to make *farrecchiata*, a polenta flavoured with garlic and anchovies.

Gnocchetti alla collescipolana

Collescipoli's small gnocchi are made with flour, water and fine breadcrumbs, giving them a more compact texture than the usual potato-based recipe. The *gnocchetti* are served with a sauce of local Terni pork sausage, tomato, chilli and cannellini beans or similar varieties, and topped liberally with grated pecorino.

Spaghetti col rancetto

This tomato-based dish from Spoleto looks a lot like the Roman amatriciana (page 155) but uses pancetta, onions and marjoram in place of guanciale and chilli. It's also served with umbricelli, a thick spaghetti.

Umbria

CENTRAL ITALY

Zuppa di lenticchie

Umbria is famous for its lentils, which are small and tender with a thin skin so they don't need to be pre-soaked. This warming soup is made with a soffritto of finely chopped celery, carrot and onion and flavoured with bay leaves and rosemary or sage. Fatty prosciutto can be added for extra flavour.

Secondi

Galantina

The star of every Umbrian Christmas, *galantina* is a terrine made with a deboned chicken which is stuffed with minced (ground) meat, boiled eggs, carrot, celery, pistachios, truffle and cheese. Once filled, it's tied with twine, wrapped in a cloth and boiled in stock. After cooling under a weight, the galantina is sliced and served cold.

Gallina 'mbriaca

This stew from Orvieto, a city southwest of Perugia, literally translates to 'drunken hen'. Chicken is marinated overnight in red wine, then cooked on the stove with the juices from the marinade and more wine until the meat is tender and falls off the bone.

Impastoiata

From *impastare*, meaning 'to knead together', the dish's name refers to the union of its two main elements, polenta and beans. To bring them together, a bed of smooth, creamy polenta is topped with a stew of borlotti (cranberry) beans, lardo and tomato.

Palomba alla ghiotta

Palomba is a type of wild pigeon with a strong flavour, rarely found outside of Umbria. Its interiors are cooked in a pan with red wine, garlic, olives and herbs to create a luscious, glossy sauce, the meat roasted on a spit or in the oven.

Sedano nero di Trevi ripieno

Trevi is famed for its black celery, which has a more pronounced flavour than the regular variety. In this dish, the whole head is briefly boiled and filled with mixed minced (ground) meats and sausage. Tied with string, it is dipped in flour and egg and fried in oil, then baked covered with tomato sauce and cheese.

Dolci

Ciaramicola

Perugia's symbolic Easter cake dates to the 1400s. The large, doughnut-shaped sponge is tinged red with alchermes liqueur while the meringue topping is bright white, echoing the city's coat of arms (a red shield with a white griffin) and symbolising love (red) and purity (white). Young women used to offer this cake to their suitors on Easter Sunday.

Crescionda

Every family in Spoleto has their own recipe for this renowned Carnevale cake, but the consensus is that it has three layers: a base of almond amaretti, a creamy centre of eggs and milk, and a topping of dark chocolate.

Pinoccate

To make these diamond-shaped sweets associated with Christmas, pine nuts and lemon zest are added to a thick sugar syrup. The mixture is poured onto a flat surface to set, and while it cools, the *pinoccate* are cut. Once ready, they're individually wrapped in brightly coloured paper. The lemon may be swapped for cocoa to make a 'black' version.

Rocciata

A round, strudel-like cake also known as *attorta*, rocciata has a crisp, flaky pastry exterior filled with apple, raisins and nuts. Its distinctive pink colour comes from the coating of alchermes added after baking.

... and to drink

Wine is an essential, ancient part of Umbrian cuisine. The area's climate is influenced by the Apennine Mountains, which run through Umbria, producing one of Italy's colder regions. With cool winters and warm summers, the weather is ideal for viticulture, as is the soil, which comprises a diverse mix of clay, sand and limestone. Together, these create grapes with unique flavours.

Production here is mostly centred around three areas: the Tiber River Valley, the hills around the town of Montefalco, and the region of Orvieto. Umbria has over a dozen distinct DOC regions, which include Assisi, Colli Altotiberini, Colli Amerini, Colli del Trasimeno, Colli Martani, Colli Perugini, Lago di Corbara, Montefalco, Orvieto Classico, Rosso Orvietano and Torgiano.

Like nearby Lazio and Marche, Umbria is more famous for its whites. Its well-known varieties are produced from grechetto grapes – especially those in the Orvietto area. The popular Orvieto DOC is made from grechetto and trebbiano grapes: a refreshing and crisp wine with notes of citrus and minerality that pairs well with seafood dishes.

Antinori and Lungarotti wineries are among the more popular brands exporting Orvieto DOC whites outside of Italy, while red wine vintners, such as Arnoldo Caprai, Colpetrone, Antonelli, Bea and Tabarrini, brought Sagrantino di Montefalco to the world's attention. This full-bodied red is known for its intense notes of dark fruit: a perfect pairing for hearty foods, such as roasted meats or aged cheeses.

Umbria is also home to several lesser-known varieties that are worth trying. These include Torgiano Rosso Riserva, a red wine made from sangiovese and canaiolo grapes, and the elegant Trebbiano Spoletino.

Umbria offers more than just wine, though. In a nod to a long history of foraging, the region's many shrubs, herbs and spices (and even truffles!) are used to produce some high-quality liqueurs, amari and grappa, including *nocino*, infused with walnuts and chocolate. In the Assisi area, you can find Rosolio Franciscan, the oldest available *rosolio*, a liqueur made with rose petals.

The region is also known for beer, like the award-winning Birra Perugia. Craft beer is having a bit of a moment here, with small breweries on the rise. In the town of Nocera, for instance, Birrificio San Biagio is located in a centuries-old monastery where they specialise in high-end craft brews.

Umbria

CENTRAL ITALY

Culinary experiences

Whether you're looking for a castle retreat or a spot of truffle hunting, or you want to live out your childhood chocolate factory fantasies, Umbria will leave an indelible mark on your memory.

Experience life in a 1,000-year-old castle and explore the Umbrian countryside

Set in the tranquil and picturesque Umbrian landscape lies the magnificent Castello di Reschio, a grand castle steeped in history that dates to 1050. This remarkable fortress has been thoughtfully and meticulously converted into a charming rural retreat, offering a perfect escape from the bustle of modern life. Inside the castle, you'll find spacious and elegant rooms adorned with tasteful and modern design elements that harmoniously blend with the building's ancient features. Surrounded by verdant hills and meadows, the hotel boasts a spa, pool and activities to suit all tastes. You can choose from nature hikes and wildlife watching to foraging expeditions and truffle hunting. If you'd like to stay in, they also offer on-site cooking classes to learn all about the local cuisine.

RESCHIO.COM

Truffle hunting, olive oil tasting and aperitivo in ancient caves

Local agency Umbria con Me has worked solely in this region for more than two decades and offers culinary tours and customised experiences, from truffle hunting to cellar tours and olive oil tastings. They run cooking classes at local farms and even offer a food and wine tasting or aperitivo in the underground caves of Orvieto. Be fully immersed in Umbria's food and wine heritage and meet the local artisans and tastemakers working behind the scenes.

UMBRIACONME.COM

Explore the food (and chocolate) of Perugia

Indulge in Perugia's history with a tour of tasting locations within the historic centre. Sample classic Umbrian flavours at restaurants, cafes and markets. You'll taste local flatbread, pasta, cheeses and a whole lot more. Stroll medieval streets and learn about the city's ancient architectural gems, its museums, food artisans and arts scene. Perugia-based Via del Vino runs these tours almost daily, all year round. Afterwards, satisfy your sweet tooth by discovering the secrets of chocolate-making on a tour of the Perugina Chocolate Factory. Learn about this iconic brand from master chocolatiers and witness the magic, sampling plenty of chocolate along the way!

VIADELVINO.COM, PERUGINA.COM

Foraging and forest bathing at a chic hotel

Just an hour from the medieval city of Perugia lies Vocabolo Moscatelli, a charming design hotel in a restored 12th-century monastery. The cosy getaway was the brainchild of hoteliers Frederik Kubierschky and Catharina Lütjens, who set out to create a little slice of paradise. Their restaurant offers a fusion of modern Italian cuisine with international flair, influenced by the renowned chef Yotam Ottolenghi. Hospitality goes further here, with their philosophy of connecting with the local community. To have a truly soulful Umbrian experience, you can enjoy foraging, wine tasting, truffle hunting, forest bathing and pottery classes.

VOCABOLOMOSCATELLI.COM

Stay and eat at a farmhouse in medieval Todi

Danish chef couple Lisbeth and Thomas worked in hospitality for years before opening this dream property in the gorgeous hilltop town of Todi. A stay at their farmhouse is about the seasons, local produce and slow life. The on-site cooking school boasts a rich program of lessons with varying themes and duration, but they'll happily tailor your experience. Visiting a local wine producer and challenging yourself with a hike or a truffle hunt are just some of the activities on offer. This fantastic couple are the friends in the Italian countryside you always wished you had!

ILGHIOTTONEUMBRO.COM

SAGRE

FEBRUARY

Sagra del Tartufo,
Black truffle festival, Norcia

Cioccolentino,
Chocolate festival, Terni

MARCH

Eurochocolate, Perugia
(twice annually)

MAY

Porchettiamo,
Porchetta festival, San Terenziano

SEPTEMBER

I Primi d'Italia,
First courses festival, Foligno

Festa della Cipolla,
Onion festival, Cannara

Uwine, Umbrian wine festival, Perugia

OCTOBER

Eurochocolate, Perugia
(twice annually)

Mostra Mercato dello Zafferano, Saffron festival, Cascia

NOVEMBER

Festa dell'Olivo e della Bruschetta, Olive and bruschetta festival, Spello

Festa del Vino Novello e della Castagna, New wine and chestnut fair, Narni

Palomba alla ghiotta

Umbrian roasted wild pigeon

Nothing represents Umbria more than pigeon, and this dish,
which roasts the bird in the oven, takes you straight to the region.
Chef Lorenzo Cantoni, of monastery turned design resort
Vocabolo Moscatelli, was so kind to share this recipe with me.
It's close to his heart, as he says it was one of the first recipes
he learned as a chef. This age-old dish is typical of the medieval
town of Todi, particularly in the warmer months, when it features
on restaurant menus. Keep some fresh bread handy *per fare
la scarpetta* (to mop up the juices).

Umbria

SERVES 4

200 g (7 oz) pork sausages

1 tablespoon finely chopped
rosemary leaves

7 sage leaves, finely chopped

50 ml (1¾ fl oz) extra virgin
olive oil

2 garlic cloves, crushed

2 wild pigeons or 4 large quails
(about 160 g/5½ oz each),
prepared by your butcher

30 g (1 oz) lardo, finely sliced

6–7 juniper berries

175 ml (6 fl oz) red wine, plus
extra if needed

crusty bread, to serve

Preheat the oven to 170°C (340°F) fan-forced.

Squeeze the meat from the sausages into a bowl and
stir in the rosemary and sage. Add the olive oil, garlic, salt
to taste and a generous crack of black pepper, and mix
well. Stuff the pigeons or quail with the sausage mixture.
Truss the legs together with kitchen twine.

Drape the lardo over the breasts of the pigeons or quail
and place them in a clay pot or ovenproof dish with the
juniper berries and red wine. Cover with foil and roast
for 20 minutes, then remove the foil and cook for a
further 15–20 minutes, until golden and cooked through.

Serve with crusty bread.

CENTRAL ITALY

Basilicata

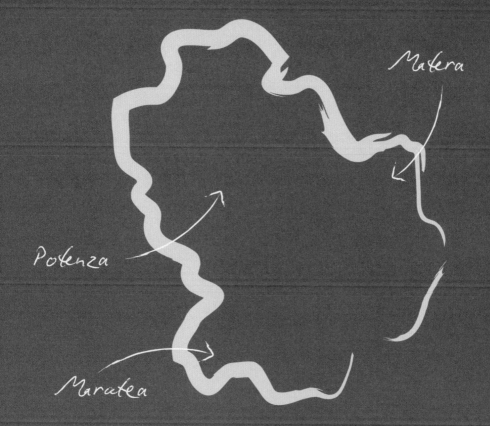

Matera

Potenza

Maratea

Regional produce

Basilicata's rural landscape and agricultural
traditions keep its larder well stocked
with rustic ingredients that symbolise the
region's cuisine. Expanses of wheat fields
contribute to local pasta and breadmaking,
while sheep and pig farming bring lamb,
pork, mutton and pecorino into the
mix. The culinary symbol of Basilicata
is undoubtedly the *peperone crusco*
(dried pepper) from Senise, which is used
in a multitude of dishes to add a uniquely
local flavour.

- Baccalà
- Caciocavallo cheese
- Horseradish
- Lamb
- Lucanica sausage
- Matera bread
- Moliterno's Canestrato
- Pork
- Red chilli pepper
- Rotonda's red eggplant
  (aubergine)
- Pecorino di Fillano
- Pezzente salami
- Sarconi beans
- Senise's peperoni cruschi
- Vincotto

Matera

One of Italy's most southern regions, Basilicata takes up real estate in the arch of the boot. From the coast, the region leads all the way up to the inland borders of Apulia, Campania and Calabria.

International tourism has increasingly spread across the peninsula's south over the last decade, and Basilicata is finally having its moment in the global spotlight. Destinations include Matera in the region's east: one of the oldest inhabited cities in the world, with rock-cut caves that the locals used to live in. It was named a UNESCO World Heritage Site in the 1990s, and became the European Capital of Culture for 2019. Not bad for a city that was once called the 'shame of Italy'.

Entire families, sometimes with livestock, used to live in Matera's cramped spaces. And we're not talking back in the Middle Ages, but within living memory. Extreme poverty and widespread disease in its ancient Sassi districts led to the compulsory relocation of residents in the 1950s, and so the crumbling neighbourhood, one of the oldest in the world, lay empty for the first time in 10,000 years.

More than half a century later, investments had helped makeover this belle for the ball. After the city received years of funding and attention, Hollywood came knocking: Matera became the backdrop for Mel Gibson in *Passion of the Christ* and Daniel Craig in *No Time to Die*.

I visited in 2018, a year before the city's new fame earned it its 2019 title. Nowadays, the historical centre is strikingly beautiful, but there's something unnerving about it: there's still an echo of Matera's impoverished and unstable past. But even so, I saw signs of its renaissance everywhere: in the boutiques run by young locals, in the contemporary wine bars and, especially, in the tourists who wouldn't have been caught dead in this part of Italy not long ago. Although the families

that were forced out never returned, many of their descendants came back to open hotels and restaurants.

While it's a region that challenges itself to look to the future, this context is critical to understanding Basilicata's ties to its history, its land and its cuisine.

If Basilicata was a food, it would definitely be the *peperone crusco*. Touted as the 'red gold' of the region, this dried bell pepper (capsicum) is a local specialty. Prepared with the certified indigenous Senise variety, which is sweet, the peppers require a labour-intensive process. It takes place over rugged terrain in the hot summer months, when the peppers ripen and develop their bright red colour. Once ripe, they are picked, hand-strung on vertical wreaths and left to dry in the sun for a month.

When the peppers are thoroughly dried and slightly shrivelled, they are flash fried for seven seconds (no more!) in local extra virgin olive oil and packaged with a light

Basilicata

SOUTHERN ITALY

dusting of sea salt, producing a deliciously crunchy, uniquely flavoured snack. Across the region you'll find it in fillings, crumbled on pasta dishes and tossed through vegetables in *contorni* (side dishes). It is the pride of the *lucani* (the locals' name for themselves, taken from Basilicata's ancient name of Lucania) and a perfect example of the cucina povera that characterises this land. La cucina lucana is more than this humble pepper, but a conversation about food in these parts couldn't be had without it.

Vegetables hold the same importance as meat in Basilicata's cuisine, with an abundance of characteristic produce, such as eggplants (aubergines, including a red variety), artichokes, tomatoes, broccoli rabe, potatoes, *lampascioni* (wild hyacinth bulbs), peppers, chicory and broad (fava) beans. Legumes such as chickpeas (garbanzo beans) and lentils are also commonly grown and appear in most household recipes. Chestnuts and mushrooms feature as well, found along with a range of herbs in the expansive Pollino National Park that spans across Basilicata and Calabria.

Basilicata is also known for its spicy dishes. In fact, Basilicata has the second highest amount of chilli consumption per person in Italy, after neighbouring Calabria. The most common varieties of *peperoncino* (chilli peppers) are Diavolicchi and Sigarette. As is common throughout the South, many homes have strings of dried chillies hanging in the kitchen, ready to use.

Because the region's cuisine still embraces an austere kind of simplicity, pasta and bread are staples here. Handmade pasta comes in various imaginative shapes, typically made from just flour and water, without eggs – elsewhere a prized ingredient. Among the popular pasta shapes are *strascinati* (with indentations made using two or three fingers), *tagliolini* (thin spaghetti), *orecchiette*

The Aliano badlands

(small pasta shaped like ears), *tapparelle* (large orecchiette), *lagane* (wide, thick tagliatelle) and *ferrettini* or *fusilli* (strips rolled around a thin metal rod).

In the capital of Potenza, *cavatelli* (small, shell-shaped pasta) are usually served with beans, while lagane are cooked with chickpeas. Strascinati are tossed through peperoni cruschi dust and a grating of *cacioricotta*, the local hard cheese. As for orecchiette, they may be prepared with tomatoes, cheese and lamb to create *orecchiette alla materana* (page 228).

Although fresh fish is readily available in coastal areas, particularly around Maratea (not to be confused with Matera), meat dishes are more popular inland, commonly made with pork, goat, beef and lamb. However, as was the case in many communities around the world in the past, meat was once an expensive rarity only served at special occasions, and even today locals are not huge meat eaters. Materani would traditionally only eat meat two or three times a year (at times of festival) and often, on those occasions, they would make *la pignata*.

This mixture of broth, potatoes, onions, celery, tomatoes and some local cheese is prepared with the main ingredient: mutton. It's traditionally cooked very slowly in a large earthenware pot in a wood oven. Sometimes it's made with bread dough covering the top of the pot, acting as a seal. The idea is that the bread is then broken into the stew, creating a hearty secondo. And speaking of bread, you won't want to miss the Pane di Matera, which is a country-style sourdough made with semolina using ancient techniques.

Young lamb is a delicacy here and was once thought to have medicinal properties. Today, it is often served for special family meals at Easter and Christmas. During the latter, all families, regardless of income, prepare up to 13 different dishes for their feasts in reference to the last supper shared by Jesus and his 12 apostles. Families also raise pigs, which are roasted whole during festivities or used to make sausages and

salumi (like the popular salsiccia lucanica and salsiccia di Cancellara), which can be mild or *piccante* (spicy, from added chillies).

Butter rarely makes an appearance in these dishes. Extra virgin olive oil is a prized product in several parts of Basilicata, and it is used extensively instead throughout the region.

Basilicata is also known for its cheeses – especially the exceptional *caciocavallo podolico*, formed in the shape of a giant teardrop. Other cow's milk cheeses include provolone, scamorza, burrata, mozzarella and caciotta. Sheep's and goat's milk cheeses are also popular, including Pecorino di Filiano, moliterno and the salted cacioricotta.

From its cuisine to its history, including Matera's renaissance as a cultural capital, Basilicata is finally getting the recognition it deserves on the global stage. Where poverty and disease were once the norms, the Lucani have persevered to emerge stronger than ever, and their humble cuisine gives you a real taste of the land and the region's story of struggle, resilience and passion.

If Basilicata was a food, it would definitely be the peperone crusco. Touted as the 'red gold' of the region, these dried red bell peppers (capsicums) are a rare specialty.

MARIA'S TOP 10 DISHES OF BASILICATA

1 BRODETTO LUCANO

A beloved part of Basilicata's annual Easter feast, the local *brodetto* (also known as *tortino di asparagi e carne d'agnello* and, in dialect, *vredett*) unites the springtime ingredients of lamb, wild asparagus and eggs, which are baked to create a kind of pie flavoured with wild fennel.

2 CIALLEDDA MATERANA

Invented to utilise old bread, a basic *cialledda* combines tomatoes, onions and the local Matera bread, which is soaked in water to soften it and seasoned with olive oil and oregano. Also known as *colazione del mietitore* (harvester's breakfast), the dish may include other ingredients, such as cucumber and olives. There is a winter version, served hot, which includes eggs and seasonal vegetables such as chicory and broccoli rabe.

3 CIAMBOTTA

Similar to caponata (page 308), *ciambotta* is a medley of eggplant (aubergine), bell peppers (capsicums), tomatoes, onion and potato. It was originally prepared by the wives of farmers and shepherds for their husbands, placed in a large, hollowed-out loaf of bread for transport to work.

4 FUCUAZZA CU LA PRMMARORA

Closer to a pizza than a focaccia, this bread consists of a flat, crunchy base topped with olive oil, tomato sauce and oregano. You can make it without tomato, or with cheese and vegetable, but nothing beats the classic version.

5 FUSILLI AL FERRETTO CON PEPERONI CRUSCHI

Basilicata's *fusilli* are twisted around a *ferretto* (metal rod). This method, used throughout the South, is famously typical of this region. The fusilli are often paired with peperoni cruschi and cacioricotta cheese.

6 MUNNULATA

Autumnal ingredients collide in this soup of Castelsaraceno, which is prepared in the countryside as the evenings begin to cool down. Made with chestnuts, borlotti (cranberry) beans, peperone crusco and sometimes potatoes, it pairs well with bread, which soaks up the flavours.

7 ORECCHIETTE ALLA MATERANA

Matera's baked pasta dish consists of orecchiette that are first cooked, then mixed with a sauce of minced or diced lamb and tomato. The pasta is layered with chunks of mozzarella and grated pecorino before being baked in the oven until the cheese melts and the top is crunchy and golden.

8 PASTA CON RAGÙ ROSSO POTENTINO

Legend has it that the recipe for Potenza's signature pasta sauce was invented when a piece of salame pezzente fell into a traditional meat ragù: it was agreed that the sauce tasted better with this addition. Usually served with strozzapreti or strascinati, the sauce is often topped with fresh, spicy red chilli, chilli powder or a grating of fresh horseradish – a relatively uncommon ingredient in Southern Italy.

9 STRAZZATE MATERANE

Matera's *strazzate* are made at Christmas and resemble cantucci. Made with toasted almonds, cinnamon, cocoa and lemon, they can be hard and crunchy or soft and delicate. They're often eaten after a meal, dipped in a glass of *passito* (sweet wine).

10 TIMBALLO DI RISO AL FORNO

This layered, savoury cake has a base of rice topped with minced meat, sausage, chicken livers, provola, pecorino, eggs, tomato sauce and breadcrumbs. It is covered with a layer of rice and baked until the top is crisp and the inside is gooey.

Other dishes to look out for

From dense regional bread to simple stews and, of course, a heaping finish of chilli, the cuisine of Basilicata wears its complex history and unique landscape on its sleeve.

Street food

Carchiola

It takes just three ingredients and a touch of magic to make *carchiola*: a mixture of cornmeal, boiling water and salt. It is rolled into a flat circle and cooked over fire, and can be stuffed or served with vegetable soup.

Gnummareddi

Found all across Southern Italy and known by many names, Basilicata's *gnummareddi* are made with mixed lamb or kid offal encased in tightly wrapped intestines and seasoned with parsley and wild fennel seeds.

Scarcédda / Picciddata

A typical Easter treat that exists in both sweet and savoury versions. Either is recognisable by the whole eggs baked into the dough. The savoury pie uses fresh ricotta, pecorino and lucano sausage, while the sweet version uses sugar, lemon and vanilla.

Strazzata

Hailing from the town of Avigliano, this doughnut-shaped focaccia is made with plenty of black pepper and is often served stuffed with salami, vegetables or cheese. There is also a sweet version filled with chocolate or jam.

Primi

Cappucci e cicorie

This soup starts with a slow-cooked stock made by boiling a pig trotter and pork rind. Locally grown white cabbage and wild chicory are then added and everything is cooked together with aromatic fennel seeds.

Cauzunciedd

Basilicata's version of ravioli are stuffed with sheep's ricotta, egg and a touch of mint. They are typically served with a simple tomato sauce, topped with grated pecorino.

Crapiata materana

Dating back centuries, this traditional Materan soup is a symbol of community, which celebrates the end of the harvest. Mixed vegetables, grains and legumes are slowly cooked together: these commonly include lentils, beans, peas, spelt, onion, celery, carrots, tomatoes and new potatoes.

Frascatula

The polenta of the South, *frascatula* is found in the mountainous areas of the region. It is made with ground cornmeal cooked until thick and usually served with vegetables, offal or less prestigious cuts of pork.

Tumact me tulez

Originating in Barile, this dish from the Arbëreshë community of Albanian-Italians is found all over the South. To make it, fresh tagliatelle is tossed in a sauce of tomato and anchovy and topped with toasted breadcrumbs and chopped walnuts.

Secondi

Anguilla di Pantano

A local specialty, eel are found in the rivers around Lucano and in the picturesque lake of Pantano di Pignola, from which this dish takes its name. The eel is stewed with chilli, tomatoes, mint, bay leaf and potato, and topped with fresh mint.

Baccalà all'aviglianese / alla lucana

Until relatively recently, the only fish available in inland Basilicata was *baccalà* (salt-dried cod). This recipe puts a Basilicata stamp on the fish by adding the ever-present peperone crusco, which are cooked until crispy and served with the pan-fried fish.

Zucca lunga sposata / Cocuzza logna maritata

The long, pale green variety of zucchini (courgette) found in Sicily and Southern Italy are given a Lucanian twist in this recipe. Chunks of zucchini are cooked with onion until silky soft and *sposata* (married) with small meatballs and a touch of tomato.

Contorni

Insalata di lampascioni

This salad is synonymous with Basilicata's Christmas season. *Lampascioni* (wild hyacinth bulbs) are soaked and boiled to soften their texture and remove their bitterness, then seasoned with garlic, oregano, olive oil and a dash of vinegar. They are occasionally served mixed with eggs, peperoni cruschi, sausage or tomatoes.

Patate alla laurenzanese

In this dish from the town of Laurenzana, potatoes are stuffed with a mix of sausage, cheese, eggs and sometimes breadcrumbs, then baked. A little horseradish can be added for extra flavour.

Dolci

Lagana chiapputa

This unusual dessert features lagane as its base, covered with walnuts, almonds, pine nuts, raisins and vincotto, which is commonly used in the region.

Scorzette

These sweets hail from the medieval town of Bernalda. Almond meringue is shaped into ovals and curled up at the edges before baking, then spread on one side with melted dark chocolate.

Torta di ricotta

Baked to celebrate the return of spring, this ricotta tart is commonly eaten at Easter and was historically made to use up the abundance of milk at this time of the year. A light pastry casing is filled with a cream made from fresh cow's ricotta, eggs, sugar, cinnamon and lemon and cooked until lightly golden.

... and to drink

Basilicata isn't really a name that crops up when it come to wine. One of Italy's smallest regions in terms of production, it boasts just one DOCG and four DOCs, which comprise only two per cent of the wine produced here. The remaining 98 per cent is sold as less prestigious local or table wines.

Despite being overlooked, the region does have a rich winemaking history that dates back more than 1,000 years. While winemaking in Central and Northern Italy was pioneered by the Etruscans and Romans, here in the South it was largely undertaken by seafaring Greeks.

The heart of the region's viticulture lies in the volcanic soil of the Vulture Mountains to the north. In this area, the town of Rionero is home to over 1,000 underground wine cellars. While challenging mountainous terrain and harsh winter conditions make growing vines a challenge, the area still enjoys an abundance of sunshine throughout the growing season and cool temperatures around harvest, thanks to climatic variations. Cool Balkan breezes and the Apennines also help moderate temperatures.

In Basilicata's vineyards, aglianico, known also as ellenico, has been the leading grape for centuries. It was possibly introduced during the late Middle Ages under Aragonese rule, and today, the Aglianico del Vulture appellation is particularly well known for its reds made from this grape; the established DOCG Aglianico del Vulture Superiore has gained an excellent reputation for producing some of Italy's finest wines.

But while Aglianico is the undisputed star, other varietals are taking centre stage, thanks to greater flexibility in local regulations. Two other DOCs – Matera and Potenza's Terre dell'Alta Val d'Agri –

produce excellent wines from indigenous grapes, as well as merlot and cabernet sauvignon. The region's other wines include Moscato, Malvasia, Primitivo, Sangiovese, Montepulciano and Bombino Nero.

While Basilicata's wines may not be household names, everyone in Italy knows the famous Amaro Lucano: the pride of this region. This iconic name came to life in 1894 through a closely guarded recipe that has been meticulously upheld by the Vena family, who remain at the helm of the company to this day. Crafted from a masterful blend of over 30 herbs, the liqueur is not just a delightful digestif, but also serves as an exquisite foundation for creating cocktails. With its rich amber hue and distinctive bold flavour, it's perfect for any occasion. Locals drink it mostly chilled, over ice or with a twist of orange peel to elevate the drinking experience.

Basilicata

SOUTHERN ITALY

Culinary experiences

With chances to stay in ancient caves or the Coppola family's palazzo between cooking lessons and swims at the beach, Basilicata is full of reasons to visit.

Basilicata

Eat, cook and unwind in a luxury ancient cave

Discover the most unique resort, built within the caves of Matera. Step back in time at Sextantio Le Grotte della Civita and look out to the spellbinding Sassi cliffs. Relax with a massage or soak in a hot tub in your luxe cave suite and dine under candlelight at the deconsecrated 13th-century rock-cut church. Then embark on a gastronomic tour of the region and enjoy a wide host of activities, like wine tastings and visits to vineyards, oil and honey experiences, cooking classes and cheesemaking lessons. Why not take a hot air balloon ride over this UNESCO marvel or enjoy a guided night tour of the Sassi? Or let the size-inclusive Stellavision Travel take you on a female-only multi-day tour of the region.

SEXTANTIO.IT, STELLAVISIONTRAVEL.COM

Learn about Matera's bread and make it, too

During this immersive and educational workshop, you'll visit a traditional bakery in the historic city of Matera, where you'll learn the art of making the local bread from expert bakers. With their guidance, you'll get to try your hand at shaping and mounding a loaf using time-honoured techniques that have been passed down for generations. Once your bread is ready, you'll get to enjoy it with local focaccia and wine. Run by Martulli Viaggi or Terrachevive, this sensory experience will leave you with a newfound appreciation for a unique and delicious local staple.

MARTULLIVIAGGI.COM, TERRACHEVIVE.COM

Culinary delights at Francis Ford Coppola's hotel

Immerse yourself in the opulence of Palazzo Margherita, the breathtaking 19th-century palazzo owned by legendary filmmaker Francis Ford Coppola, which is situated in the town where his grandfather was born. Enrol in their four-day cooking course, where you venture out to local markets and prepare a different menu each day, or spend a few hours at a local *masseria* (farmhouse), tasting wine and learning to make pizza. Located close to the coast in Bernalda, about 40 minutes south of Matera, this baroque escape is the ultimate in Italian retreats. Adorned with intricate frescoes that transport you to a bygone era, the luxurious suites, designed by the Coppola family, will leave you in awe. With the rustic dishes and family-like atmosphere, you will feel right at home – here, you're not just a guest, but an honorary member of the Coppola dynasty.

THEFAMILYCOPPOLAHIDEAWAYS.COM

Discover the treasures of an ancient wine legacy

Explore Barile, a picturesque village nestled in the Vulture Mountains area. This hidden gem of Arbëreshe origin is known for its rich heritage, religious traditions and unique dialect, which have been preserved for centuries. Discover the town's legacy as a renowned home of olive oil and wine on this experience offered by Istar Viaggi. It will take you to the iconic wine caves on Sheshë Hill, where the legendary Aglianico del Vulture wine is stored, to sample wine and local specialties. Bike Basilicata also run multiple day trips biking through the Vulture wine territory.

ISTARVIAGGI.COM, BIKEBASILICATA.IT

Relax in Amaro Lucano's birthplace

Experience stunning Pisticci, the picturesque 'white town' perched on three hills. Enjoy panoramic views of the Ionian Sea and the surrounding valleys, canyons and white dunes. Explore the white houses, Mother Church and noble palaces, hike the trails, visit beaches and, importantly, drink Amaro Lucano, right here in its birthplace. Stay at Torre Fiore Hotel Masseria, a boutique property in a fortified former farmhouse surrounded by fields of grain and wildflowers. Relax in a spa, swim in the pool, eat traditional cuisine and take a chef-led cooking class.

HOTELTORREFIORE.COM

SAGRE

JULY

Sagra dell'Albicocca,
Apricot festival, Rotondella

AUGUST

Sagra della Crapiata,
Crapiata festival, Matera

Sagra delle Orecchiette,
Orecchiette festival,
Nova Siri

Porklandia,
Lucanica festival, Picerno

*Sagra della Soppressata
e del Caciocavallo,*
Soppressata and
caciocavallo festival, Rapone

Sagra del Canestrato,
Canestrato festival,
Moliterno

U Strittul ru Zafaran,
Peperoni cruschi festival,
Senise

Sagra del Baccalà,
Baccalà festival, Avigliano

SEPTEMBER

Sagra della Strazzata,
Strazzata festival, Avigliano

Sagra della Salsiccia,
Sausage festival, Cancellara

OCTOBER

Sagra della Varola,
Chestnut festival, Melfi

Tumact me Tulez,
Aglianico wine festival, Barile

NOVEMBER

Sapori d'Autunno,
Autumn festival,
Pietrapertosa

Cialledda materana

Matera-style bread salad

Nunzia, the cook at Sextantio le Grotte della Civita, kindly shared this beautifully simple dish with me. I visited the stone caves turned boutique hotel in 2018, and it remains one of the most unique properties I've ever stayed in. The dishes in and around Matera are emblematic of its peasant and impoverished past and this cialledda materana is as simple as it is hearty. Of course, there, they use the local bread, which, historically, was baked in the home and made to last days. That's why, to not let it go to waste, the bread was soaked in water to soften and refresh it.

Similar to a panzanella, this bread salad is full of fresh summer flavours. Feel free to swap any of the below ingredients with what you have on hand, and adjust the amounts to suit your personal taste.

Basilicata

SOUTHERN ITALY

SERVES 4–6 GENEROUSLY

250 g (9 oz) stale Matera bread (or any rustic white bread with a dark crust)

250 g (9 oz) cherry tomatoes, roughly chopped

½ large long cucumber (or 2 short green cucumbers), sliced

2 celery stalks, roughly chopped

1 small red onion, finely sliced

handful of Materane olives (or any black olives)

100 ml (3½ fl oz) extra virgin olive oil

handful of oregano leaves (or 1 tablespoon dried oregano)

Cut the bread into large chunks, place in a bowl and cover with cold water to soften. Squeeze out the excess water and put the bread in a large salad bowl. Add the tomato, cucumber, celery, onion and olives, and toss everything together. Season with the olive oil, oregano and a sprinkle of salt.

Place the cialledda in the fridge for 30 minutes for the flavours to develop, then serve.

Calabria

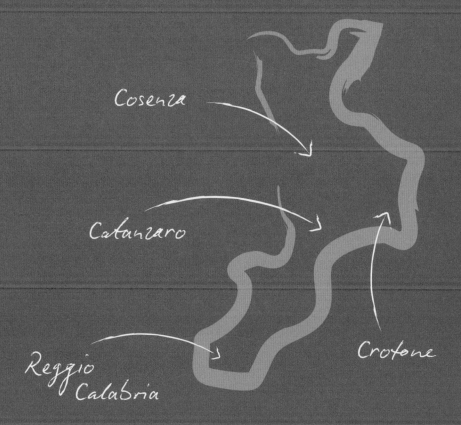

Cosenza

Catanzaro

Reggio
Calabria

Crotone

Regional produce

Calabria, the toe of Italy's boot, is known for its wild landscape of plains, mountains and rugged coastline, which produce a robust cuisine bursting with colour and flavour. Preserving produce is imperative in the hot, dry inland areas, where cured meats and cheese are produced, while the waters of the Tyrrhenian and Ionian seas provide plentiful seafood. Fresh, local Mediterranean vegetables are bulked out with legumes, while Calabria's ubiquitous chilli is applied liberally to give everything a signature spicy kick.

- Bell peppers (capsicums)
- Caciocavallo Silano cheese
- Cedro
- Chilli
- Eggplant (aubergine)
- 'Nduja
- Pecorino
- Pork
- Reggio Calabria's bergamot
- Rossano's liquorice
- Sila's potatoes
- Soppressata salami
- Stockfish
- Swordfish
- Tropea's red onions

Castello Aragonese, Le Castella

The food of the Italian South is widespread in countries where mass Italian immigration occured and a large diaspora remains. My childhood in Australia with a Calabrian aunt exposed me to this region's cuisine long before I visited it as a young adult. Family parties and feast days were filled with baked pasta dishes and salty, fried *zeppole* (a savoury doughnut of sorts; page 242). When I think of Calabria, my mind is filled with food memories that seesaw between spicy and sweet. The diversity of its landscape is echoed in its cuisine and bound to a history of invasion, colonisation and occupation.

Calabria forms the so-called toe of Italy's boot. Its long history and reputation for organised crime, known as the *'Ndrangheta*, have long overshadowed its magnificent landscapes and dynamic cuisine. As a result, it remains one of the country's least popular destinations with international travellers. But not with me! I first came more than a decade ago looking for its famed robust and piquant cuisine, but I found so much more.

My first bite into a *tartufo di Pizzo* (page 242) was at a bar in Tropea on a hot August night, and I knew right then that Calabria and I would get along just fine. This cocoa-dusted, dome-shaped delicacy, which is made of artisanal chocolate gelato, originated in the 1950s in the nearby town of Pizzo Calabro, dubbed the region's gelato capital. This was only the beginning of my journey through Calabrian cuisine.

That trip I ate my body weight in *pesce spada* (swordfish), as well as the local handmade fileja pasta topped with a luscious pork sauce (page 242), frittata with the famed local *cipolla rossa di Tropea* (red onion) and *surici fritti* (page 245), which is made with the pearly white, delicately flavoured razorfish that's found in the southern Tyrrhenian and Ionian seas, and in the Sicilian Channel in the warmer months.

And the iconic, spicy *'nduja* (page 242) – Italy's most famous spreadable salami – was never far away. Produced in Spilinga, between the slopes of Monte Poro and Capo Vaticano, this humble specialty has a fascinating past and is symbolic of Calabria's history of invasion. In the 19th century, the French, under Napoleon Bonaparte, wrested control of Calabria from the Spanish, and it's thought that 'nduja originated during this transitionary period. Among the multitude of ways it's used in the region, I loved it on toasted bread and mixed into a rustic tomato sauce atop fileja.

On my trips back to this untouched southern gem, I explored magical places, such as coastal Sibari, known for its high-quality rice, and Reggio Calabria, where I tasted one of the best gelatos of my life. I spent long, sun-soaked days at the beach, swimming in the turquoise waters of Capo Vaticano after fish-filled lunches, and in Scilla I ate a *spaghetti alle vongole* (with clams) that has stayed in my memory for years. This charming town is known for its beaches, its castle, a mythical Greek monster and the fishing village of Chianalea, which is referred to as the 'Venice of the South', because fishermen once used its small network of narrow canals to bring their catch to shore. Nowadays, the canals are lined with brightly coloured houses and eclectic seafood restaurants.

The Calabrians take much pride in their culinary, fishing and agricultural heritage, and it's felt throughout towns like this. In Tropea, those famous onions are braided together by their stalks and hung in beautiful displays outside store fronts. (The locals claim they are sweet enough to be eaten like apples!) They're displayed alongside another of Tropea's specialties: *peperoncino* (chilli peppers), which hang in bundles, drying in the sun, alongside plaits of garlic. Together, they look like works of art proudly showcasing the gastronomic culture of the area.

Whether you come to swim, ski,
    learn or indulge in the delectable local cuisine,
Calabria is sure to captivate and enchant.

Calabria is made up of five provinces: Catanzaro, Cosenza, Crotone, Reggio di Calabria and Vibo Valentia. The region is bordered by Basilicata and sandwiched between the Ionian and Tyrrhenian seas, with the narrow Messina Strait separating it from Sicily. With so much coastline, no matter where you are in the region, the sea is never more than 50 km (30 miles) away. Unsurprisingly, seafood has long been an essential part of the local cuisine. Popular dishes include *baccalà alla calabrese* (page 244), a sweet and salty dish made with salt-dried cod, and *involtini di pesce spada* (page 245), which stars stuffed swordfish.

Beyond the sparkling sea, the land – and, as such, the food – is defined by mountain ranges and three national parks: Aspromonte, Pollino (which is the largest in the country) and Sila. This rich and rugged terrain is the source of age-old dishes and much-prized produce such *soppressata*, the salami that's the pride of the region. This delicacy is prepared from lean cuts of pork seasoned with black pepper or chilli. Then there's *spianata*, which is prepared with finely ground pork, lard and chillies.

The Sila mountain ranges and plateau stretch out across the provinces of Catanzaro,

Cosenza and Crotone and, like much of Calabria, it is a land of ancient customs and practices, where authentic cuisine and flavours have endured through the ages. The area is home to native chestnuts and prized porcini mushrooms. The latter are celebrated each year at a festival in Camigliatello Silano, an alpine-like village just a short drive from Cosenza, which was once a stop on the Italian Grand Tour taken during the 17th and 18th centuries by affluent European men. Today, the village is both a food lovers' paradise, famous for its wonderful wild mushrooms, and a fantastic base for exploring the lakes and forests of the Sila National Park.

The region is also home to the humble potato, hence the Cosenza classic *pasta e patate ara tijeddra* (page 244), a potato, tomato and pasta bake, and *patate 'mpacchiuse* (page 242), in which potatoes are pan-fried. Other simple dishes include *mpanata*, a soup crafted from ricotta, hot whey and hard bread.

Goat, pork and wild boar are also on the menu in these parts, often served together in a hearty sauce with *macaroni al ferretto* (the local name for fileja) or 'mparrettati pasta. Meat here also comes in the form of sausages, often served in a panino or in recipes like *pasta alla silana* (page 244), a dish which also includes guanciale.

Other produce that puts this region on Italy's gastronomic map includes *cedro* (citron), bergamot and liquorice. Bergamot – used in cooking, as a juice and in liqueurs – is typically from Reggio Calabria, but there's a lot of debate around the origins of liquorice. Nowadays it's produced across the whole region – at the height of summer, the bright yellow flowers of liquorice plants cover huge swathes of the countryside – but most agree that the town of Rossano is probably where it all began. Along with coffee, these ingredients are used to make local juices and carbonated drinks.

Brasilena is a coffee-flavoured sparkling drink that gives you a quick caffeine pick-me-up, while *cedrata* is a refreshing soft drink: sweet with a hint of sourness and full of the cedar fruit's citrus aroma.

So much collides in the enigmatic and intriguing Calabria, which offers visitors a rich combination of history, natural beauty and cultural experiences. You have the allure of stunning beaches, cathedrals and Byzantine churches, with a wealth of vibrant frescoes, ancient castles and majestic mountains. Whether you come to swim, ski, learn or indulge in the delectable local cuisine, Calabria is sure to captivate and enchant. And one thing's for sure – you definitely won't leave hungry!

MARIA'S TOP 10 DISHES OF CALABRIA

1 CUDDRURIEDDRI / ZEPPOLE

A fried specialty of the Christmas period, Cosenza's *cuddrurieddri* are made from a dough of potato and flour which is then shaped into lengths or rings and deep-fried until crunchy on the outside and light and fluffy on the inside. The dough can also be combined with anchovy and rolled into balls for an extra-savoury variation.

2 FILEJA

To make this thick maccheroni-style pasta, a sheet of dough is rolled around a thin metal or wooden rod known as a *ferretto* (or *dinaculu* in dialect). It is a skill that is passed down through generations of Calabrian families. The finished pasta is usually served with a sauce of goat or wild boar.

3 'NDUJA

Calabria's quintessential product, *'nduja* enjoys fame in kitchens around the globe, thanks to its punchy, spicy flavour and wide versatility. A large, spreadable sausage, it is made from a mixture of minced pork offcuts and hot Calabrian chillies, packed into a sausage casing and smoked. Sold as a salami or packed into jars, it can be spread on bread or added to pasta for a fiery kick.

4 PASTA CA' MUDDICA

A great example of 'less is more' that uses up stale bread. Pasta – usually spaghetti – is tossed in oil and anchovies and then topped with fragrant toasted breadcrumbs to add a touch of crunchiness and texture.

5 PATATE 'MPACCHIUSE

An easy side dish to serve with meat or fish, here potatoes are peeled and thinly sliced, then pan-fried with lots of olive oil until they turn golden and stick together. Variations add onion, pancetta, mushrooms and *pipi* (roasted bell peppers/capsicums).

6 PATATI, PIPI E SOZIZZU / PATATE, PEPERONI E SALSICCIA

A simple yet tasty comfort food featuring the classic elements of Calabrian cuisine. Chunks of potato, slices of bell pepper and sausages are fried together in olive oil until soft and succulent. Perfect with a slice of crusty bread to mop up the juices.

7 PESCE SPADA ALLA GHIOTTA

Swordfish is the most popular and utilised fish in Calabrian cuisine, and this is a common way to prepare it. Thick steaks are covered with a tomato sauce of capers, olives and slices of the celebrated red onions from the town of Tropea.

8 PITTA 'MPIGLIATA

Hailing from the town of San Giovanni in Fiore, the rose-shaped *pitta 'mpigliata* was initially prepared as a wedding cake, with its origins dating to the 1700s. Small rosettes of pastry are filled with nuts, dried fruit, honey and spices, then arranged in a circle before baking. The result is a delectable combination of chewy and crunchy textures, and sweet and nutty flavours.

9 STRONCATURA

This Calabrian version of linguine started life as a way to use the flour and bran that ended up on the floor during wheat milling. Nowadays it's produced in a more hygienic way, but *stroncatura* has maintained its rustic appearance and wholewheat flavour and is usually served with local ingredients, such as anchovies, garlic, capers, olives, chilli and toasted breadcrumbs.

10 TARTUFO DI PIZZO

Named for its similar appearance to a *tartufo* (black truffle), this dessert from the seaside town of Pizzo is in fact made of hazelnut and chocolate gelato that is filled with melted chocolate and coated with a dusting of cocoa powder.

Other dishes to look out for

With the mountains and the coastline serving up riches, Calabrian food is a luscious marriage of land and sea. So grab a hunk of local bread, slather it in 'nduja or sardella, and dive in.

Street food

Gliommarieddi

Gliommarieddi is the local dialect for a dish widespread across Italy's Centre and South. These morsels of lamb or goat interiors (usually liver, kidney and lungs) are wrapped in their own casings and fried or grilled over a fire.

Polpette e crespelle / Purpetti e frittelle

From grandmothers' homes to restaurants, *polpette e crespelle* are eaten all day. Their name is the umbrella term for a host of fried delights that utilise seasonal ingredients and local meat and fish. Common interpretations are meatballs, battered fish or fishcakes, potato croquettes and deep-fried zucchini (courgette) flowers.

Antipasti

Pitta maniata

A type of focaccia traditionally made only with the hands (*maniata* comes from *mani* or 'hands'), this rustic bread is studded with pieces of salami, pork scratchings and provola or caciocavallo cheese before baking. A richer version adds boiled eggs and ricotta.

Polpette di melanzane

The region's abundance of eggplant (aubergine) makes these easy-to-prepare fritters a staple in most households. Cooked eggplant is mixed with old bread, eggs and grated cheese before being baked or fried for a quick snack or meal.

Sardella

Also known as 'Calabrian caviar', *sardella* is made from sardines or whitebait combined with sweet or spicy chillies and herbs, such as wild fennel seeds, to form a thick spread – a fish version of 'nduja. It is eaten atop local bread or used as a sauce for pasta. A recent call for varieties of whitebait to be restricted for sustainability reasons means similar ice or noodle fish are substituted in some cases.

Primi

Cicoria cotiche e fagioli

In keeping with the Calabrian tradition of cucina povera, this *minestra* (thick soup) takes simple ingredients and magics them into a delicious, warming dish. Bitter, iron-rich wild chicory is cooked with white cannellini beans and pork rind and flavoured with a hit of zingy red chilli. It's served with crusty bread to soak up the juices.

Lagane e cicciari

Pasta with chickpeas (garbanzo beans) is a time-honoured dish in most of Southern Italy, and the Calabrian version is made with *lagane*, a kind of wide tagliatelle made with just flour and water. The chickpeas are cooked with a little tomato, garlic and sometimes a hint of chilli until they're soft and creamy before being stirred with the silky pasta.

Licurdia / Zuppa di cipolle

Tropea's famous red onions and caciocavallo
cheese are the stars of this comforting
soup which champions Calabrian produce.
The onions are slow-cooked and combined
with chunks of potato and cubes of cheese to
create the perfect balance of sweet and salty.
The soup is served poured over toasted bread
and seasoned with grated pecorino and
flakes of dried red chilli.

Pasta alla silana

The mountainous region of the Sila gives
its name to this pasta dish, which uses local
ingredients that may vary slightly from
recipe to recipe. Pasta, often fileja, is tossed
in a tomato sauce made with dried Calabrian
sausage, guanciale or pancetta, porcini
mushrooms, caciocavallo and, of course,
a hit of chilli.

Pasta e patate ara tijeddra

This potato and pasta bake from Cosenza
sees thin slices of potato layered with pasta
(usually penne), passata (pureed tomatoes)
and parmigiano, before being cooked until
the top is crunchy. Mozzarella or caciocavallo
may be added for extra substance.

Ragù alla calabrese

Calabria's signature *ragù* is a combination of
pork, beef and sausage which is slow-cooked
in a tomato sauce to create a rich ragù
flavoured with bay leaves, basil and parsley.
Its lengthy cooking time makes it a popular
recipe for Sunday lunch, when it is served
with traditional pasta, such as fileja.

Secondi

Alici 'arriganate'

In Calabria, where fresh anchovies are easy
to come by, this dish is a favourite. Cleaned
anchovies are layered with garlic, oregano
and crushed tomatoes, then covered and
cooked on the stove until the flavours have
melded. The finished dish is served with a
grating of lemon zest for extra zing.

Baccalà alla calabrese

Fillets of *baccalà* (salt-dried cod) are gently
cooked in a stew with potatoes and sweet
red bell peppers, sometimes with the
addition of onions and olives. The result
is a soft, comforting blend of sweet and
salty flavours in a succulent sauce.

Baccalà fritto con peperoni

One of many ways that baccalà and stockfish
are prepared in the South. Fillets are coated
in flour and fried them until golden. They're
served with crispy fried red and green peppers.

Cuccìa

A dish made from boiled wheat, goat and pork, *cuccìa* is traditionally cooked in a terracotta pot known as a *tinìellun* and eaten to celebrate saints' days in the Cosenza area. There is also a sweet version, with chocolate, cinnamon and orange zest, made in honour of Santa Lucia on 13 December.

Frittuli

From the Reggio Calabria area, this dish uses the skin and left-over meat and interiors of pigs. These are boiled together in pork fat for five hours before being eaten hot. Leftovers are often eaten in a panino for Saturday lunch.

Involtini di pesce spada

Swordfish from Calabria's pristine seas features extensively in local recipes. In this one, thin slices of the fish are rolled around a filling of breadcrumbs, garlic and herbs, sometimes with parmigiano or capers. They can be coated in breadcrumbs and baked, pan-fried, or cooked in a tomato sauce.

Morzeddhu / Morzello

A symbol of Catanzaro, *morzeddhu* was devoured as a mid-morning snack by the city's workers throughout the 19th century. This stew, also known as *spezzatino di trippa* and *cuore, fegato e polmoni*, utilises offal from cows cooked with tomato puree and spicy peppers. It's served in a round bread known as a *ruota di carro* (cartwheel).

Pipi chini / Peperoni ripieni

As with many stuffed vegetable dishes, Calabria's recipe for *pipi chini* (stuffed bell peppers) varies between households but generally involves filling the peppers with minced (ground) meat and cheese and then baking or frying them. Eggplant can be used, with the scooped-out pulp mixed with tomato sauce and local cheese or, alternatively, with stockfish.

Stocco alla mammolese

This hearty stew, from the small town of Mammola, used to be a staple for poorer workers who could not afford the luxury of fresh fish. These days it's a famous dish in which pieces of stockfish and chunks of potato are cooked until soft, along with onion, tomato, olives, capers and chilli for an explosion of flavour.

Surici fritti

Found in the Mediterranean, pearly razorfish (also known as cleaver wrasse, or *assurici* in Calabrian dialect) are often used in local cuisine. Noted for their bright white flesh, they are best prepared simply coated in flour and deep-fried in oil until crisp and golden.

Dolci

Crocette di fichi

Calabria's delicious sun-dried figs are split open and filled with walnut or almond kernels and citrus zest, then formed into the cross shape from which they get their name. They are baked, then sprinkled with sugar and cinnamon to create this treat.

Cuzzupa

Baked to symbolise Lent's end, Calabria's Easter cake has many names and forms. Rings, animals, hearts and letters are all popular shapes, but the cake is always dotted with whole eggs for good luck. Traditionally, it was given to a future son-in-law by the mother of his betrothed, the number of eggs conveying a message; nine meant the engagement would be extended, while seven signified he should prepare for marriage.

Nacatole / Ciambelle fritte

These deep-fried doughnuts, flavoured with a hint of aniseed or lemon, are made chiefly during Christmas in the province of Reggio Calabria. They're often braided or twisted to recall the shape of Jesus' cradle, and are dusted in icing (confectioners') sugar.

Nepitelle

Once prepared during the Easter period, *nepitelle* can now be found throughout the year. A sweet ravioli, these half-moons of pastry are filled with chocolate, jam, nuts, honey and spices before being baked until crisp and golden.

Pignolata calabrese

Calabria's version of Campania's struffoli (page 262) were originally prepared for the period of Carnevale. Small balls of fried pastry are tossed in warm honey and formed into cones or pyramids to set, then decorated with sprinkles or citrus zest. Sometimes liqueur, lemon or bergamot is added.

Sanguinaccio calabrese

Created to utilise the blood of a pig collected during its slaughter, *sangunazzu* (its name in dialect) is a spreadable cream of blood, chocolate, honey, cinnamon and vincotto, which is eaten with bread or cookies.

Scalille

The distinctive shape of these festive treats represents a ladder, signifying the ascension of Jesus into heaven. The dough is rolled into a thin strip and wrapped around a metal rod. After frying, it is coated in honey or a sugar glaze.

Turdilli

A Christmastime sweet from Cosenza, *turdilli* are made with sugar, oil and vincotto, which are formed into small, gnocchi-like shapes. Traditionally they are fried and then tossed in hot fig honey before being decorated or sprinkled with cocoa or cinnamon.

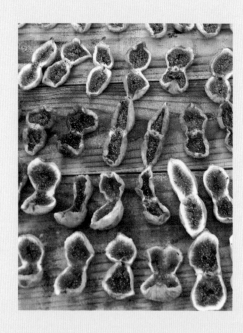

Calabria

SOUTHERN ITALY

... and to drink

Calabria's wines haven't yet made their mark on the world stage, but the region produces drops worth discovering. It stands out not only for its unique grape varieties but also for the distinctive winemaking techniques used locally. One of these methods is the 'gobelet' training system, which involves growing vines without support. This technique enhances the vines' exposure to sunlight and airflow, leading to healthier grapes with richer flavours.

Calabria's viticultural origins lie with the Ancient Greeks. Today, more than 90 per cent of wine produced in the region is red, primarily coming from the gaglioppo grape variety. It is used in the production of Ciró, a DOC wine that is considered one of the best reds of Southern Italy. Produced in the province of Crotone, it has a deep ruby-red colour with aromas of red fruit and spices.

Calabria is also known for greco nero. Grown in the province of Cosenza, this red wine grape is used to make Terre di Cosenza DOC, a full-bodied red wine with intense aromas of dark fruit, spices and chocolate that pairs well with the grilled meats and hearty stews of this area.

While Calabria is mainly known for its reds, the region does produce some lovely white wines. One of the most popular white grapes is greco bianco, aptly named after the region's Greek origins. Used in the production of the Cirò Bianco DOC, it makes for a dry white with a straw-yellow colour and aromas of citrus and flowers that pairs well with seafood and light pasta dishes. The region is also home to the mantonico grape, used to make Mantonico Bianco DOC with its intense aromas of tropical fruit and honey.

As for amaro, Vecchio Amaro del Capo – one of Italy's most popular – is produced here. The secret recipe has been passed on from generation to generation in the Caffo family, and features more than 30 medicinal herbs, flowers, fruits and roots. It is enjoyed locally ice cold in small glasses. You may also want to keep an eye out for Amaro Silano and Jefferson, two other amaro brands.

Culinary experiences

Discover all Calabria has to offer, from modern viticulture and an art resort on the coast to sustainable farming and dining.

Visit Tenute Ferrocinto and do a wine tasting

Located on the edge of the Pollino National Park, Tenuta Ferrocinto's vineyards benefit from an ideal grape-growing microclimate. The history of the vineyard can be traced back to 1855, when the first vines were planted. In 2003, the winery was renovated to incorporate the latest oenological practices. The winemaking process at Tenuta Ferrocinto combines innovative and traditional fermentation techniques, the maturation and storage of wine taking place in wooden barrels under the watchful eye of the winemaker. During a tour of the property and a tasting of their red, white and sparkling wines, you'll see how Calabria's winemaking history and future coexist.

STRADEDELGUSTOCALABRIA.IT/LISTING/TENUTE-FERROCINTO/

Enter the world of organic farming and gourmet cuisine

There is so much to stimulate the senses at the Ceraudo family's biodynamic farm, not least of which is the Michelin-starred restaurant, helmed by one of Italy's youngest chefs, Caterina Ceraudo, inside an old mill. Caterina has one goal with her elegant cooking – to bring traditional Calabrian cuisine into the 21st century, and that she does. Most dishes are prepared with produce that comes direct from the farm, where you can stay the night (or longer!). It comprises 50 acres of vineyards, 91 acres of olive groves and seven acres devoted to citrus trees and vegetable gardens: essentially a textbook example of biodiversity and sustainability. Book your meal directly with the Ceraudo group or an entire immersive experience with operator Wine Tourism.

DATTILO.IT, WINETOURISM.COM

Explore the Ionian coast and an art resort

Praia Art Resort is a five-star resort created by local artisans. It borders the protected marine area of Isola Capo Rizzuto: an ideal spot for exploring the region's natural beauty. Located just 20 m (65 ft) from a private white-sand beach, Praia is a luxury hideaway. A degustation at the on-site Pietramare Natural Food is a deep dive into the region's maritime and rural traditions, and the resort's culinary voyage takes you beyond your table and into the *orto dei profumi*: an aromatic garden home to herbs and 30 varieties of *peperoncino* (chilli pepper). Enjoy a private wine tasting, a cooking lesson with the chef, or experience waterfalls, ancient trees and the rare flora and fauna of nearby Valli Cupe Nature Reserve on a private foraging excursion with the in-house botanist.

PRAIAARTRESORT.COM

Get to the real heart of Calabrian produce

The local Calabrian liquorice, known as 'black gold', is said to be one of the world's best varieties. Though there are other producers, Amarelli is synonymous with liquorice in Calabria and around the world. In business since the 18th century, the family was the first to industrialise a method of extracting juice from the root. Still located in Rossano, you can visit their museum, sample liquorice and buy some to take home. Further south in Reggio Calabria, the Bergamot Museum tells the 300-year-long story of this special citrus. Visitors can sample essential oils and teas before indulging in a scoop of bergamot gelato.

MUSEODELLALIQUIRIZIA.IT
MUSEODELBERGAMOTTOEDELCIBO.COM

Cook, eat and drink your way through Calabria

Born in Australia to Calabrian parents, Tania Pascuzzi has spent a large part of her life in Tropea. Here, she creates culinary itineraries for visitors to her beloved Calabria. From wine tasting and home-style cooking classes to multiple-day tours where you'll meet food experts, each experience fully immerses you in this part of Italy. Tours can be customised and Tania also offers ancestry tours for those looking to connect with their Calabrian heritage.

INITALYTOURS.COM

SAGRE

MARCH

Sagra dei Piselli,
Fresh peas festival,
Montegiordano

MAY

Festa del Pane,
Bread festival, Altomonte

JULY

Gran Gala' di Pescespada,
Swordfish festival,
Bagnara Calabra

Sagra del Pesce Azzurro e della Cipolla Rossa, Bluefish and red onion festival, Tropea

AUGUST

Sagra della 'Nduja,
'Nduja festival, Spilinga

Sagra della Cipolla Rossa,
Tropea red onion festival, Ricadi

Sagra dello Stocco,
Stockfish festival, Mammola

Sagra del Polpo,
Octopus festival, Joppolo

SEPTEMBER

Peperoncino festival,
Chilli pepper festival, Diamante

OCTOBER

Festa del Cioccolato,
Chocolate festival, Cosenza

Sagra del Fungo,
Mushroom festival,
Camigliatello Silano

NOVEMBER

Sagra della Castagna,
Chestnut fair,
Sant'Agata di Esaro

Pasta con mollica

Pasta with breadcrumbs

He might be an international, star-studded and award-winning chef, but I'm proud to call Anthony Genovese my friend. His outstanding talent inspires me (his Il Pagliaccio in Rome has long held an impressive two stars in the Michelin Guide), but it's our mirroring migrant experiences that make us resonate on many levels. He was born in France to a Calabrese family. I was born in Australia to an Abruzzese family. And we connected in our beloved Rome. Anthony shared this recipe from the heart with me and says it's the dish that brings everyone together. You make it when you don't know what to cook, when you're in a hurry but still want to eat something delicious. Anthony says, 'It's the story of evenings spent eating and drinking with lifelong friends. Knowing how to prepare pasta with breadcrumbs was a must for us Calabrian kids, so as not to disturb our sleeping mothers. For me, *pasta ca muddica* – as we would call it – is the quintessential pasta!'

Calabria

SOUTHERN ITALY

SERVES 4

70 ml (2¼ fl oz) extra virgin olive oil

2 garlic cloves

70 g (2½ oz) fresh breadcrumbs

1 bird's eye chilli, finely chopped

4 anchovy fillets in oil, drained

320 g (11½ oz) stroncatura pasta (or spaghetti)

2 teaspoons crusco pepper powder (or other sweet chilli powder)

Heat the olive oil and garlic cloves in a frying pan over medium heat. Add the breadcrumbs and cook, stirring frequently, for 5–6 minutes, until toasted and golden.

Turn off the heat, discard the garlic and use a slotted spoon to transfer the breadcrumbs to paper towel to drain, leaving any excess oil in the pan.

To the still-warm pan of oil, with the heat off, add the chilli and anchovy fillets. Stir for 2–3 minutes, until the anchovies begin to break down.

Cook the pasta in salted boiling water until al dente. A few seconds before the pasta is ready, reheat the pan of oil and anchovy and stir in the crusco pepper powder.

Drain the pasta and toss it through the sauce. Add the toasted breadcrumbs, stir quickly and serve.

Campania

Benevento

Avellino

Caserta

Napoli

Salerno

Regional produce

Campania's vast areas of pasture
and fertile soil have been celebrated
since ancient times. The countryside
and coastline produce many staples
of Mediterranean cuisine, from plump
vegetables and citrus to cow's and
buffalo's cheeses. Add the bountiful fresh
seafood along the coast and plenty of
livestock inland, and you have a region
that is full of flavour and history.

- Amalfi lemons
- Annurca apples
- Buffalo mozzarella
- Cilento's cacioricotta and
  white figs
- Colatura anchovy extract
- Friarielli
- Hazelnuts
- Paestum's artichokes
- Provolone del Monaco
- Rabbit
- San Marzano tomatoes
- Sorrento's lemons and walnuts
- Vesuvius' Piennolo
  cherry tomatoes

San Francesco di Paola Basilica, Naples

See Naples and die, they say. It's only when you visit the Campanian capital that you truly understand this expression.

The first time I visited, I could feel Naples' energy pulsing through my veins. This is a city with heart. It's passionate, proud and yes, it's often been described as lawless and dirty, yet it's magical – often all at the same time. For me, Naples represents everything that is beautiful and grotesque about Italy. Yes, there's organised crime (here it's *la Camorra*), there have been garbage crises and soccer scandals, and simple things like road rules don't always seem to apply. But the other side of the coin? A rich culture with a history of poetry, music and art. Throughout the early 2000s, a clean-up effort has tidied the streets and transformed some underground metro stations into works of art – especially the water-themed Toledo stop. And in some neighbourhoods, world-renowned street artists (Banksy, to name one) have created a vibrant new edge. It's also a ridiculously delicious city.

Food is Naples' lifeblood. After all, this is the birthplace of pizza – the city's gift to the world! Pizza is a way of life here, the aroma wafting along the streets of the Centro Storico, where crowds of locals form, waiting for what they'll tell you is the best pizza in town, if not the world. I've never left Naples without eating one, like the *pizza a portafoglio*, an on-the-run variety folded and wrapped in paper; the *pizza fritta* (page 258), my favourite, which is fried and usually stuffed with ricotta and crispy pork bits or salame; and the classic of classics, the margherita.

Naples serves up way more than pizza, however. The *sfogliatelle* – orange- and cinnamon-spiced, ricotta-filled pastries – will blow your mind. Its coffee is regarded as some of the country's best (if you take yours without sugar, let the barman know, as it comes sweetened at many old-school bars).

And then there's Italy's other gift to the world – Mozzarella di Bufala. If the milk doesn't drip while you're eating it, you really don't know what you're missing out on.

As Naples is a port, fishing has always been critical to the local economy, so expect exceptional seafood, from octopus salad to seafood pasta like *spaghetti allo scoglio* (with shellfish). In terms of pasta, this is durum wheat heartland, with Pasta di Gragnano (from Gragnano, south of Naples) renowned as one of the best durum wheat pastas in the world. One of the most heart-warming dishes is *pasta mista* or *mischiata* (mixed pasta shapes), which was born at a time when pasta was often sold loose instead of in bags. If a small amount of a pasta was left over, it was mixed with other types and then prepared with simple ingredients like potato and provola to make the luscious pasta *patate e provola* (also known as *pasta e patate*; page 258). This former home-cooked dish is now served at all levels of Campanian restaurants as a nostalgic nod to the past.

And when in Naples, we can't forget street foods like *fritti* – fried anything! (page 259) – and tripe, the quintessential dish of cucina povera. Naples is a working-class city at heart, which you can feel throughout the Centro Storico, where markets bustle, selling every thing from fish to fruit to electronics – sometimes at the same stand!

Then there's the *babà* (rum-soaked sponge; page 262), which I never loved until I tasted the real deal. This iconic sweet is said to have arrived in the 18th century. Its origins are debated, but most accounts credit Polish king Stanislao Leszczyński, father-in-law of Louis XV of France, for its invention. Monsù chefs brought the babà to the Neapolitan court, which ruled this part of the peninsula from 1282 to 1816. This period's cultural legacy is reflected in untouchable culinary classics like the elaborate sartù (page 260), the potato gattò (page 258) and Naples' famous ragù (page 260).

Campania

SOUTHERN ITALY

Of course, there's more to Campania than Naples. In Capri, I learned how to make torta caprese (page 262) and ravioli capresi (page 260), and I tasted the best mussels of my life in Ischia. I ate my first *delizia al limone* (lemon cream sponge; page 258) in Sorrento and my first *melanzane al cioccolato* (chocolate eggplant/aubergine) in Amalfi.

It was here on the coast that I started my love affair with *frittata di maccheroni* (spaghetti or pasta frittata), which I ate whenever and wherever I could get my hands on it. And then the spaghetti. All the spaghetti: *alle vongole* (with clams; page 258) on the pebbled shoreline of Conca dei Marini, *al limone* (with lemon) in Positano and *alla Nerano* (with fried zucchini/courgette and Provolone del Monaco or caciocavallo; page 261) in Nerano.

Campania has a long history to match its never-ending list of culinary delights. Sitting south of Rome, the region is inextricably tied to Italy's capital. It was part of the Roman Republic from the 4th century BCE, and an important part of the empire for centuries. The Romans always valued Campania for its vast pastureland and nutrient-rich soils; its volcanic earth produces some of the world's best tomatoes!

As you move inland, there is ample grazing land available for livestock, which means cheese and meat dishes are more common. The Irpinia area and cities like Avellino are particularly famous for cheeses, such as caciocchiato, caciocavallo and scamorza, along with soppressata salami and prosciutto di Trevico, as well as quality produce like chestnuts, hazelnuts and truffles.

Closer to the mountains, the area around Benevento is known for small farms that produce olive oil, wine, fruits (especially apples and cherries), nuts, legumes and some of the finest durum wheat. Legend has it that the city was a meeting point for witches, which is how the famous local liqueur, Strega (witch), got its name.

The Apennines cut right through the area, and to the eastern side you have the Sannio Hills. Straddling Benevento and Avellino, this abundant land has beautiful medieval villages and olive groves with ancient roots. The prized Sannio Caudino Telesino extra virgin olive oil is produced in 35 towns across the rolling hills, which vineyards and apple groves share. Touted as the 'queen of apples', the Melannurca Campana grows here.

In this part of the region, you'll find handmade pasta served with seasonal vegetables or legumes and even *cotica* (pork rinds). Soups like *zuppa di cardone*, made with broth and cardoons, are often prepared at Christmas. And meats, including beef, lamb and goat, are served as roasted or flame-grilled prime cuts, their offal used to make a variety of dishes – particularly *ammugliatielli* (grilled lamb innards).

Palazzo dello Spagnolo, Naples

Food is Naples'
Lifeblood. After all,
this is the birthplace
of pizza.

South of Naples and the Amalfi Coast, you'll find the Cilento Coast, which could very well be the region's best kept secret. It combines the picturesque coastline of the Tyrrhenian Sea, the rugged beauty of the Cilento and Vallo di Diano National Park and historic, sites such as the Greek temples at Paestum. Importantly – beyond the area's historical significance – Paestum and nearby towns like Battipaglia and Eboli are renowned for their Mozzarella di Bufala.

As I reflect on my time in Campania, I can't help but smile and think of Naples. If I close my eyes, scooters zoom by and boisterous Neapolitans spill out of bars, along with the intoxicating scent of coffee. It's loud. It's colourful. It's a complete feast for all the senses: a delicious, in-your-face mess, and the perfect initiation to dynamic Campania. The locals live with a contagious thirst for life, which is fitting for people who live in the shadow of Vesuvius: one of the world's most famous volcanoes and a good enough reason to live like there's no tomorrow.

MARIA'S TOP 10 DISHES OF CAMPANIA

1 ALICI MARINATE

In this common antipasto, fresh anchovies are marinated in white wine vinegar, sometimes with lemon juice or wine, which cures the fish. They're dressed with garlic, herbs and chilli and served with bread to soak up the tangy juices.

2 DELIZIA AL LIMONE

This delight from Sorrento is made with the huge, tangy lemons of the Amalfi area. Domed sponge cakes are soaked in limoncello syrup and filled with a light lemon cream. The cakes are covered in white lemon icing and decorated with swirls of whipped cream and sprinkles of lemon zest.

3 GATTÒ DI PATATE

A savoury cake with a name derived from the French *gateau*. Mashed potatoes are combined with eggs, parmigiano and cubes of meat and other cheeses, such as salami, prosciutto, provola and scamorza. The mix is pressed into a tin, topped with butter and grated parmigiano and baked.

4 GRAFFE

These ring doughnuts from Naples are typically made for Carnevale, but they are found across the region year round. Their distinction from similar doughnuts is the boiled potato that's added to the dough, making them even lighter and fluffier.

5 PARMIGIANA DI MELANZANE

With layers of fried eggplant (aubergine), tomato sauce, basil and mozzarella baked together until soft and oozing, this dish uses the South's fresh ingredients to their maximum potential.

6 PASTA E PATATE

Pasta and potatoes is much more than the sum of its parts. Quick, tasty and satisfying, the two main ingredients' starch combines to create a cross between a pasta dish and a thick soup. In Naples, parmigiano rind is often added, along with provola cheese and pancetta for extra heft.

7 PIZZA

Pizza was born in Naples, and its production in the city is recognised on UNESCO's Intangible Cultural Heritage List. Strict rules ensure quality: the base should be thin, with a large, puffy, raised *cornicione* (crust). The tomatoes must be from San Marzano or the slopes of Vesuvius, and the cheese must be either cow's milk fior di latte from Agerola or local Mozzarella di Bufala.

8 PIZZA FRITTA

During World War II, many of Naples' pizza ovens were destroyed. Paired with the scarcity of ingredients, this meant pizza was an unattainable luxury. In response, *pizza fritta* was born. The dough is shaped into a kind of calzone and filled with cheaper ingredients, such as ricotta and pork scratchings, before being fried until golden and puffy. During the war, housewives became the principal purveyors of pizza fritta, cooking it at home and selling it from their doorsteps.

9 SPAGHETTI ALLA COLATURA DI ALICI

The seaside town of Cetara is famous for its anchovies and especially for its *colatura di alici*, a concentrated sauce made with fermented anchovies that's like liquid gold. The intense flavour is best appreciated with a simple plate of spaghetti, garlic, parsley and chilli.

10 SPAGHETTI ALLE VONGOLE

Campania is home to the world-famous *spaghetti alle vongole*. In this simple dish, the flavour of the sweet, briny clams shines: all that's needed is olive oil, garlic, a splash of white wine and, perhaps, a little chilli or a few cherry tomatoes.

Other dishes to look out for

Campania is a vibrant and gourmet cornucopia: think effervescent lemons, baskets of seasonal vegetables, creamy fresh cheeses and fried, golden street food.

Street food

Cuoppo napoletano

A paper cone filled with a mix of *fritti* (fried snacks). It can be *di mare*, with fried seafood and *frittelle di alghe* (seaweed dough balls), or *di terra*, with potato croquettes, *palle di riso* (rice balls), mozzarella balls, *pasta cresciute* (fried pizza dough) and zucchini (courgette) flowers.

Frittatina di pasta

These deep-fried fritters of spaghetti or bucatini can be grabbed on the go on Naples' streets. The pasta is cooked, mixed with bechamel and stuffed with a mixture of peas and ham. It's then shaped into medallions, dipped in batter and fried.

Pane

Casatiello

In Campania, Easter wouldn't be the same without this savoury cake. Made with lard-infused bread dough to which pieces of cheese and salami are added, the cake is ring-shaped in reference to Jesus' crown of thorns. Whole eggs are baked into the surface, encased under crosses of dough.

Panino napoletano

These savoury delights, born as a way to use up left-over pizza dough, are a popular snack in Naples. The dough is enriched with lard, topped with a mix of cheese, salami and eggs and rolled up before being sliced and baked.

Parigina

Named for Queen Margherita of Savoy (*parigina* comes from *per la regina* or 'for the queen'), this dish is a rectangular pizza base topped with tomato, cheese and ham and covered with a layer of puff pastry. A little cream and egg is brushed over the surface and the pizza is baked until golden.

Antipasti

Capitone

Eel, cut into chunks and fried in oil, is a symbolic Christmas Eve dish. As the eel is said to represent the biblical serpent of the Garden of Eden, consuming it signifies the triumph of good over evil.

Impepata di cozze

Requiring just two ingredients, this recipe lets the freshness of the mussels do the talking. They're put into a hot pan with a generous crack of black pepper and then covered and left to open in their own steam. The pot is brought straight to the table with lemon and parsley.

Insalata caprese

Echoing the three colours of the Italian flag, Capri's famous salad is a true taste of Campanian summer. It only has a few ingredients, so quality is key. The mozzarella must be moist and milky, the tomatoes sweet and juicy, and the basil fresh and fragrant. A drizzle of good olive oil and a dash of salt are all that's needed to complete the dish.

Primi

Cardone di Benevento

A cardoon soup hailing from Benevento which is often prepared for Christmas. A whole chicken is boiled with water and vegetables, then the meat is removed and shredded and the liquid is strained. Pieces of the tender inner stems of cardoons are added to the simmering stock, along with small veal meatballs and a handful of pine nuts. When it's ready, the chicken is added, along with a mixture of beaten egg and parmigiano.

Cicatielli

This pasta from Irpinia is made with flour and water. The story goes that a wife, angered by the betrayal of her husband, decided to quell her rage by making pasta: she rolled dough into short shapes between her index and middle finger with the gesture used for someone who is cheating. *Cicatielli* are usually served with a fresh tomato sauce with local wild mint leaves.

Pasta alla genovese

Despite its name, this ragù originated in Naples in the 15th or 16th century. Pieces of beef are slow-cooked with lots and lots of sliced onions, wine and stock, creating a sweet, rich sauce. It is usually served with paccheri, candele or ziti, which can hold the weight of the ragù.

Pettolelle con fagioli

In Italy, pasta and beans comes in many guises. In Caserta, the dish is made with a local pasta shape known as *pettolelle* – sheets of pasta cut into irregular angular shapes. The pasta is added to a soupy sauce of cannellini beans cooked in a tomato sauce with a little guanciale and onion.

Ragù alla napoletana

Beef, pork ribs and sausage are cooked for hours in a tomato sauce and red wine to create a Neapolitan ragù. Unlike in the Bolognese variety, the meat is left in large pieces and removed after cooking to be eaten as a second course, the left-over sauce used in dishes like lasagne and sartù. At Carnevale, it's made with rich ricotta, tiny meatballs and hard-boiled eggs – an epic celebratory dish.

Ravioli capresi

This ravioli dish celebrates the tasty trinity of mozzarella, tomato and basil. The small pasta parcels are filled with drained mozzarella (or caciotta campana cheese, which releases less water), parmigiano and basil. Once cooked, they are tossed in a sauce of sweet cherry tomatoes and fresh basil.

Sartù di riso

An extravagant timballo of rice, *sartù* was once prepared for the Neapolitan nobility. It has many separate elements, the rice forming a base to which tiny meatballs, boiled egg, cheese, sausage, peas and meat ragù are added. The whole thing is baked and turned onto a plate for serving.

Scialatielli all'amalfitana

Scialiatelli are luscious ribbons of pasta similar to but shorter than fettuccine. Native to the Amalfi Coast, where they are served with a rich sauce made with fresh seafood, such as clams, mussels and prawns, often combined with tomatoes, garlic, olive oil, white wine and fresh herbs.

Spaghetti alla Nerano

Zucchini stars in this pasta dish from Nerano. It's sliced into rounds and fried in olive oil until it starts to colour. Cooked spaghetti is added to the pan, along with the zucchini, grated Provolone del Monaco and a splash of pasta water, creating a creamy sauce.

Spaghetti allo scoglio

This pasta uses the treasures of Campania's coastline. Ingredients vary depending on the day's catch but usually include mussels, clams, prawns (shrimp) and calamari. Before it is al dente, the pasta is drained and finished in the seafood sauce to absorb the juices. A few halves of sweet cherry tomatoes and a scattering of parsley are added for freshness.

Sugo alla puttanesca

Found throughout Italy, this Neapolitan dish throws together tomatoes, olives, capers, garlic and chilli for a salty, punchy sauce. Anchovies can be added to the mix, which is traditionally served with spaghetti.

Secondi

'A meveza 'mbuttunata

Salerno's stuffed spleen is traditionally prepared for the feast of the town's patron saint, Matthew, on 21 September. The spleen is packed with chopped parsley, garlic and chilli before being re-closed. It's then seared on both sides, covered in red wine, vinegar and wine must, and cooked for an hour. After cooling, the spleen is sliced and served cold.

Coniglio all'ischitana

A staple in the restaurants and homes of Ischia, this stew uses local island ingredients, cooking a jointed rabbit with white wine, tomatoes, stock and aromatic fresh herbs for a succulent, tender result.

Contorni

Cianfotta

A medley of summer vegetables, *cianfotta* is prevalent across the South, albeit with different regional names. Potatoes, eggplants, onion, tomatoes, zucchini and bell peppers (capsicums) are cooked in olive oil with basil and oregano. This colourful dish pairs well with the fish and meat of the region.

Friarielli

From the same family as Apulia's broccoli rabe, Campania's leafy *friarielli* are characterised by their tender stems and bitter taste. Usually boiled, drained and swirled with olive oil, garlic and red chilli, they go hand in hand with sausage, acombination often found in panini or on pizza.

Peperoncini verdi di fiume

These sweet green peppers are cultivated in areas along the Sebeto and Sarno rivers in the Campania region; they are fried whole with salt and garlic. Fresh tomatoes are added halfway through to create a succulent sauce.

Scarole con olive e capperi

Leafy escarole is a versatile vegetable with a slightly bitter taste which is often added to soups, stews and rustic, savoury tarts. As a side dish, it is commonly served boiled and mixed with olives and capers, with pine nuts and anchovies sometimes added.

Dolci

Babà

A specialty of Naples' pastry shops, *babà* are individual domed sponge cakes dried and then soaked in a syrup flavoured with rum or liqueur and citrus. Sometimes they are brushed with apricot jam for an extra glossy sheen, and occasionally you'll find large ring-shaped varieties.

Pastiera

A sweet tart made for Easter, *pastiera* has a shortcrust (pie) case with a lattice topping. Inside, you'll find a creamy filling of cooked wheat, ricotta, honey, candied fruit and orange flower water. The cake is usually made on Holy Thursday to allow time for the flavours to develop before Easter Sunday.

Pigna

Otherwise known as a sweet casatiello (page 259), *pigna* is a yeasted Easter cake from the area of Benevento. Proved for many hours to ensure a light texture and height, the cake is flavoured with citrus zest, orange blossom water and Strega liqueur. Once baked, the cake is covered with white icing and topped with colourful sprinkles and painted eggs.

Sfogliatella

This gem of Campanian pastries may be the classic *riccia* (made with flaky layers of puff pastry) or *frolla* (made with shortcrust pastry). It usually has a filling of ricotta, semolina and orange zest, but there are variations with chocolate, cream custard and almonds. In the Salerno/Amalfi area, you'll find the Santa Rosa version of a riccia topped with custard cream and sour cherries.

Struffoli

These small balls of sweet dough are fried and coated in warm honey and citrus zest, then arranged into rings or cakes and left to set. Made for the Christmas period, they are decorated with brightly coloured sugar sprinkles.

Torta caprese

Legend says that the eponymous cake of Capri was invented in 1920 when a chef to the king of Naples forgot to add flour to a chocolate cake. Made with just dark chocolate, almonds, eggs, butter and sugar, the dessert's lack of flour ensures it is moist and soft inside, with a firm, crunchy exterior.

... and to drink

Falerno, one of Italy's most ancient wines, is still produced in Campania, where viticulture dates to the 12th century BCE, with influences from the Greeks, Romans and Byzantines.

This region's name comes from *campania felix*, a Latin phrase roughly meaning 'happy land'. Its diverse terroirs, from volcanic soil near Mount Vesuvius to the unique Sannio and Irpinia hillsides to the coastline, offer the perfect conditions for cultivating more than 100 native grape varieties. These produce incredibly diverse wines, including many DOC and DOCG labels.

Two of the region's most prominent reds are Taurasi and Aglianico del Taburno, made from the aglianico grape variety. Often referred to as the 'Barolo of the South', Aglianico is a full-bodied wine with long aging potential. Noteworthy white grapes include fiano di avellino and greco. Fiano is unique to Campania and produces a crisp, aromatic, fruity wine with hints of nuts and apple. Greco is known more for its high acidity, minerality and aging potential. Asprinio, coda di volpe and Ischia's biancolella are other varieties of note.

The Benevento province and its surrounds produce half of the region's wine. Within this area, the Valle Telesina wine district is one of the most beautiful stretches, while the Sannio area is home to Campania's most extensive wine production.

When it comes to liqueurs, there's few more famous than limoncello, in both Italy and the world. The entire Amalfi Coast is known for its limoncello – particularly Sorrento.

In Campania, it is often served very cold in decorative glasses, and is used nowadays in cocktails and desserts. Other liqueurs that have taken off along Campania's coasts include *meloncello* (rockmelon/cantaloupe liqueur) and *crema di liquore al pistacchio* (pistachio cream liqueur).

Liquore Strega, one of Italy's most famous liqueurs, has been made in Benevento by the Alberti family since 1860. With its secret recipe of more than 70 different herbs and spices, it is enjoyed both after dinner and in local desserts. And finally, *nocino* (*nocillo* in Naples) is a liqueur made with walnuts.

It's not just about alcohol here, though: the Neapolitans are quite obsessed with coffee, from the water to the roasting (they like it strong and bitter) and the grinding of the beans. Famously, Naples has a longstanding tradition of the *caffè sospeso*, which involves paying for a coffee to be given to someone in need later. The practice is rooted in the belief that coffee is a fundamental part of daily life in Naples, and everyone should have access: a simple and heart-warming example of community spirit.

For those looking for something fresh, the city is also known for its *acquafrescai*: stands selling freshly squeezed juices and lemonade, as well as kiosks that make *limonata a cosce aperte* (open-your-legs lemonade). Basically, this is lemonade with baking soda added, which makes it extra effervescent. To avoid spilling it all over themselves, locals lean over and stand with legs wide apart to drink it.

Culinary experiences

Whether you're in an ancient lemon grove or on a boat off Capri, there's no end of magical locations in Campania for trying its specialties.

Cook and dine in a private garden villa on the isle of Capri

While Capri's majestic waters and landscapes don't need too much of a sales pitch, Australian Holly Star and her Caprese husband, Gianluca D'Esposito, have found a unique way to showcase the island's authentic food. At their villa and garden in Anacapri, they offer bespoke and sustainable culinary activities: think private garden dining or making ravioli capresi or torta caprese and limoncello in a tailored cooking class. Enjoy a tasting of local wines and their very own extra virgin olive oil. If cooking isn't your thing, you'll have the garden to yourself while they cook for you. They can even create a gourmet hamper for a day on the boat or a picnic in one of their secret spots around the island. They'll pick you up in private transportation at the port, so all you need to do is arrive hungry!

CAPRIMICHELANGELO.COM

Experience a luxury stay in pizza heartland

Indulge at the luxurious Aquapetra Resort & Spa in Telese Terme with treatments and thermal spring bathing. In-house dining showcases the best of Campania's Sannio territory – especially the starred Locanda del Borgo restaurant – and the team can book you into experiences, such as vineyard picnics. This is the perfect base for exploring this food heartland and two of the best pizzerias in the country (and, recently, the world): Pepe in Grani in Caiazzo and I Masanielli in Caserta. Franco Pepe has created digital itineraries and workshops to explore the area, also known as Pizza Hub, and, nearby, you have Michelin-starred Krèsios, with its tasting menu at the whim of Chef Giuseppe Iannotti.

AQUAPETRA.COM, PEPEINGRANI.IT, KRESIOS.COM, PIZZERIAIMASANIELLI.IT, PIZZAHUB.VIATORIBUS.COM

Taste wines from the Amalfi Coast and Vesuvius

Le Vigne di Raito is Patrizia Malanga's boutique organic winery near Vietri sul Mare, the gateway to the Amalfi Coast. If you stop in for a tasting of certified wines, you can add on a lunch or dinner or even a pizza or cooking class – all while taking in incredible sea views! In Positano, husband and wife duo Cristian and Jenny of Swirl the Glass run tastings and vineyard tours. From Furore to Pompeii, Vesuvius to Taurasi, their small-group tours introduce you to local producers, and many include lunch.

LEVIGNEDIRAITO.COM, SWIRLTHEGLASS.COM

Lemon groves and mozzarella-making

This half-day experience, which includes a visit to a working organic farm high above the Sorrento coastline, starts with a tour of an ancient lemon grove. Here you get to taste freshly squeezed lemonade and homemade marmalades before you learn how to make limoncello from scratch. Then you'll ride up to a cattle farm in the hills on the iconic Ape Calessino, where, after meeting the cows, you'll see how mozzarella is made and enjoy a light lunch. The team at Casa Mia Food and Wine really know this region and can arrange anything, from picnics in Positano and lunch in Pompeii to a street food tour in Naples.

CASAMIATOURS.COM

Get to the culinary heart of Ischia

A stay at San Montano Resort & Spa on Ischia is sure to be unforgettable, and not just because of the luxury amenities (including private pools) or the breathtaking views across the San Montano Bay: it's because you leave with a suitcase full of memories. You can experience a massage in the private lemon grove, an olive oil tasting or a farm-to-table cooking class with the chef. Or what about sailing to the Aragonese Castle distillery to taste craft spirits, taking a cocktail masterclass or joining a family for the *vendemmia* (grape harvest)? Their mainland sister property, Borgo Santandrea in Amalfi, offers an equally impressive program, including limoncello classes, with a Michelin-starred restaurant on site.

SANMONTANO.COM, BORGOSANTANDREA.IT

SAGRE

JUNE

Pizza Village, Pizza festival,
Naples

Sagra del Casatiello, Casatiello
festival, Sant'Arpino

Festa a Vico, Vico food festival,
Vico Equense

JULY

Sagra del Cuoppo,
Fried food festival, Saviano

Sagra dei Limoni,
Lemon festival, Massa Lubrense

*Sagra del Caciocavallo
Impiccato,* Caciocavallo cheese
festival, San Marco ai Monti

AUGUST

Sagra del Mare, Sea festival,
Procida

Fiordilatte Fiordifesta,
Mozzarella festival, Agerola

Ciccimmaretati, Cilento food
festival, Stio Cilento

SEPTEMBER

Festa della Sfogliatella,
Sfogliatella festival,
Castel San Giorgio

Tufo Greco Festival,
Wine festival, Tufo

Gragnano Città della Pasta,
Pasta festival, Gragnano

Ischia Safari,
Ischia food festival, Ischia

OCTOBER

*Festa della Castagno e
dell'Olio,* Chestnut and olive
oil festival, Salento

Candele alla genovese

Genovese ragù with candele

Campania is renowned for its slowly cooked and closely treasured
pasta sauces, among which is the wildly debated Genovese, whose
origins continue to divide local opinion. But whether it was introduced
to Naples by the Genovese during the Renaissance, named after a
sailor called Genovese who claimed to have invented the dish in the
18th century, or inspired by the Neapolitan inns and taverns of Via dei
Genovesi, one thing's for sure – it's a crowd pleaser. I've eaten Chef
Crescenzo Scotti's version on the magical terrace of Borgo Santandrea
and, combined with Amalfi Coast sea views, it was just perfection.

SERVES 4

100 ml (3½ fl oz) extra virgin
olive oil, plus a little extra

700 g (1 lb 11 oz) beef (chuck
or braising steak)

1.25 kg (2 lb 12 oz) onions
(preferably Montoro variety),
finely sliced

200 ml (7 fl oz) vegetable stock

400 g (14 oz) candele
pasta (or you could use ziti,
casarecce or any thick-tube
pasta such as rigatoni)

1 teaspoon softened butter

handful of grated parmesan

40 g (1½ oz) grated pecorino
(preferably di Grotta, but the
finest quality available to you
will work)

alfafa sprouts or a few sprigs
of small basil leaves, to serve
(optional)

Heat the olive oil in a large saucepan over medium heat
and brown the beef on all sides for about 5 minutes,
until caramelised. Cover the beef with the sliced onion,
add the stock and cover with a lid or layer of baking
paper, leaving a small hole on one side to allow the steam
to escape.

Reduce the heat to low and cook, stirring occasionally,
for 3–4 hours, until the meat is tender. Leaving the onion
in the pan, remove the meat and place it in the fridge.

Once cold, cut the meat into four cubes of about 70 g
(2½ oz) each (one per portion) and add any left-over
meat trimmings back to the pan with the onion.

Reheat the onion mixture over medium–high heat
for a further 15–20 minutes, until the onion is soft and
caramel-coloured and the mixture has reduced to a sauce-
like consistency. If necessary, add a pinch of salt to taste.

Meanwhile, cook the pasta in plenty of salted boiling
water until al dente. Drain, then return the pasta to the
pan and toss in the butter, along with the parmesan.
Stir to combine.

Reheat the beef in a frying pan over high heat
with a little olive oil. Serve the pasta topped with the
caramelised onion sauce and with the beef on the side.
Sprinkle the pasta and beef with the grated pecorino
and garnish with alfalfa sprouts or small basil leaves,
if desired.

Campania

SOUTHERN ITALY

Puglia

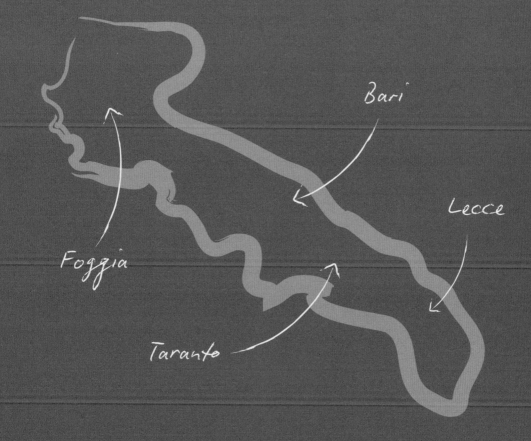

Bari

Lecce

Foggia

Taranto

Regional produce

Apulia's flat swathes of landscape are
covered with farms that produce huge
amounts of olive oil and the durum wheat
that's used in the region's numerous
breads and pastas. In this historically
poor area, meat plays a less important
role than fresh vegetables, which are
bulked out with local beans, cereals and
lentils, while a long stretch of coastline
ensures plenty of fresh seafood.

- Andria's burrata
- Altamura's bread
- Black chickpeas
  (garbanzo beans)
- Brindisi artichokes
- Canestrato cheese
- Clementines
- Dried figs
- Horse meat
- Lampascioni onions
- Martina Franca's capocollo
- Pork
- Shellfish
- Turnip top greens
- White beans

Grottaglie

I visited Apulia long before Justin Timberlake famously got married there, and way before another wedding on popular soap opera *The Bold and the Beautiful* put it on the tourist map. It still attracts fewer American travellers than the Amalfi Coast or Tuscany, but I'd say it's not far from catching up. And for very good reason. From an aesthetic, cultural and gastronomical standpoint, it's hard to fault Apulia. If you told me I'd have to spend the rest of my summers there, I'd be okay with that! I'd find a way to manage.

I remember noticing how relatively flat the region is on one of my first trips there. A driver explained to me that this flatness makes Apulia perfect for olive trees – some 60 million of them (including some that are over 4,000 years old). This region produces 40 per cent of the country's olive oil – more than any other region – because it's blessed with some magical combination of sun, sea, soil and ancient tricks. Here in the South, olive trees thrive in the Mediterranean climate, hence why some of Italy's best oil is bottled here. As you probably guessed, not only do the Pugliesi take extreme pride in their olive oil, but their cuisine is completely fuelled by it!

I have so many Apulia food moments etched in my memory, like a spaghettata on a boat sailing the Salento coast during the Italian Ferragosto holiday in August. The crew kept dishing out plates of spaghetti al pomodoro and, dripping wet from a swim in the turquoise waters, I ate it all up and then washed it down with a glass of Negroamaro. One year, there was a lunch feast with my family in Alberobello, where dish after dish of locally sourced produce just kept arriving until there was no space on the table: cured meats like salami and *capocollo* (a dried, cold cut made with pork shoulder), luscious cheeses like burrata and caciocavallo, seasonal grilled and pickled vegetables, and then orecchiette (page 274) to finish.

I'll never forget dinner in Lecce at Trattoria Le Zie (The Aunts); as the name suggests, you feel like you are dining at a relative's home. On my visit, it was an orecchiette and pan-fried *polpette* (meatballs) affair. It was also in Lecce that I had my first *rustico leccese* (page 274). *Rustico* is the blanket term for savoury pastry, and this bechamel-filled one is a beauty. And I'll long remember my first *tiella barese* (page 274), a rustic yet luscious rice, potato and mussel hot pot of sorts.

But from all my Apulian food memories, if I had to choose one thing to eat here all day, it would be burrata. Originating from the farming town of Andria over a century ago, this glossy and bulbous fresh cheese is a hand-stretched mozzarella with a creamy, luxurious centre of stracciatella.

There are countless culinary options to choose from in Apulia, however. This region sprawls over the entire heel of the boot, with around 800 km (500 miles) of coastline. The Adriatic Sea is to its east and the Ionian Sea to its south. With its coast and fertile plains, the region is a historical centre for agriculture and fishing, with a long history of settlement. Apulia has been inhabited by Greeks, Romans, Normans and other groups, all of whom left their mark on the region's food. For example, the Greeks introduced olive trees, which the Romans expertly cultivated, laying the foundation for Apulia's wealth of olive groves.

Apulia's cuisine is deeply rooted in tradition, and particularly in cucina povera. The climate is ideal for growing fruit and vegetables, and so many traditional dishes feature locally grown produce, such as tomatoes, bell peppers (capsicums), artichokes, broad (fava) beans and eggplants (aubergines), as well as herbs like oregano and basil, and, of course, olives.

As you'd expect in a region so large, the cuisine varies in different parts. Apulia's capital, Bari, and its surrounds are famous for orecchiette, and you'll still find women rolling the pasta outside on the streets of the city's old town. It's usually served with *cime di rapa* (broccoli rabe) or a tomato sauce with caciocavallo. And while you're exploring the streets, keep an eye out for *panzerotto* (deep-fried, stuffed turnovers; page 274).

Bari is also known for its seafood – particularly *crudi* (raw seafood; page 275). It's not uncommon to see fishermen at the port repeatedly slapping octopus onto the concrete to tenderise it. Calamari, mussels, sea urchins: you name it. If they can catch it, you'll eat it fresh and raw across Bari or on the spot at the port market.

The city also offers one of the most well-known focaccias within Italy. You can find variations across Apulia, but the Barese variety (page 274) is a standout. Meanwhile Altamura, southwest of Bari, is home to the region's famous bread – *pane di Altamura* – which is naturally leavened and made from remilled durum wheat semolina, the result similar to sourdough.

In the northern parts of Bari province and through to the Barletta area, it's very common to find horse meat on the menu, in the form of either sausages or a ragù served with pasta. Meat becomes more common as you travel inland, with popular products on offer in the Foggia area like *muschiska*: a cured, dried meat made from sheep, goat or veal. And once you reach the Itria Valley to the southeast, between Brindisi and Taranto, meat is king. Yes, seafood is still prominent here because of the coastline, but valley towns like Martina Franca and Cisternino are famous for their prime cuts and salumi – particularly capocollo. I loved dining in butcher's stores in Cisternino where you choose your meat cuts, including the bite-sized bombette (page 274): they're cooked on the spot and delivered piping hot to your table.

Heading back west to the Salento coast, you'll find seafood dishes like the ancient *scapece gallipolina* (page 276), but there

are also street foods like the *puccia* flatbread and the soaked crispbread *frisa salentina*. These parts are also known for *pasticciotto* (page 274). I especially love this custard-filled sweet alongside the local *caffè leccese*: an iced coffee, prepared with hot espresso, ice cubes, sugar syrup and almond milk.

And it would be hard to talk about food in Apulia without mentioning *taralli* (page 274). This ring-shaped cracker of sorts is served as a snack at any hour and can be found in various incarnations.

Of course, what is a culinary trip to Apulia without a visit to the north's Gargano Peninsula, which comprises a national park? Its hills are covered with olive groves, citrus orchards and grapevines, which are bordered by a spectacular coastline. The area is unique to the central and southern parts of the region: yet another example of Apulia's beautiful diversity.

As I said before, if I had to spend every summer here, I would manage. As I write, the tunes of the Apulian folk dance *pizzica* play in my mind: the soundtrack to a region known around the world for its exceptional olive oil, burrata and orecchiette, but one that will keep you coming back for so much more.

Puglia

This region produces 40 per cent of the country's olive oil — more than any other region — because it's blessed with some magical combination of sun, sea, soil and ancient tricks.

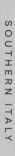

SOUTHERN ITALY

MARIA'S TOP 10 DISHES OF PUGLIA

1 ACQUASALE / FRISELLE

Old bread is given new life in *aquasale*, which is made by pouring tomatoes, onions, olive oil and herbs over chunks of stale bread to soften it. Other ingredients such as egg, bell peppers (capsicums) and cucumbers can be added. The mixture can be served with *friselle*, a hard, crispy, doughnut-shaped bread native to Apulia.

2 BOMBETTE

These little bombs of flavour are eaten as a hearty street food or second course and are sold in the region's inner countryside, where each butcher closely guards their signature recipe. Rolls of pork meat, usually capocollo, are stuffed with local caciocavallo cheese and (often) a slice of pancetta. The bombette are usually cooked over a grill to ensure an oozy cheese centre.

3 FOCACCIA BARESE

Inviting to both the palate and the eye, Bari's focaccia begs to be devoured. The dough incorporates semolina flour and boiled potato to create the perfect balance between a cloud-soft centre and crunchy edges, while the surface, studded with black olives and cherry tomatoes and dusted with oregano, is pretty as a picture.

4 ORECCHIETTE

Apulia's 'little ears' are a symbol of the region and are served up in a variety of ways, most commonly with cime di rapa cooked with anchovies, garlic and chilli. They are also found with horse meat ragù or topped with caciocavallo cheese. In the town of Foggia, they're accompanied by a tomato-based sauce made with potato and peppery rocket (arugula).

5 PANZEROTTO

Panzerotti are made all over Italy, but they were born in Apulia. These fried turnovers, filled with gooey mozzarella and tomato passata (pureed tomatoes), are a perfect street food snack.

6 PASTICCIOTTO

Salento's breakfast pastry of choice, *pasticciotti* are small, oval pies made with a sweet shortcrust (pie) pastry and filled with a dense creme patissiere. They're brushed with egg yolk and baked until they're a deep, glossy brown. You can sometimes find them filled with jam or chocolate.

7 PATATE, RISO E COZZE / TIELLA BARESE

Bari lays claim to this recipe of rice, potatoes and mussels which are layered, uncooked, along with slices of tomato and onion. The dish is topped with grated Pecorino Romano, then baked in the oven, where the juices from the mussels and tomato permeate the rice and potatoes, while the cheese topping becomes crisp and golden.

8 RUSTICO LECCESE

Now found all over Apulia, Lecce's savoury *rustici* are a hugely popular street food. These rounds of flaky puff pastry are stuffed with a tasty filling of bechamel, tomato and mozzarella, and they're delicious straight from the oven or cooled.

9 SPAGHETTI ALL'ASSASSINA

A dish truly unique to Apulia, the 'assassin' differs from any other pasta dish in that, rather than being boiled, the spaghetti is cooked directly in the pan. Using the same concept as a risotto, a watery tomato broth is gradually added. As the pasta absorbs the liquid, the underside becomes burnt and crunchy. Fiery red chilli is added at the end to finish off the mix of soft and crisp textures and smoky, spicy flavour.

10 TARALLI

Eaten as a snack or as part of an aperitivo, Apulia's *taralli*, now found all over Italy, are crunchy little rings of savoury dough often flavoured with chilli, black pepper, fennel and poppy seeds, garlic and herbs. There's also a sweet variety that can be dipped in wine.

Other dishes
to look out for

From the freshest catch to local pastas that sauce perfectly clings to, Apulia's long stretch of coast and its abundance of olive groves shine in its cuisine.

Street food

Calzone barese

Less of a calzone and more of a savoury pie, this recipe from Bari uses *sponsale*, a local type of spring onion (scallion) with an undeveloped bulb which imparts a delicate, leek-like flavour. A sturdy pastry crust holds a filling of onion, tomato, olives and cheese, sometimes with anchovies and capers or raisins mixed in.

Gnummareddi / Turcinielli

Found all over Southern Italy, in Apulia, these rolls of grilled offal go by many names, depending on the town. They feature lamb or kid interiors encased in tightly wound strips of the animal's gut, flavoured with grated pecorino and leaves of fresh parsley.

Puccia leccese

Salento's puccerie shops, which specialise in this typical panino, are the best places to try them. *Pucce* are hollow bread rolls cooked in a wood-fired oven: ideal for stuffing with local ingredients such as cured meat, cheese, grilled vegetables or even meat stew.

Antipasti

Crudi di mare

Apulia's enviable coastline offers a host of treasures straight from the sea, and one of the best ways to kick off a meal is with a mixed selection of raw seafood. Large platters of shellfish, including mussels and oysters, are served with calamari, prawns (shrimp) and tartare of fresh fish dressed with local olive oil and a squeeze of lemon.

Cozze arraganate

Using just a few ingredients to achieve maximum flavour, the name of this mussel dish refers to the dialect term for 'topping with breadcrumbs'. The mussels are arranged in a single layer and individually topped with a mixture of grated pecorino, beaten egg and finely chopped parsley. The dish is covered with breadcrumbs and olive oil and then baked.

Frittata di lampascioni

Lampascioni are wild bitter bulbs, similar to onions, that are found across Apulia. For this dish, they are soaked in water and boiled to remove any unpleasant bitterness. They are then cooked with eggs and pecorino to create this frittata that showcases their flavour and aroma.

Puglia

SOUTHERN ITALY

Muschiska

Easy to transport and consume, *muschiska* was created for local shepherds who would take it on their long journey of transhumance. Strips of mutton or goat are seasoned with garlic, chilli and fennel seeds, then threaded on string and hung to dry in the sun for 15–20 days.

Scapece gallipolina

During medieval times, when their town was regularly under siege, the people of Gallipoli found ways to preserve and conserve their local ingredients for the periods when they were trapped within the city walls. One such solution was this dish, in which small, deboned bluefish are fried and packed between layers of vinegar-soaked bread. Saffron, which is mixed with the vinegar, gives the dish its distinctive bright-yellow colour.

Primi

Cavatelli

There are many types of small, curled pasta found all over the southern regions. They have many names, including *cavatelli* in Apulia, and are served with many sauces. However, one thing they all have in common is an interior cavity (their namesake), which traps the accompanying sauce.

Ciceri e tria

In this Apulian spin on the classic *pasta e ceci* (pasta and chickpeas/garbanzo beans), fresh twisted pasta is divided, a portion boiled and the rest fried until crunchy. The pasta is then combined with chickpeas cooked with bay, rosemary, chilli and garlic.

Fave bianche e lagane

Just a handful of ingredients go into this Apulian version of pasta and beans. Dried white beans are left to soak for 12 hours, then cooked with a little water and onion until the beans begin to fall apart. Olive oil is then added to achieve a thick cream. Flat lagane pasta is tossed with the bean puree and a drizzle of oil tops things off.

Macco di fave e cicoria

Apulia's classic *fave e cicoria* is a vegetable dish hearty enough to eat as a secondo. Dried broad (fava) beans are soaked and boiled until they break down into a dense puree, while fresh chicory leaves are boiled and drained. The two elements are then served side by side with a swirl of olive oil.

Sagne 'ncannulate

A typical pasta from the Salento area which gets its name from the dialect for 'twisted'. A dough of flour and water is rolled and cut into strips, which are twisted around a finger. Left to dry out, the sagne are then served with a simple tomato sauce, basil and a grating of hard cheese, such as ricotta salata.

Strascinati

A wider and flatter form of orecchiette, *strascinati* are well known in the town of Taranto, where the pasta dates to the 1500s. There, they are more commonly known as *chiancaredde*. Just like orecchiette, they are often cooked with broccoli rabe, meat-based sauces or a simple accompaniment of tomato and basil.

Zucchine alla puviriedda

An easy dish that invigorates the zucchini (courgette) of Apulia. The zucchini is sliced into rounds that are spread out and left to dehydrate in the heat of the sun. Once dried, they are quickly fried in plenty of olive oil until they begin to colour. They're then drained, dressed with vinegar, garlic and fresh mint, and left to absorb the flavours before serving.

Secondi

Brasciole

An old-school Sunday lunch dish, *brasciole* are traditionally made with horse meat, though nowadays it is commonly substituted with beef or veal. The meat is rolled in garlic, pecorino and parsley and secured into parcels before gently simmering in a tomato sauce until tender. Any extra sauce is saved to serve with pasta – often orecchiette. When prepared with beef, this dish is known as *braciole pugliesi*.

Cozze alla tarantina

The coast of Taranto is famous for its mussels, and this local recipe truly lets them shine. After the mussels are opened in a hot pan with white wine and garlic, they are dressed with a tomato sauce flavoured with parsley and a hint of red chilli.

Melanzane ripiene

Apulia's plump, shiny eggplants (aubergines) are halved and the flesh scooped out to make a stuffing with cherry tomatoes, capers, olives and breadcrumbs. Sprinkled with cheese, they're baked for a delicious taste of summer.

Pitta di patate

Two layers of mashed potato flavoured with pecorino sandwich a filling of tomatoes, capers, onion and olives. Topped with breadcrumbs, the pitta is baked until golden and may be eaten hot or cold.

Polpo alla pignata

From the Salento coast, this octopus dish is named after the *pignata* (the terracotta dish it was traditionally made in). The octopus is slowly cooked with a tomato sauce, preserving its flavour, with some recipes adding cubes of potato. It should be served with toasted bread to mop up the sauce.

Puglia

Dolci

Biscotto di Ceglie

Ceglie Messapica is the proud hometown of these celebrated cookies (also known as *pesquett*), which are made by hand using strictly local ingredients. Toasted almonds form the base of the dough, which is shaped into squares and filled with jam made from cherries, grapes or figs. They can also be coated with a cocoa frosting called *cileppo*.

Bocconotti

Little pies made from a shortcrust pastry shell, *bocconotti* are also found in Abruzzo and Calabria, but each region has its own local variations for the filling. In Apulia, they're stuffed with a cream of sweetened ricotta flavoured with lemon and cinnamon.

Cartellate

Apulia's *cartellate* are a crispy, crunchy, festive treat. A sweet, oil-based dough flavoured with clementine is passed through a pasta roller until thin and then cut into strips with a serrated roller cutter. These are rolled around themselves and pressed together to create a rose before being fried. After cooling, they're covered with warmed vincotto or honey.

Sospiri di Bisceglie / Tette delle monache

The origin of this delicious cake lies with 16th-century Poor Clare nuns from the town of Bisceglie, though legend has it that eating it promotes fertility due to its voluptuous shape. Whatever the case, the light sponge is filled with vanilla cream custard and covered with a delicate white glacé icing.

... and to drink

Apulia's fertile soil and dry, hot climate with cool sea breezes make the region perfect for growing grapes. It produces many excellent wines – mostly notably full-bodied reds and rose.

The millennia-old wine culture in Apulia started with the Greeks, who brought vines across the Adriatic around the 7th century BCE. It has been a prominent agricultural region with a winemaking heritage since then, but until recently very few people – even in the business – were aware of Apulian wine. This is primarily because quantity, not quality, was the focus of production. But around the turn of the 21st century, this started to change, thanks to some major producers. Today, award-winning wines from Apulia can be found on tables around the world. It currently has 29 DOC and four DOCG wine regions, mostly concentrated in the Salento region at the southern part of the heel.

Reds are the bread and butter of Apulia, and the most well known are Negroamaro and Primitivo. *Negroamaro* translates to 'black bitter': the dark-skinned grapes used to produce this ruby-red wine have a distinct, bitter flavour. It is mainly produced in and around Lecce and Brindisi, and on a smaller scale in Taranto. Many local roses are also made from negroamaro grapes.

Primitivo is made with the zinfandel grape, which is said to have arrived in Apulia from Croatia. The name means 'early ripening' in old Italian – a name true to its typical early August harvest. Less robust than Negramaro, its flavours are pronounced and often reminiscent of very ripe dark berries, liquorice and black pepper. If you'd like to try it, look out for DOC Primitivo di Manduria.

In the Foggia and Bari area, try the elegant Nero di Troia, which is often overshadowed by the two dominant red varietals. Malvasia Nera di Brindisi and Malvasia Nera di Lecce are also both worth seeking out.

But while Apulia is most famous for red wine, its whites shouldn't be overlooked. The climate produces crisp, dry varietals that make for easy drinking. Some to look out for are Gravina, Verdeca, Bombino Bianco, Greco Bianco and Malvasia.

For those looking to try a rose, Castel del Monte is a DOC wine produced in the provinces of Barletta, Andria and Trani. And for a taste of history, look for the renowned Five Roses – first produced in 1943, it was the first rose ever bottled in Italy.

There's no shortage of liqueurs or amari here, either. *Nanassino* is a liqueur made with prickly pears, Padre Peppe is made with walnuts and Mirinello from wild cherries. The list goes on, with ingredients ranging from fennel to chocolate to bay leaves. Amaro Pugliese is a local digestif produced with around 40 herbs including absinthe, mint and aloe. Each bottle of Amaro del Gargano is said to be created with 99 olive leaves, while arancino liqueur is made with the best oranges of the Gargano area.

Puglia

SOUTHERN ITALY

Culinary experiences

If you want to return home with some serious foodie skills in your back pocket, Apulia can offer some delicious gourmet experiences, such as learning how to make cheese or the region's renowned orecchiette.

Learn how to make orecchiette (and eat them too!)'

You can't leave Apulia without trying orecchiette or seeing them rolled on the streets of Bari Vecchia, the capital's historic centre (don't miss Via dell'Arco Basso, dubbed 'orecchiette street', where local makers produce them on the daily). But why just watch when you can make the pasta yourself? Puglialy runs classes in a *masseria* (farmhouse), and if you're still hungry, focaccia and pasticiotto classes are on the menu too. And expert food guide Sophie Minchilli runs delectable week-long tours through Apulia where, in addition to the famed pasta, you'll eat a whole lot more.

PUGLIALY.COM, SOPHIEMINCHILLI.COM

Cheesemaking and tasting

You could say that Apulia is known for its cheeses. Think burrata, caciocavallo and pecorino. In the Andria area, there are many *caseifici* (cheese producers) to visit, including Caseificio Olanda, who have a cheese museum you can walk through, and Terra Che Vivi, a company who offers a range of cheese-related tours. In Altamura, don't miss the Dicecca family-run dairy farm. Book in for The Cheese Experience, a 3–4 hour immersion with a visit to their farm and the town, finished with a tasting at their cheese bar in a local forest.

CASEIFICIOOLANDA.IT, TERRACHEVIVE.COM
VITODICECCA.IT

Taste liquid gold at an olive oil tasting

Apulia produces some of the best olive oil in Italy, and travellers can visit olive groves and mills to taste the different varieties and learn about the production process. Puglialy is a local provider that runs small group and private tours with departures from a number of towns. They'll take you to an olive oil farm where you'll partake in tastings and learn about this culinary tradition that has put Apulia on the world stage.

PUGLIALY.COM

Meat lovers rejoice in Cisternino

If meat in all its varied glory is your thing, Cisternino in the Itria Valley is a great stop. There are many lodging options in the area to base yourself, and a dinner at Zio Pietro is a must. It's basically a butcher's shop with tables, as is common in this meat-loving town. Order sausages, steak cuts and especially bombette, and the guys here will flame-grill it all to perfection. Also be sure to organise a visit to Salumificio Santoro to see local cured meats, such as capocollo, being produced, and enjoy a tasting too!

FACEBOOK.COM/DAZIOPIETRO
SALUMIFICIOSANTORO.COM

Luxury meets ancient traditions

Despite the rapid increase in tourism and luxury hotel investment over the last decade, Apulia has somehow remained pretty authentic. Part of that is due to the number of restored masserie: farmhouses offering activities aimed at exposing travellers to the region's rich past. Many have turned into boutique properties where you can stay and take part in wine tasting, cooking classes and even folk dancing. One of the most luxurious stays in the area is at Masseria Torre Maizza, a Rocco Forte Hotel. Located in Savelletri, it's the perfect base for exploring the surrounding area. There's a host of activities on site, from learning how to make focaccia to a mixology class, a sunset picnic or a private dinner under the stars.

ROCCOFORTEHOTELS.COM/IT/HOTELS-AND-RESORTS/
MASSERIA-TORRE-MAIZZA

SAGRE

JULY

Sagra del Polpo, Octopus festival, Mola di Bari

Te la Uliata, Black olive bread festival, Caprarica di Lecce

AUGUST

Orecchiette nelle 'nchiosce, Orecchiette festival, Grottaglie

Sagra del Caciocavallo, Cicatielli e Acc', Festival of caciocavallo cheese, cavatelli and celery, Monteleone di Puglia

Sagra della Bombetta e della Bruschetta al Tartufo, Bombette meat and truffle bruschetta festival, Cisternino

Sagra dell'Olio e del Vino, Olive oil and wine festival, Cisternino

Sagra della Trippa, Tripe festival, Cisternino

Sagra degli Gnumerèdde Suffuchète, Stewed rolls of intestine and tripe festival, Locorotondo

OCTOBER

Fish Experience, Seafood festival, Polignano a Mare

NOVEMBER

Sagra del Fungo Cardoncello, Mushroom festival, Ruvo di Puglia

Festa del Vino Primitivo e Cece Nero, Primitivo wine and black chickpeas festival, Acquaviva delle Fonti

Orecchiette con cime di rapa

Orecchiette with broccoli rabe

Regarded by his peers as one of Italy's finest chefs, Fulvio Pierangelini guides every aspect of gastronomy at each Rocco Forte Hotel around the world. The beautiful simplicity of his approach includes a profound respect for excellent produce combined with local tradition, and so the food of each outlet reflects its surrounds. Masseria Torre Maizza in Savelletri is no different, and it really doesn't get much more 'Apulia' than orecchiette con cime di rapa. If I close my eyes tightly, I'm back on the restaurant terrace eating this rustic pasta dish with broccoli rabe, sourced from the on-site veggie patch.

Puglia

SOUTHERN ITALY

SERVES 4

250 g (9 oz) fine durum wheat semolina flour, plus extra for dusting

1.5 kg (3 lb 5 oz) broccoli rabe

40 ml (1½ fl oz) extra virgin olive oil, plus extra for drizzling

1 garlic clove, peeled

½ bird's eye chilli

6 anchovy fillets in oil, drained

grated pecorino, to serve (optional)

Place the flour on a work surface and make a well in the centre. Gradually pour in 120 ml (4 fl oz) of lukewarm water and use your finger to gradually mix the ingredients together, then knead until you have a smooth and elastic dough – this will take 12–15 minutes.

Form the dough into a ball, cover with a damp, clean cloth and leave to rest for 15 minutes.

Divide the dough into four pieces and roll each into a long, thin sausage shape about 1 cm (½ in) thick. On a lightly floured surface, cut each length of dough into 1 cm (½ in) pieces.

To form the orecchiette, drag a smooth-bladed knife over each piece of dough to make a rounded shell shape, then turn the shape 'inside-out' to form the orecchiette. Continue until all the dough has been used.

To make the sauce, trim and separate the broccoli rabe into three parts: the large outer leaves and tender stalks, the middle leaves, and the interior with the unopened flower buds, setting a few sprigs aside for garnish.

Bring a large saucepan of lightly salted water to the boil and cook the rabe outer leaves and stalks for 7–8 minutes, until softened but still green. Leaving the water in the saucepan, use tongs to remove the leaves and stalks and plunge them into iced water. Squeeze out the excess water, then roughly chop.

Heat a drizzle of olive oil in a large frying pan over medium heat, add the chopped rabe and cook for 1–2 minutes, until warmed through. Remove from the heat, then blend the rabe in a food processor or blender, adding a sprinkle of salt and a drizzle of olive oil to form a smooth cream.

Return the water to the boil and add the orecchiette. After 2 minutes, add the middle leaves from the rabe and cook for 3 minutes or until the orecchiette is al dente. Drain, reserving 250 ml (1 cup) of the cooking water.

Meanwhile, heat the olive oil in a large frying pan over medium heat. Add the whole garlic clove, chilli and anchovy fillets and cook, stirring, for 2 minutes. Using the back of a fork, press the anchovies into the oil to help them break down and dissolve. Add the remaining uncooked broccoli rabe and cook for a couple of minutes, adding a few tablespoons of the reserved pasta cooking water to stop the pan drying out.

Add the pasta mixture to the frying pan. Remove the garlic and chilli and toss everything until well combined.

To serve, spread the rabe cream across the base of four plates. Top with the orecchiette and rabe sprigs, drizzle with olive oil and sprinkle with pecorino, if desired.

Sardegna

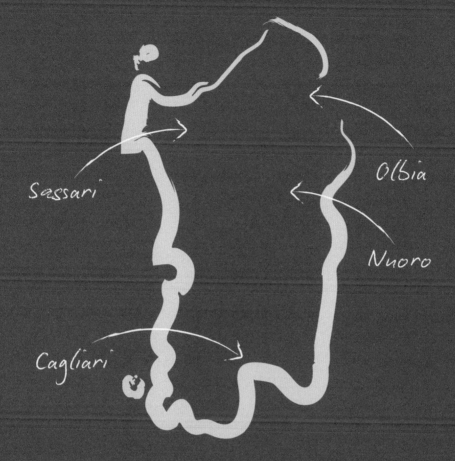

Sassari

Olbia

Nuoro

Cagliari

Regional produce

Surrounded by sea, Sardinia naturally
has a huge range of fish-based dishes,
but move inland to the wild, unspoiled
countryside and you will find a heavier,
meat-orientated cuisine. With millions
of sheep roaming the farmland and
pastures, lamb is at the forefront of
menus, alongside sheep's milk cheeses,
which are used in both savoury and
sweet recipes.

- Almonds
- Bottarga
- Casizolu cheese
- Casu marzu cheese
- Fiore Sardo cheese
- Honey
- Lobster
- Pecorino
- Pompia citrus
- Olbia's mussels
- Saffron
- Sea urchins
- Spiny artichokes
- Suckling pig
- Wild fennel

San Pantaleo

S ardinia: what a majestic landscape! That sweeping ruggedness, adorned with untamed prickly pears and myrtle bushes, all set against a breathtakingly blue sky.

After Sicily, this is the second-largest island in the Mediterranean Sea, located west of the Italian peninsula. Its diverse geography includes mountainous regions, fertile plains and stunning coastline, with rugged cliffs and sandy beaches. The island is home to several major cities, including the capital, Cagliari, situated south and known for its historic architecture and bustling port. Other notable cities include Sassari in the northwest, renowned for its cultural heritage, and Olbia in the northeast, a hub for tourism and commerce.

Sardinia's population is concentrated along the coasts and in urban areas, the interior characterised by smaller towns and villages. In some parts, the roads are rough, and the signage even rougher, but the people throughout are hospitable and as warm as the Mediterranean climate. And when it comes to lifestyle, the Sardinians must be doing something right: they are some of the longest-living people in the world, with many medical experts attributing this, in part, to their diet.

Sardinians prioritise their regional identity, seeing themselves as Sardinian above all else, due to the island's unique history, language and culture, which distinguish it from the mainland. Their past is defined by foreign occupation and the many different cultures that settled here, including the Phoenicians, Romans, Genovese and Spanish: each left their mark on the island and its cuisine. The Phoenicians founded the city of Nora in the 8th century BCE and introduced the cultivation of wheat and the production of bread. The Romans conquered the island in the 3rd century BCE and brought new fruits and vegetables, such as figs and pomegranates. The Spanish, who ruled

Sardinia from the 14th to the 18th century, eventually introduced new ingredients, such as tomatoes and bell peppers (capsicums), which are now local staples.

These cultures also brought their languages, which produced the local dialect. Until the 1960s, when Italian began its radical diffusion through TV and radio, the region's language, Sardu, set the island apart from the rest of Italy with its distinct vocabulary characteristics: an archaic Romance tongue with no close relation to any Italian dialect. Nowadays, though, the younger generations – who are predominantly Italian monolinguals – don't identify with the indigenous tongue, which is reduced to memory: the language of their grandparents.

However, much of Sardinia's culture – and cooking – remains true to tradition, with dishes unchanged even in the face of foreign influences. Just take the roasted suckling pig *porceddu* (page 290): its recipe is said to be 1,000 years old.

My first meals on this eclectic island read like a jumbled shopping list: cheese, honey, pork, pasta, clams, fregula, shellfish, lamb and more cheese. It sounds like a mishmash, I know, but if you take a deeper dive into this glorious region, you start to put the pieces together.

My first stop here was in 2006, on a visit to the medieval seafront city of Alghero, in the island's northwest. Our small group was hit by a stomach bug and we spent most of the trip in our hotel. My long-held hopes of sampling the local Catalan-style lobster were dashed. But then, on the hunt for dry crackers, I stumbled upon the local flatbread staple, *pane carasau* (page 290). So began my foray into the island's cuisine, which included sampling many local specialties such as *fregula con le arselle* (with tiny clams), which I ate at a beach club near Villasimius in the south. This dish became the source of my fregula addiction.

Sardegna

ISLANDS

I've eaten *culurgiones* (page 290) all around Sardinia, but especially on the eastern part of the island, where they're said to have originated. This stuffed pasta is filled with a mix of pecorino, potato and mint and is usually served with a tomato sauce and grated pecorino. These stuffed delights have ancient origins, likely dating back to the Nuragic civilisation, which flourished on the island from around 1800 BCE. Still made today, the pasta's wheat-like appearance is so ornate that each culurgione looks like an expert tailor has hand-sewn it. They were created this way to appease the year's wheat crop and are believed to protect families from hardship like a talisman. When visiting, I also try not to miss *malloreddus* (page 290). These little ribbed, shell-shaped pasta, often called *gnocchetti sardi*, are usually served with a pork sausage sauce.

A short visit to Cagliari, the island's capital, gave me my first taste of *seadas* (page 290). Originally crafted by shepherds and peasants, possibly as a main or only course, the treat is now symbolic of Sardinia. In its modern form, it is a type of fried dumpling with a lemony pecorino filling and generous drizzling of honey. This melding of flavours and textures encapsulates this melting pot of an island, but there is much debate among locals around the dessert's origins. One theory claims it dates to the 15th century when the region was under Spain's rule, because the word *seada* is taken from Spanish. Others argue that the term stems from the Latin word *sebum*, tied to the traditional use of animal fat or lard in the pastry. While debate may exist, the simplicity of seadas' ingredients remains undisputed, and the treat reigns as Sardinia's dessert par excellence.

In a sense, Sardinia's diversity is reflective of Italy. The island lies basking in the Mediterranean Sea, so you'd expect a cuisine of seafood, but farming is at the heart of this region's ancient gastronomy. Dining here, you may well be more likely to feast on suckling pig, lamb, goat and wild boar than the day's catch. I love these peculiarities and contrasts. On the one hand you have the Costa Smeralda, a playground of the rich and famous, and on the other you have sheep: an island of designer stores and shepherds, if you like!

Thanks to Sardinia's isolation from the mainland, it's a region that's historically been self-sufficient, with a strong agricultural tradition. This includes its ancient sheep-breeding tradition, which led to the island's reputation for cheese production. In fact, it's the largest producer of pecorino in Europe, and dairy production here can be traced back to the Bronze Age. Currently, the island has three cheeses made with sheep's milk that are protected under the DOP designation: Pecorino Sardo, Pecorino Romano and Fiore Sardo. There's also a revered delicacy known as *casu marzu*, which is a fermented sheep's milk cheese infested with live maggots (the name translates literally to 'putrid' or 'rotten'). Commercial sale was deemed illegal by the Italian government in 1962, but it's still beloved on the island, even though it's quite difficult to source. Locals once gave me a tip that if you were nice to your wait staff at a restaurant or a deli worker, they might give you some intel on where to find some.

The prevalence of Sardinian sheep might be surprising: as I said, one might naturally assume that seafood reigns supreme on the second-largest island in the Mediterranean. However, the region's reliance on farming stems from the little-known fact that malaria wreaked havoc on the coast during the Carthaginian invasion of 215 BCE, and it persisted until after World War II. Inhabitants were forced to move inland to escape the disease, resulting in a diet that was less reliant on fish.

These days, though, seafood has made a comeback and is a much-loved delicacy. Dishes that now feature as essential parts of the island's diet include *spaghetti alle vongole* (with clams) and *sa merca* (page 293), a deliciously herby way to prepare mullet. The island is a big producer of *bottarga* (dried and cured mullet roe), which is often served thinly sliced and accompanied by lemon and olive oil, or grated over pasta to add a briny flavour.

Vegetables and legumes also play a significant role in Sardinia's cuisine, with artichokes, broad (fava) beans and chickpeas (garbanzo beans) among the most common ingredients. *Minestra di fave e piselli* (broad bean and pea soup) is a popular springtime dish, found in the countryside, along with *minestra di ceci e finocchi* – a chickpea and fennel soup, which can also include tomatoes, pork and small pasta or potatoes.

Bread is a staple here, too: in addition to *pane carasau* and *pane frattau* (page 290), there's *pane guttiau*: a baked pane carasau topped with oil, salt and often rosemary. And then you have *pane civraxiu*, a hearty, dense sourdough made with durum wheat flour and a starter that was traditionally passed down through generations. This round loaf has a dark crust and a compact texture, making it perfect for bruschetta.

In recent years, the island's cuisine has garnered international recognition, its dishes featuring in festivals and exhibitions worldwide. Today, many chefs incorporate traditional Sardinian ingredients and cooking techniques into their cuisine, showcasing the island's culinary heritage.

As Sardinia moves forward, its cuisine will undoubtedly continue to shape its cultural identity and cement its place in the world of gastronomy. So, come for the breathtaking landscape, stay for the warm hospitality and fall in love with a cuisine that is as rich and diverse as the island itself.

On the one hand you have the Costa Smeralda, a playground of the rich and famous, and on the other you have sheep: an island of designer stores and shepherds, if you like!

MARIA'S TOP 10 DISHES OF SARDEGNA

1 CULURGIONES

These ravioli-like pasta dumplings from Ogliastra are typically stuffed with potato, pecorino and mint, although fillings can vary depending on the area. They are distinguished by the intricate twists that close them, designed to recall the pattern of an ear of wheat.

2 FAINÈ SASSARESE

Found in Sassari but with roots in Genoa, this is a Sardinian version of *farinata genovese* (page 54), a savoury cake made of chickpea (gram) flour. Often served plain, with plenty of freshly ground black pepper, *fainè* can also come with sausage, onion, vegetables or cheese added to the mix.

3 FREGULA

Fregula (or *fregola*) is a Sardinian pasta made with semolina flour. The dough is formed into tiny balls that are dried and toasted before cooking. They are used in multiple ways but are most famously served with tiny telline clams in the dish *sa frègula de cociùla*.

4 MALLOREDDUS

Sometimes called *gnocchetti sardi*, *malloreddus* is actually a pasta made of water and semolina flour. Shaped into 2 cm (³⁄₄ in) long shells, they have ridged exteriors which, along with the inner cavities, capture the accompanying sauce. In one popular recipe, they are prepared *alla campidanese* (with a sauce of sausage, tomato and saffron).

5 PAELLA ALL'ALGHERESE

Alghero's Catalan influences come to the fore in this dish, which was created in 2003 to celebrate the 900-year anniversary of the founding of the city. Similar to its Spanish counterpart, *paella* contains seafood, sausage and chicken but, in a nod to Sardinian tradition, the usual rice is substituted with fregula.

6 PANE CARASAU

This thin flatbread's thin transparency gives it its other name, *carta da musica* (music paper). It is rolled into a large sheet, then baked until it puffs up. Sliced horizontally, it is returned to the oven to dry out and become crispy. This preserves its longevity: a perfect meal for shepherds of the past. It is usually eaten like a cracker, along with cheese and cured meats. (If not returned to the oven, it is known as *pane lentu*, which is soft and malleable and is often filled and rolled up to form a panino.)

7 PANE FRATTAU

Similar to pane salìtu chin bagna, *pane frattau* would traditionally have used the pieces of pane carasau left over after a day of work. The bread is soaked in meat stock and layered with tomato and cheese, then topped with a poached egg.

8 PIZZETTA SFOGLIA CAGLIARITANA

These pastry rounds filled with tomato, capers and anchovy fillets were originally conceived by bakers to utilise left-over scraps of puff pastry during World War II. Today, they are a local favourite and are often eaten for breakfast.

9 PORCEDDU

A whole suckling piglet either roasted on a spit over a fire or wrapped in myrtle leaves and slow-cooked in the embers, *porceddu* (also known as *porcetto sardo* or *maialino*) is a symbolic festive food of the countryside inland. The piglet, which should be no older than 40 days to ensure a tender meat, is cleaned, deboned and infused with herbs and spices before cooking.

10 SEADAS / SEBADAS

Sardinia's most famous dessert plays with the sweet and savoury flavours of the island. It's a large, circular, deep-fried pastry, filled with local pecorino cheese and lemon. It is served hot and oozing, drizzled with warm honey.

Other dishes to look out for

Signature pastas, seafood stews, cheesy breads and famous sweets – the cuisine of Sardinia is as rich and full of surprises as the island itself.

Street food

Pane salitu chin bagna

Layers of pane carasau, tomato sauce and pecorino are constructed like a lasagne. The crisp bread is soaked in water or stock before the ingredients are layered to soften it and allow the flavours to penetrate through.

Sa coccoi prena

Tangy sheep's cheese, potato and mint make up the tasty filling for these individual focaccias from Ogliastra, which have a star-like shape from the pinched edges.

Antipasti

Cardi sott'olio

Cardoons, which are found all over Sardinia during winter, are cut into pieces and placed in jars with olive oil, vinegar and garlic and pickled for several months. They are often served with cheese and cured meats.

Lumache al sugo

An autumnal dish usually served as an antipasto or first course. Snails are soaked, cleaned and boiled to loosen the meat from the shell. They are then cooked in tomato sauce with garlic and a little red chilli.

Primi

Favata

Pork and beans, Sardinian-style. *Favata* is made with broad (fava) beans and cabbage, cooked with pork rind, ribs and sausage and flavoured with wild fennel. It is traditionally served on top of pane carasau.

Li puligioni

Ravioli from Gallura with a filling of sheep's milk ricotta, lemon and a spoonful of sugar. The filling's sweetness is balanced by the fresh tomato and basil sauce the ravioli are served with, as well as the salty, tangy Sardinian pecorino grated on top.

Macarrones de busa

Named after the *busa* tool used to shape it, this traditional Sardinian pasta is made from flour and water. The time-consuming preparation sees the dough divided into small balls and rolled around a metal rod, similar to a knitting needle. The finished pasta is usually served with a tomato and meat ragù.

Pasta alla carlofortina

Carloforte is the only town on Isola di San Pietro, a small island off the southwest coast of Sardinia. The town was founded by families from the Genoa area, and its cuisine features many influences from Liguria, including this pasta dish. In it, the pasta is served with a sauce of fresh tuna, cherry tomatoes and Genoa's typical basil pesto (page 54).

Su succu

This vibrant yellow pasta dish is made with very fine tagliolini, which are added to a rich meat stock, along with saffron and grated aged pecorino. Topped with fresh, acidic sheep's cheese, such as casu axedu, the pasta is baked until the stock is absorbed and the top layer of cheese melts. In some parts of the region, like Logudoro, su succu is made with fregula.

Zuppa gallurese

More a dense pie than a soup, this dish layers stale bread with grated pecorino or casizolu cheese. Lamb or mutton stock is poured over, followed by a last layer of cheese before the dish is baked in the oven until golden.

Secondi

Agnello alla sarda con uova e limone

To make this dish, hunks of lamb left on the bone are cooked slowly until tender. A mixture of beaten egg with lemon is then carefully added to the pot over a low flame to create a light, creamy sauce.

Burrida a sa casteddaia

Local catshark is served with a sauce of its own liver mixed with walnuts, garlic and vinegar. Pieces of the small shark are boiled and then left to marinate in the sauce for 12–24 hours to absorb the flavours of this popular Cagliari dish.

Indattari olbiesi

Olbia is famous for its mussels, known locally as *indattari*, and many of the city's dishes feature them, including this zuppa di cozze. Cooked with garlic and parsley until they open, the mussels are served in their own juices with plenty of bread.

Ispinadas

Ispinadas refers to the short skewers shepherds would carry with them to grill meat over a small fire. The dish is a kebab made with alternating pieces of lean and fatty mutton.

Panada di anguille

This pie, from the southern town of Assemini, is often made for special occasions, with layers of eel and sliced potatoes, and a seasoning of garlic, parsley and sun-dried tomatoes, all encased inpastry.

Pecora in cappotto

With a name that means 'sheep in a coat', this hearty stew features hunks of mutton (usually shoulder on the bone), which are slowly cooked covered in water with a mixture of vegetables, including potatoes, onions, carrots, celery and sun-dried tomatoes.

Sa cassola

At least seven types of fish and seafood must be included in this Cagliari stew, including scorpion fish, squid, mussels, scampi, bream and octopus. The fish is delicately cooked with a sauce of onion, garlic, tomatoes, basil and parsley, and served with a side of pane carasau or toasted bread.

Sa cordula

In Sardinian cuisine, meat never goes to waste, resulting in plenty of recipes for lamb, goat and calf interiors. *Zimino* is a way of cooking veal offal over a fire from Sassari. This method is used to prepare *sa cordula*. In this dish, lamb or goat innards are laboriously braided together and cooked on a spit or in a pan with peas.

Sa merca

Using ancient salt preservation techniques, chunks of mullet are boiled in salted water and then wrapped in a local marsh grass called *obione*, similar to salicornia or glasswort. The process of boiling and salting preserves the fish for several days, while the grass lends the mullet a herby flavour.

Contorni

Carciofi e patate

Sardinia's prized spiny artichokes are a much-loved ingredient during the winter and spring. Here they are trimmed, cut into chunks and cooked together with potatoes, garlic and parsley to form a tasty side dish for meat or fish.

Mazza frissa

A dish of the poor shepherd community, *mazza frissa* consists of just sheep's cream boiled and mixed with fine semolina until thick. Traditionally, it would be eaten with honey. Nowadays, it is used as a sauce for gnocchi or served with fresh broad beans in springtime.

Sardegna

Dolci

Acciuleddhi

Twisted Carnevale treats, *acciuleddhi* are made from a sweet dough which is intricately braided and fried in oil. They are then coated in warm honey and grated orange zest and decorated with colourful sugar sprinkles.

Arrubiolus

Made from a ricotta dough flavoured with orange, lemon and saffron, these delicious fried balls are made for Carnevale. After frying, they are rolled in white sugar or dusted with icing (confectioners') sugar.

Gattò de mendula

Although the name suggests a cake, *gattò de mendula* is actually a crunchy brittle made with almonds, sugar, honey and lemon. After the sugar and honey are heated to a caramel, the almonds, lemon juice and zest are added and the mixture is poured onto a work surface coated in lemon juice, flattened and left to cool. It is cut into irregular, angular shapes that are each placed on a lemon leaf to serve.

Pardulas

Pastry cases enclose a light, creamy filling of ricotta, saffron and lemon in *pardule*, (or *pardulas*), which are typically made during the Easter period. They may take the form of circular buns, but are more commonly found as tarts that are pinched around the edges to make the shape of a star.

S'aranzada / Sa cuffettura

Now enjoyed all year round, these citrus treats were once served at important occasions like weddings. They feature just three ingredients, but require plenty of time and care. Orange zest is peeled, cut into thin strips and left to soak for a couple of days, the soaking water regularly changed

to remove any bitterness. The strips are then boiled and left to dry overnight. The dried peel is added to warm honey, along with thin pieces of toasted almond, then divided into individual paper cases, decorated and left to cool.

Sos papassinos

Traditional Sardinian cookies, *sos papassinos* (also called *papassini*), are made for Ognissanti (All Saints Day) on 1 November. Recognisable by their diamond shape and white glacé icing topped with colourful sugar sprinkles, they are made with raisins and almonds.

Torta de menjar blanc

Menjar blanc (Catalan blancmange) arrived in Alghero in the 14th century along with the Aragonese occupation. Here, the custardy filling is flavoured with lemon and enclosed in a sweet pastry tart.

In 2015, botanists discovered 15,000 well-preserved grape seeds from the Middle and Late Bronze Age in Sardinia: evidence of early viticulture in the area. That same year, chemists found tartaric acids on a 2,800-year-old wine press, confirming that the Nuragic civilisation was making wine from grapes well before Phoenicians took over the island.

Given this evidence, Sardinia is now known to be one of the oldest viticultural sites in Europe. Both local scientists and winemakers are eager for DNA testing to determine whether the island's primary grapes were imported or were indigenous and spread throughout Europe from the region.

Despite the island's long history of viticulture, Sardinia's wines are not all world famous. However, the island boasts a diverse number of very good drops. One of the most well known is Cannonau, a bold and full-bodied red wine made from the cannonau grape. It's characterised by notes of black fruit, spices and herbs, and pairs well with grilled meat and strong cheeses. Perhaps the most popular varietal is Vermentino, a crisp and refreshing white wine. It has flavours of citrus, tropical fruit and herbs, and is a great match for seafood, salads and light pasta dishes. Meanwhile, around Cagliari, Nasco is a favourite white.

Carignano is another notable red. While it is produced throughout the Mediterranean, Sardinia is one of the few places the grape is made into a single-varietal bottle. These wines are bold and tannic, with flavours of dark fruit, tobacco and leather that pair well with hearty meat dishes, stews and aged cheeses. Other Sardinian wines include whites such as the light and crisp Nuragus and the aromatic yet dry Vernaccia di Oristano, and reds such as the fruity Monica, and Bovale and Nieddera. Sweet varietals include Malvasia and Moscato.

The local beer and pride of the island is Ichnusa, with the distinct red, black and white regional flag on the label. And of course, Sardinia has its spirits, including the classic digestif, *mirto*. This go-to amaro is a tangy, bittersweet myrtle liqueur that is the perfect end to any meal, at home or in a restaurant. It's generally found in two varieties: red mirto, which is made with berries; and green (or white) mirto, which is made with the leaves. Then you have *filu 'e ferru* (local dialect for 'iron wire'), which is a highly potent and transparent distilled liqueur with a fennel flavour. Also known as the *acquevite* (water of life) of Sardinia, it has a dangerous reputation, thanks to alcohol concentrations that reach up to 45 per cent. Its origins date to prohibition in the late 1800s, when containers were hidden underground and tied with iron wires during clandestine distillation. Today, the quality product is highly regarded and produced legally under a few brands, including Silvio Carta and Zedda Piras, though many households still produce it illegally.

With such a wild landscape, Sardinia is also known for its botany and therefore its herbal teas. Look out for all types of infusions and mixes, with ingredients like saffron, myrtle, sage, wild fennel and rosemary. They are often enjoyed as a natural remedy for digestion and relaxation.

Sardegna

ISLANDS

Culinary experiences

Sunset aperitivos, bedding down in a vintage camper van in an olive grove, luxing it up with your own private plunge pool or learning how to make local cheese… have you booked your flight to Sardinia yet?

Explore the inland food heart of the island

Run by Sardinian Samuel Lai, Domu Antiga is a small boutique guest house in the sleepy town of Gergei, just north of Cagliari. At this haven for food lovers, you can learn some of the secrets of traditional Sardinian cuisine by taking a breadmaking course or a cheese workshop. In 2022, Samuel launched Sinnos, a project dedicated to producing natural sheep's cheese; visitors to the site can sample the Sa Mola olive oil–infused pecorino in the garden courtyard. Just up the road, Samuel's sister Giulia has her own delightful property. From her Mario Cesare cottage, Giulia works closely with the area's artisans, including bakers and small food store owners, to serve up local produce that you can enjoy for breakfast under the cottage's fig tree. Nearby, you have the town's beautiful vineyard, Olianas, which champions natural farming and low-intervention winemaking.

DOMUANTIGA.IT, MARIOCESARE.IT, OLIANAS.IT

Go glamping in an ancient olive grove

Sa Mola Experience allows you to stay in an ancient olive grove in this aperitivo-meets-glamping hotspot. For four generations, the Cadoni family has been crafting exquisite extra virgin olive oil in the quaint village of Escolca (about an hour north of Cagliari). During the pandemic, the younger family members hatched an innovative plan to showcase their legacy, embracing the outdoors: an evening aperitivo affair among the verdant groves. As the sun sets, guests indulge in regional wines paired with a delectable assortment of olives, cheeses, artisanal breads and expertly cured meats. Then you retreat for the night in your glammed-up tent or 1970s-style camper van.

OLIOSAMOLA.COM/SA-MOLA-EXPERIENCE

Slow down at a luxury eco resort

Spread over 90 acres of olive groves, organic kitchen gardens and fragrant shrubs, the Cascioni Eco Retreat is an oasis of calm and minimalistic elegance. Each of the 15 stazzo suites in former farmhouses has a private plunge pool and garden. The resort features a rejuvenating organic spa and an oak-scented wine cellar. The estate produces its own extra virgin olive oil – perfect for drizzling on fresh flatbread while dining alfresco in the garden-to-table restaurant. Explore the traditions of Gallura, learn about the olive harvest, make traditional jams at their workshop or enrol in a cooking class.

CASCIONI.COM

Meet a shepherd and taste local cheeses

Locals Claudio and Bea run Sardinia Slow Experience, offering a range of culinary experiences, including cooking classes and tasting workshops. For cheese lovers, they offer the chance to embark on a fun exploration of sheep farming and cheesemaking. Meet a shepherd, explore a local farm and witness the production of pecorino and ricotta, from the milking of the sheep all the way to the aging process. The shepherds will reveal their cheesemaking secrets and, depending on the season (usually March to July), you may get to participate in the process. After the tour, enjoy cheese and Sardinian delicacies in the peaceful countryside setting.

SARDINIASLOWEXPERIENCE.COM

Taste Italy's rarest pasta in Nuoro

Su filindeu ('the threads of God' in dialect) is a rare pasta which is folded to produce 256 delicate strands that form a large sheet. The ancient recipe has been passed down by only a few families, and today it remains with only a handful of people in Nuoro and the few people they've taught around the island. It is traditionally served in a lamb or beef broth, but the difficulty of making it means it seldom appears on tables. Only three restaurants serve it, and usually only on special occasions. Visitors can try their luck at Trattoria Il Rifugio in Nuoro, ChiaroScuro in Cagliari or Arieddas in south Sardinia.

TRATTORIARIFUGIO.COM, ARIEDDAS.IT,
CHIAROSCURODIMARINARAVAROTTO.EATBU.COM

SAGRE

APRIL

Sagra del Torrone,
Nougat festival, Tonara

MAY

Porto Cervo Wine & Food Festival, Porto Cervo

JUNE

Girotonno, Tuna festival,
Carloforte

Sagra delle Ciliegie,
Cherry festival, Burcei

AUGUST

Sagra del Carciofo,
Artichoke festival, Uri

Calici di Stelle, Wine festival,
various towns

Sagra del Vermentino,
Vermentino wine festival, Monti

SEPTEMBER

Sagra del Pesce, Fish festival,
Santa Teresa Gallura

Autunno in Barbagia,
Art, culture and food festival,
Barbagia area

NOVEMBER

Sagra dello Zafferano,
Saffron festival, Villanovafranca

Fregula risottata allo zafferano con polvere di finocchietto e ragù di polpo

Saffron fregola risotto with wild fennel and octopus ragù

I've never not eaten fregula on my trips to Sardinia. This tasty pasta, made from hard durum wheat flour, is lush and nutty and the ultimate comfort food. This recipe is by Chef Claudio Sadler, who has won just about every culinary award available, and whose cuisine is known for precision and elegance. His historic restaurant, Sadler, is in Milan, but he also has an outpost in north Sardinia. This dish turns fregula into a creamy risotto with flavours of saffron and wild fennel and a tasty octopus sauce. I know it will become your Sardinian-inspired dinner-party hit!

Sardegna

ISLANDS

SERVES 4

2 tablespoons extra virgin olive oil

1 small carrot, finely diced

½ celery stalk, finely diced

1 small onion, finely diced

1 shallot, finely diced

3 cm (1¼ in) piece of ginger, finely diced

1 garlic clove, peeled

1 bird's eye chilli, finely diced

150 ml (5 fl oz) white wine

100 g (3½ oz) fresh tomato sauce or tomato passata (pureed tomatoes)

large handful of basil, leaves picked and finely chopped, plus extra sprigs to serve

handful of parsley, leaves picked and finely chopped, plus extra sprigs to serve

Octopus

750 g (1 lb 11 oz) whole octopus, cleaned (ask your fishmonger to do this for you)

1 carrot, roughly chopped

1 celery stalk, roughly chopped

1 onion, peeled and left whole

1 small bunch of flat-leaf parsley

2 fresh bay leaves

To prepare the octopus, place the ingredients in a large saucepan of water and bring to the boil. Reduce the heat to a simmer and cook, uncovered, for about 1½ hours, until the octopus is tender at its thickest part when pierced with a skewer. Remove the pan from the heat and leave the octopus in the liquid to cool. Once cooled, peel the octopus and discard the skin and suckers. Cut the octopus into 5 mm (¼ in) dice.

Heat the olive oil, carrot, celery, onion, shallot, ginger, unpeeled garlic clove and chilli in a frying pan over medium–low heat. Add the octopus, increase the heat to high and cook for 5 minutes or until the octopus starts to caramelise on the base of the pan. Pour in the white wine and cook for a further 5 minutes or until the liquid has almost evaporated.

Reduce the heat to low, add the fresh tomato sauce or passata and slowly bring to the boil. Season with salt and pepper and, at the last moment, stir in the basil and parsley. Remove the pan from the heat and discard the garlic.

Meanwhile, to prepare the fregula, add 25 ml (¾ fl oz) of the olive oil, the shallot and a splash of water to a large saucepan over medium–low heat. Cook the shallot for 3–4 minutes, until softened, then add the fregula, 900 ml (30½ fl oz) of the vegetable stock, the saffron and fennel. Cook, stirring occasionally, for 9–10 minutes, until the fregula is tender, adding a little more stock if needed to stop the mixture drying out. Stir in the remaining 50 ml (1¾ fl oz) of olive oil, the butter and Grana Padano to thicken slightly. Add a drizzle of soy sauce and the chopped red chilli, to taste.

If you'd like to make the cuttlefish ink air, pour all the ingredients into a large bowl and blend with a stick blender to incorporate air and create a light foam.

Divide the fregola among plates. Use a circular mould or large cookie cutter to place the octopus ragù on top, and finish with a few sprigs of basil and parsley and a spoonful of the cuttlefish ink air (if using).

Fregula

75 ml (2½ fl oz) extra virgin olive oil

1 shallot, finely chopped

350 g (12½ oz) fregula

1 litre (4 cups) vegetable stock, approximately

½ teaspoon saffron threads

2 teaspoons ground fennel

25 g (1 oz) butter

25 g (1 oz) Grana Padano, grated

soy sauce, to taste

chopped red chilli, to taste

Cuttlefish ink air (optional)

150 ml (5 fl oz) fish stock, chilled

1 teaspoon cuttlefish ink

½ teaspoon soy lecithin granules

Sardegna

ISLANDS

Sicilia

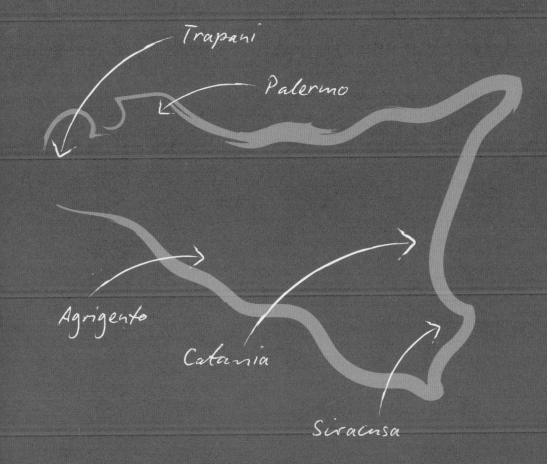

Trapani

Palermo

Agrigento

Catania

Siracusa

Regional produce

This sun-kissed, fertile land has many dimensions, including its volcanoes and mountains, coastlines, and fields of crops and vineyards. Travelling through, you notice the terrain and how it changes with altitude, pistachio trees appearing as you head up Etna's volcanic slopes. This enigmatic region has a glorious bounty of ricotta and citrus and an abundant coastline, with offerings changing through the seasons.

- Almonds
- Blood oranges
- Bronte's pistachios
- Candied fruit
- Capers
- Eggplant
- Lemons
- Mazara del Vallo prawns (shrimp)
- Modica chocolate
- Nebrodi black pork
- Prickly pears
- Ricotta salata
- Swordfish
- Tomatoes
- Torrone

Beach in Scopello

As cliched as it sounds, I've never found a place, or a meal, that I didn't like on this magnetic island, from brioche dipped in granita (page 312) on the western tip in Trapani to the largest ricotta cannolo (page 308) of my life in medieval Erice. There's nothing like the couscous (page 310) in San Vito Lo Capo, or the Baroque architecture of Noto and Syracuse, visited between trips sailing the Aeolian archipelago eating pane cunzato (page 309) topped with tomato, mozzarella and capers. And you'll never forget diving into the majestic jewel and hot mess that is Palermo for the first time, with its arancine (page 308) and luscious gelato (page 312). Sicily's capital is one of the world's most electric cities and it has me falling in love more and more with each visit.

I continue to travel around Italy, and the world, but I just keep coming back to Sicily, with its distinct identity of contrast and diversity. This region that was once a kingdom has a long history that's both regal and corrupt, home to kings and a mafia stronghold that's no secret. But it's this mixed past, if anything, that gives Sicily so much character and soul, which is reflected beautifully in the variety and depth of its cuisine. Yes, eating is a way of life in Italy, but it seems that the Sicilians, with their fiery passion, take it a little more seriously.

The Mediterranean's largest island has been shaped by the Greeks, Spanish, French, Arabs and Normans, among others, who have all left traces of their influence on Sicilian food. Take the region's street food: it originated with the souks that Arabs introduced during their rule in the 10th century. Today, we have the markets of Palermo, including Ballarò, one of the city's oldest: a walk through is an unforgettable jumble of sights, sounds and sensations. There's fruit and vegetable stands, panelle (page 308) frying and octopus being flung onto hot grills, all to the tune of vendors bantering loudly and

commercial pop music blaring. And then there's the scents: a mix of frying oil and the day's catch.

Inside Sicily's kitchens, cucina povera is common: particularly in the home, where families sit together at the table, often accompanied by neighbours, friends and relatives. Many of the meals I've enjoyed in Sicily fall into this category – moments that combine simple ingredients, no-fuss dishes and copious amounts of wine.

Sicily's third type of cuisine is known as *cucina dei Monsù*, which is tied to Naples (Sicily's sister kingdom), and the cuisine of the 17th-century French aristocracy. Cucina dei Monsù is rich in flavour and history, combining the techniques of French haute cuisine with the fresh, seasonal produce of the South. The dishes are visually appealing (with taste to match), layering textures and colours to create treats like *timballo* and *anelletti al forno* (two of many variations of pasta bakes; page 311). While nowadays this cuisine can be found across the island,

Sicilia

ISLANDS

in the Sicilian home, the more complex and extravagant recipes are usually reserved for special occasions.

If there was a thread that connected these culinary traditions, it would be this region's one true constant: diversity. On this magical island, there's an abundance of histories to explore and colourful traditions that keep Sicily in flux, cementing it as one of Italy's most exciting food destinations.

The produce that underlies these traditions comes from a disparate mix of rural and intensely cultivated land stretching across hills, coastline and active volcanoes. Etna is one of the most famous and active in the world, and there isn't a Sicilian you'll meet on your travels who can't tell you a story about it.

The region's geography actually extends beyond the island to ... more islands, including the stunning Aeolian archipelago off the northeastern coast. This area is known for its volcanic landscapes, crystal-clear waters and charming fishing villages, where dishes showcase seafood and bountiful produce. On my visits, I ate copious amounts of swordfish, caponata (page 308) and, specifically on Salina, capers touted as some of the best in the world. Then you have the Egadi Islands off the western coast, which include Favignana, Levanzo and Marettimo. These islands have a strong fishing tradition, with Favignana famous for a tuna fishery and its *bottarga* (dried and cured mullet roe), along with sensational coves. Back on the western side of the Sicilian mainland, the clearest link to the region's Arab heritage is the prevalence of couscous. The dish even has its own annual festival in San Vito Lo Capo!

This meld of land, sea and volcanoes makes up a microclimate that sets the stage for culinary magic, which includes Etna's aromatic white wines and plump tomatoes. These are renowned as some of Italy's best

Eating is a way of life in Italy, but it seems that the Sicilians, with their fiery passion, take it a little more seriously.

Noto Cathedral

produce, raised in a special blend of mineral-rich, volcanic soil. Nearby, the sea provides the perfect climate: for the wine and the tomatoes, but also for the prized red prawn (shrimp) of Mazara, the capers of Salina, tuna from Favignana and extra virgin olive oils – particularly the drops and infusions from around the area of Ragusa and the Iblean Mountains.

The island's abundance of sheep means pecorino is a staple, as well as ricotta, which is why it's not only possible, but totally acceptable, for you to eat a cannolo at any time of day, anywhere across the island!

Which takes me to dessert: the Sicilians are famous for it. From marzipan works of art (page 312) to gelato and granita to those cannoli filled with ricotta and topped with pistachios, candied fruit or chocolate chips. Made famous in pop culture and in *The Godfather* with the famous line 'Leave the gun, take the cannoli', this dessert is the region's pride and joy.

Gluttony is perhaps an unavoidable sin on Sicily: even in the Church. *Dolci conventuali* (convent sweets) are famous here, comprising desserts (often featuring almonds or marzipan) made by convent nuns. To this day you can find them selling their wares in cloisters and convents from Trapani to Palermo, with proceeds supporting their livelihood or restoration works. Dolci conventuali provide a beautiful example of the intersection of food and culture, and how dishes live on through generations.

Similar examples can be found throughout the region: a melding of age-old traditions, contemporary kitchens and the Sicilians who live here today. So whatever you come for, pasta topped with pistachios, wine grown in the shadows of volcanic slopes and brioche for your granita will all be waiting for you.

Hungry yet? Welcome to Sicily!

MARIA'S TOP 10 DISHES OF SICILIA

1 ARANCINI / ARANCINE

Sicilians have two names for these fried rice balls stuffed with tomato ragù and peas or cheese and prosciutto, and you'll get extra points (and avoid hearing a debate) if you learn the difference. On the eastern shore, they go by their masculine name, *arancini*, while on the western coast, you'll find the feminine *arancine*. These snacks are patriotically tied to the island, their shape said to resemble Mount Etna – particularly the ones made in the Catania area. But why two names? Arancine are usually rounder, their shape said to resemble an orange, which is a feminine noun in Italian: *arancia*.

2 BUSIATE CON PESTO TRAPANESE

Originating in Trapani, *busiate* are long, spiral pasta shapes. They are served with pesto which, in these parts, is made with tomato, toasted almonds, garlic, basil and grated pecorino.

3 CANNOLO

So many instalments of this age-old classic exist, but the most common is a crunchy, fried shell of pastry stuffed with sweetened ricotta and sometimes topped with candied orange, chocolate or chopped pistachio. Traditionally, the real deal is filled on the spot so that the shell doesn't soften.

4 CAPONATA

Caponata is a symbol of the working class. Its name derives from *capone*, a fish seasoned with a sweet and sour sauce that was prized by Sicily's aristocracy. The masses who couldn't afford the fish replaced it with eggplant (aubergine), evolving the dish. Today, it is a rich and versatile pan-fried delicacy of eggplant, tomato, olives, capers and onion that can be served hot or cold as a sauce, a side or even in a sandwich.

5 MACCO DI FAVE

This hearty, nourishing soup or puree of crushed broad (fava) beans and fennel is comfort food at its best, sometimes topped with a little ricotta.

6 MAIALINO / SUINO NERO DEI NEBRODI

The black pig of Nebrodi is an ancient Sicilian breed, and its meat is prepared in a variety of ways: cured as a sausage or salumi, or prepared as a fillet which is slow-cooked or made into a ragù for pasta.

7 PANELLE

These fried chickpea (garbanzo bean) fritters are a popular street food typically found in Palermo. The rectangular fritters are made with chickpea (gram) flour so they have a smooth consistency and are served crispy and hot. The only problem is trying to stop at one!

8 PASTA ALLA NORMA

This is the native pasta dish of Catania, found all over the island. It combines fried eggplant, ricotta salata and fresh basil in a rich tomato sauce and is usually served with a short, tubular pasta, such as rigatoni or sedani.

9 SARDE A BECCAFICO

Golden, pan-fried sardines sandwiched together with breadcrumbs, raisins and pine nuts make for this flavour-packed recipe. It was inspired by a dish nobles once enjoyed, in which sardines were prepared to resemble stuffed birds (*beccafico* is Italian for the Orphean warbler bird).

10 TORRONE

The town of Caltanissetta is famous for its torrone, but the entire island has no shortage of almonds, so nougat is made all over Sicily. You'll find the soft, the gooey and the crunchy types, with some varieties coated in chocolate, others sold plain – the list goes on. Around Christmas, it's common to find the *giuggiulena* (also known as *cubaita*); similar to torrone, it has ancient Arab origins and is made with sesame seeds, almonds and honey.

Other dishes to look out for

From fried street snacks to crumbed and creamy seafood dishes and brioche jammed with gelato, it's impossible to take a wrong turn in Sicily.

Street food

Cipollina

A filled puff pastry delight from Catania, which is stuffed with mozzarella, ham, tomatoes and onion. *Cipollina* is a flavoursome snack that's a staple of the *rosticceria siciliana* (the deli-style menu offering) which you'll find in bars and take-out joints across the island.

Crocchè

These golden mashed potato croquettes can be found at market stands, fried food spots and bars. The potato mixture is usually seasoned with mint or parsley and then crumbed.

Frittola

This ancient delicacy is basically left-over calf scraps fried up and eaten as a street food snack. They're prepared to almost resemble pieces of crispy chicken skin and are served in a paper bag or cone, sometimes with bread.

Pane cunzato

This simple street food, local to the northwestern tip of the island and common across the Aeolian Islands, is often referred to as a 'poor man's sandwich'. It's basically a flavourful and crisp bread round, usually topped with tomato, mozzarella, anchovies or capers. *Cunzato* in Sicilian dialect means 'seasoned' or 'dressed', so you get the idea. In some parts of Sicily, *pane cunzato* refers to a filled panino.

Pani câ mèusa

When it comes to nose-to-tail cuisine, in Sicily, this dish is king. Its name translates from Sicilian dialect to 'spleen sandwich'. This gutsy *panino*, which usually comprises a sesame-topped bun filled with *milza* (boiled spleen), isn't a delicate affair, but it's the pride of Palermo, where nothing gets thrown away. It dates to the 15th century, when butchers were paid in animal scraps.

Panino con carne di cavallo

Stall holders at markets in Catania fry up horse meat on their grills and stuff it into bread rolls, ready for you to try: a much-loved local specialty. If not in a panino, you can also try the meat as *polpette* (meatballs) in these parts.

Sfincione

This classic Palermitano flatbread is Sicily's version of pizza or focaccia and is topped with tomato sauce, onion, anchovy, oregano and caciocavallo cheese. It has a layer of breadcrumbs too, which crisps up in the oven, giving the bread a gorgeous crunch and texture.

Stigghiola

Grilled skewers of lamb offal seasoned with salt, parsley and onions wrapped around a leek. They are commonly found at street markets in Palermo.

Sicilia

Antipasti

Canazzo siciliano

The colourful *canazzo* is a pan-fried or baked combination of vegetables including potato, eggplant, bell peppers (capsicums) and onion. It is similar to caponata, the main difference being the addition of bell peppers and sometimes zucchini (courgette). It is eaten hot or cold, especially in the summer.

Cavolo cappuccio in agrodolce

This fresh sweet and sour salad of green cabbage is an autumn and winter dish found in both restaurants and the home. Sugar, vinegar, pine nuts and raisins or sultanas (golden raisins) combine with extra virgin olive oil to coat the cabbage.

Scaccia

This very thin, filled pastry can be found all over Sicily, but it's a particularly popular starter and snack in Ragusa, where it's rectangular and filled with ricotta, meat and vegetables, or a tomato sauce mixed with parsley and anchovies.

Primi

Cavati e ravioli alla ragusana

This staple pasta dish from Ragusa combines two types of pasta – *cavati* (a local form of cavatelli) and ricotta-filled ravioli. The ricotta is either slightly sweetened or seasoned with marjoram. They are served with a rich *strattu* (an extract made from sun-dried tomatoes) and pork sauce.

Couscous

This dish might not come to mind when you think of Sicily, but couscous is a traditional dish of Trapani and surrounds. Topped with seafood, seasoned with cinnamon and prepared with a rich broth, it's the finest example of this island's Arab and North African ancestry.

Minestra di pasta con i tenerumi

Tenerumi are found only in Sicily. They're the leaves and shoots of a *cucuzza* (a long type of squash) and are prepared with pasta, which is sometimes tossed with mussels, or used to make soup.

Pasta al pistacchio di Bronte

The versatile Bronte pistachio is an official Slow Food and DOP product grown in Bronte near Catania. It is the king of nuts in these parts and beyond, and is used in this creamy pasta dish, which is sometimes topped with raw pink prawns (shrimp).

Pasta con le sarde

This luscious pasta dish combines some of the most iconic Sicilian ingredients. It's usually prepared with spaghetti and sardines, but the sauce has fennel, anchovy, raisins and pine nuts too.

Timballo di anelletti

Reminiscent of lasagne, this baked pasta dish is made with *anelletti* (a small ring-shaped pasta) and is covered with thinly sliced fried eggplant. A nod to the rich, opulent dishes of the cucina dei Monsù, this recipe reflects Sicily's storied noble tradition.

Secondi

Involtini alla palermitana

Bite-sized veal roulade is a tasty main course in Palermo. Veal fillets are stuffed with caciocavallo, raisins, pinenuts and parsley, then rolled, crumbed and pan-fried. A similar dish called *sasizzeddi* is found in Catania and surrounds and is often stuffed with hot salami.

Involtini di pesce spada

There aren't many parts of the island where swordfish isn't on the menu, but in Messina, Palermo and the Trapani area, they really shine. Traditionally, fillets are rolled around a mix of minced (ground) swordfish, breadcrumbs, pinenuts, raisins and capers. They're then crumbed and pan-fried or baked.

Polpette

The meatball and its many variations can be found all over Sicily. You have the more traditional style, made with beef or pork or a mix of the two, and the meatless varieties, made with either eggplant or zucchini. Either way, you'll find them *al sugo* (in tomato sauce) or crumbed and fried.

Totani ripieni

These stuffed calamari are typical of Messina and the Aeolian Islands but are popular all along Sicily's coast. They are filled with breadcrumbs and pecorino or caciocavallo and are grilled or served in a rich tomato sauce.

Zuppa di pesce

On an island, you'd expect the highest quality seafood, and Sicily doesn't disappoint. The consistency and ingredients of this dish will change slightly from city to town and coastline to coastline, but a mix of the freshest catch is usually slow-cooked in a tomato, caper and white wine sauce, served with toasted bread to soak up all that juicy goodness.

Dolci

Buccellato

This fig and nut ring cake is typically baked in the winter months and found in cake stores at Christmastime. Also considered a breakfast sweet bread, buccellato is usually topped with colourful candied fruit peels.

Cassata

A sponge cake soaked in liqueur or fruit juice and filled with chocolate-chip ricotta and candied fruit. It's usually lathered with pale or bright-green marzipan frosting. Its name comes from the Arabic *quas at* (bowl). At Easter *cassata* may be baked, the marzipan exterior replaced by a layer of shortcrust (pie) pastry.

Frutta martorana

These marzipan sweets shaped and painted like fruits (and sometimes vegetables) are symbolic creations found in pasticcerie across the region, but most commonly in Messina and Palermo. On All Souls Day, they're traditionally placed at children's bedsides to honour family members who have passed.

Gelato in brioche

It's customary across the region to fill a small brioche bun with one or more flavours of gelato. You won't find a gelateria in Sicily without brioche lining the counter. You will end up with gelato dripping down your hands, but that's the delicious fun of it all.

Granita

Served in a glass with or without brioche, *granita* is more than just a flavoured frozen delicacy. It's a ritual that brings people together – not just at breakfast and during summer, but all year round. Lemon and almond are the most classic flavours, but on the Aeolian Islands, you'll often find *fichi d'india* (prickly pear) and *gelsi* (mulberry).

Iris

Hailing from Palermo, the *iris* is a baked or fried pastry that looks like a doughnut stuffed with a rich and creamy filling. Nowadays, you'll find a bit of flirting with the filling, but the traditional variety features ricotta often dotted with chocolate chips.

Sicily has long produced wine. Legend has it that Dionysus, the Greek god of wine, winemaking and grape cultivation, brought the joy of wine to Sicily. Other accounts credit traders in 1500 BCE. Either way, the Greeks brought advanced viticultural techniques to the island in the 8th century BCE.

During the 18th century, Marsala, a town on Sicily's western coast, began production of the wine that shares its name. With its unique flavour and versatility, Marsala became a favourite with the European aristocracy and eventually spread all over the world.

Since the start of the 21st century, wine production on the island has been through a renaissance of sorts – one that hasn't gone unnoticed. Awards have come in fast, cementing Sicily as one of Italy's best wine producers. It is the region with the most land dedicated to vineyards in the country, and it is poised to expand.

While travelling around the island, it's hard to miss the most popular varietals: Nero d'Avola (a red similar to Syrah) and the crisp and aromatic Grillo. While the grape was only used to produce Marsala initially, Grillo now stands on its own as a very popular white wine. Other prominent white grapes include catarratto, with its dry but citrusy notes, and the fresh inzolia, with its notes of minerals. Carricante is the main grape variety used to make wines that are often referred to as Etna Bianco.

When it comes to reds, you'll often find the light-bodied Frappato and the elegant Nerello Mascalese, made with grapes from the slopes of Etna. And for those with a sweet tooth, some of my favourites include Malvasia, said to have arrived on the island of Salina over 2,000 years ago, Passito di Pantelleria and Zibibbo.

As for digestifs, Amaro Averna, one of Italy's most popular, is Sicilian and produced in the province of Caltanissetta. Amaro Gerlando is another local name to look out for, as is the almond-flavoured Amaretto di Girgentian. For a real taste of the land, keep an eye out for grappa, amari and liqueurs made with prized local produce, such as fico d'india, oranges, pistachio and cinnamon.

Besides Amaretto di Girgentian, Sicily's abundance of almonds is used to make *latte di mandorla* (almond milk), which was born on the island. Its origins date to the medieval era, when animal-based milk would never last long and often ended up being used to make cheese.

For another thirst quencher, *spremuta* (freshly squeezed juice) is popular – particularly orange, but there are all kinds of citrus variations. Or, for something bubbly, there's *spuma* (which translates to 'foam' or 'froth'): a soft drink with a caramel flavour and a spicy aftertaste, thanks to natural infusions of ingredients, such as orange, elderflower, cloves, rhubarb and vanilla. Enjoy it as an aperitivo at the bar or on the street to wash down fried food. And finally, Catania is famous for its *seltz al limone* (a sparkling lemon drink).

Culinary experiences

Saddle up for some Sicilian foodie adventures and learn how to make traditional dishes, study cheesemaking or luxe it up in a resort with views of Mount Etna.

Hike the volcano then wine and dine at an Etna wine hotel

In the area between Catania and Taormina, innovative Sicilian entrepreneurs are leading what many locals have described – with intentional use of the pun – an Etna explosion! Wineries, kitchen gardens, outstanding restaurants and boutique hotels are popping up everywhere. Check out the chic country hotel Zash, which comes complete with private pool villas and a Michelin-starred restaurant that sits in what used to be a wine press. Explore the charming luxury resort Donna Carmela, where organic food, wine and mixology reign supreme, and all rooms have views of the sea and Etna. Local expert and chef Linda Sarris, whose passion and energy for the region are contagious, hosts curated food travel programs across the island, including taking guests to Etna and beyond, with private dinners, wine tastings and villa stays.

ZASH.IT, DONNACARMELA.COM, LINDASARRIS.COM

Book in for a farm-to-table journey at the Anna Tasca Lanza cooking school

Fabrizia Lanza has dedicated her life to the preservation of Sicilian culinary traditions. The school was opened in 1989 by her mother, Marchesa Anna Tasca Lanza, and is set on 1,300 acres of vineyards. The culinary centre offers short and long immersive educational experiences, classes and programs like Cook the Farm. While visiting, you can stay at their 19th-century farmhouse, Case Vecchie, and enjoy wine, wheat and oil workshops, writing retreats, yoga and more.

ANNATASCALANZA.COM

Take on cheesemaking and chocolate

Explore the Ragusa countryside and its cheese farms and then journey to Modica, famous for its unusual grainy chocolate. As they say here, 'Methods are ancient and traditional, rhythms are slow.' At a family-run farm in Ragusa, you'll see the entire cheese production, from the curdling of the milk to the shaping of fresh provola and Ragusano DOP, and the preparation of ricotta. In Modica, you'll taste chocolate and learn about its preparation. There are olive groves and vineyards across both areas, making it the perfect corner for culinary expeditions. Casa Mia Food and Wine can coordinate a day trip from anywhere in Sicily.

CASAMIATOURS.COM

Learn how to make arancini at a cooking class

On your travels through Sicily, why just eat arancini when you can learn how to make them? Catania and Palermo are both great places to book in for a cooking lesson, with a wide offering available. You'll also find classes in cities like Taormina and Syracuse. Sicilying offers a wide range of classes for all levels across the region.

SICILYING.COM

1920s glamour in Italy's street food capital

Enter another world at Villa Igiea, a Rocco Forte Hotel. This majestic 19th-century villa will captivate you and it's the perfect base from which to eat your way through Palermo. This city's cuisine begins in the bustling food markets, and the Villa Igiea concierge team will curate a private market walk, complete with a ride in a vintage Piaggio Ape truck. You'll eat street food along the way, like sfincione and arancini, with pani câ meusa for the adventurous. Complete your trip with a drive south to Sciacca to visit their sister property, Verdura Resort. In addition to a unique dining offering, the vast property produces its own extra virgin olive oil and hosts a series of curated and seasonal Italian culinary retreats.

ROCCOFORTEHOTELS.COM

SAGRE

MARCH

Mandorlo in Fiore,
Almond blossom festival,
Agrigento

APRIL

Sagra del Carciofo,
Artichoke festival, Cerda

Sagra della Ricotta e del Formaggi, Ricotta and cheese festival, Vizzini

Sagra del Cannolo,
Ricotta cannolo festival,
Piana degli Albanesi

JUNE

Festa del Cappero,
Caper festival, Salina

AUGUST

Sagra della Cipolla,
Onion festival, Giarratana

SEPTEMBER

Sagra del Pistacchio,
Pistachio festival, Catania

Cous Cous Fest, Couscous festival, San Vito Lo Capo

OCTOBER

Sagra del Fico d'India,
Prickly pear festival, San Cono

Sagra del Tartufo,
Truffle festival, Capizzi

NOVEMBER

Sagra del Suino Nero e Porcino dei Nebrodi, Black Nebrodi pig and porcini mushrooms festival, Cesarò

DECEMBER

ChocoModica,
Chocolate festival, Modica

BY MASSIMO MANTARRO, PRINCIPE CERAMI,
SAN DOMENICO PALACE, TAORMINA, A FOUR SEASONS HOTEL

Busiate alla trapanese

Busiate with Trapani-style pesto

The second season of the HBO hit series *The White Lotus* had us all dreaming of Sicilian sunsets, infinity pools and hotel bar cocktails. Shot at Taormina's iconic San Domenico Palace, a Four Seasons Hotel, it certainly took la dolce vita and Italian old-world glamour to new heights. Their in-house Principe Cerami restaurant (with one Michelin star, no less) and executive chef and Sicily native Massimo Mantarro elevate this Trapani pasta classic with eggplant chips and a pecorino fondue to make it extra special. While you could prepare this dish with most varieties of pasta, I implore you to look for the long twisty busiate. I ate it for the first time in Trapani with the traditional rustic version of this pesto and I still think about it to this day.

Sicilia

ISLANDS

SERVES 4

200 g (7 oz) busiate

3 spring onions (scallions), sliced

150 ml (5 fl oz) vegetable stock

1 tablespoon slivered almonds

chopped parsley, to serve

Confit tomatoes

1 garlic clove, crushed

2 tablespoons thyme leaves

2 tablespoons marjoram leaves

zest of 1 large lemon

zest of 1 large orange

15 g (½ oz) sea salt

2 tablespoons icing (confectioners') sugar

500 g (1 lb 2 oz) red and yellow datterini or cherry tomatoes, halved lengthways

Eggplant cream

400 g (14 oz) eggplant (aubergine), peeled and roughly chopped

splash of extra virgin olive oil

Pecorino fondue

80 ml (2¾ fl oz) cream

80 g (2¾ oz) pecorino, grated

Eggplant and garlic chips

150 ml (5 fl oz) extra virgin olive oil

60 g (2 oz) baby eggplant (preferably perlina variety), sliced into very thin rounds

4 garlic cloves, sliced

Parsley oil

35 g (1¼ oz) parsley stalks and leaves

100 ml (3½ fl oz) extra virgin olive oil

Preheat the oven to 50°C (120°F) fan-forced or as low as your oven will go.

To make the confit tomatoes, combine the ingredients except the tomatoes in a bowl. Place the tomatoes, cut-side up, on a baking tray and scatter with the herb mixture. Cook for 3–4 hours, until soft and sweet.

Increase the oven temperature to 180°C (350°F) fan-forced.

To make the eggplant cream, toss the eggplant with a splash of olive oil. Spread half the eggplant on a small baking tray and bake for about 8 minutes, until tender. Place the remaining eggplant in a small frying pan and cook over medium–low heat, stirring occasionally, for 10 minutes or until tender. Blend both eggplants together in a high-speed blender or with a stick blender until creamy.

For the pecorino fondue, heat the cream in a small heavy-based saucepan over high heat until boiling, then add the pecorino and whisk vigorously. Strain through a fine sieve and set aside in the fridge, covered, to cool.

To make the eggplant and garlic chips, heat the olive oil in a small saucepan over medium–high heat to 130–140°C (265–285°F) on a kitchen thermometer. Add the eggplant and garlic and fry for 1–2 minutes, until crisp. Remove with a slotted spoon and drain on paper towel.

To make the parsley oil, blend the parsley, olive oil and a pinch of salt in a blender until smooth. Strain the parsley oil through a fine sieve lined with muslin (cheese cloth) and set aside. The parsley oil will keep in a sealed jar in the fridge for 2–3 days.

When ready to serve, cook the busiate in salted boiling water until al dente. Meanwhile, in two small saucepans, heat the eggplant cream and the pecorino cheese fondue separately over medium–low heat until hot.

Heat a splash of olive oil in a frying pan over medium heat, add the spring onion and cook for 1–2 minutes, until soft, then add the vegetable stock and bring to a simmer.

Drain the pasta and tip it into the pan with the spring onion and stock.

To serve, spread the warm eggplant cream across the base of four plates, add the busiate and confit tomatoes, and top with the eggplant and garlic chips. Finish the dish with a swirl of pecorino fondue, a sprinkling of almonds and parsley, and a drizzle of parsley oil.

Acknowledgements

Mangia is a work born of love, discovery and heritage. It took over a year to write but, as with most creative projects, I've kind of been writing it my whole life. That means there are so many to thank. And so, this pride and joy wouldn't be in my hands without the amazing support and contribution of the following people:

My immediate family, my true constants: distance does not separate us. Thank you to Anthony, Kali and Lara; my smallest but biggest fans, Massimo and Marco; and especially my mum and dad, Fred and Lina, for always encouraging me to dream and for instilling in me a profound appreciation of my Italian heritage. They've provided for me and always encouraged me to aim high. I am forever indebted to them.

Particular thanks to my sister Lara for existing; for enthusiastically supporting my dreams and reading every word of my books; for selflessly, unconditionally being there; for flying to my side without delay. I dedicate this and every success to you. I love you.

Massive thanks to Kate Zagorski, whose unwavering support has been invaluable. And, by default, love and thanks to Angelo Preziosi, Mimi and Dave. As I've said many times, Kate, there just isn't enough gin in the world to thank you. But I won't stop trying!

Grazie di cuore to my friend and esteemed colleague Luciana Squadrilli for taking my initial manuscript and providing valuable tips and feedback. Thank you too for your endorsement, together with Federico De Cesare Viola and Massimo Bottura (thanks also goes to Lara Gilmore).

Immense gratitude to friends who shared their insights: Natalino Gisonna, Flavia Campailla, Chiara Di Fonzo, Francesca Polla, Teresa Leone, Andrea Febo, Luca Sessa, Angela Santoro, Tania Pietracatella and Federico De Cesare Viola.

A huge thanks to every chef, restaurant, hotel, PR agency and my mum, Lina, for the recipes.

Thank you to Paul McNally of Smith Street Books for believing in my projects. Big thanks to the entire team: Jane Ormond, Avery Hayes, Lucy Heaver, Vanessa Masci, Caroline Griffiths, Deborah Kaloper, Sonny Ross and Mark Roper. And grazie to Andrea Di Lorenzo for my portraits.

To three angels (they know why): Jennifer Bogo, Marco Ricci and Andrea Beraldo. Words, thanks, love will never capture what you mean to me. I will never forget. And forever gratitude to friends and my steadfast support team: particularly the Martone sisters, Dona Daher, Max Ballo, Robyn Woodman, Mimmo Mastrodicasa, Valentina Angelini, Teresa Leone, Fernanda Menozzi, Valeria Zuppardo, Danielle Guarnaccia, Carla Andronaco, Paula Mannello-Mammoliti, Diana Tandora, Fiona Graham and especially Chiara Magliochetti. To all other friends and family in Australia and around the world. Thank you to my friend and doctor Andrea Guerriero and Salvator Mundi International Hospital's entire team, and particularly Dr Rosa Maria Lovicu and Dr Antonio Capobianco – thank you.

To longtime blog readers and thousands of social media followers, to those who've bought my books, attended my events – thank you from the depths of my heart for always cheering me on, for your kindness and for your beautiful encouragement.

I am truly grateful. I am humbled.

And finally, grazie Italia, for forever feeding, thrilling and enriching me. You are my one true love. I will forever be proud to be Italian and won't ever stop telling your stories.

About the author

Born to Italian parents in Melbourne, Australia, Maria always knew Italy was her destiny.

Graduating with degrees in Arts (political science and history) and Public Policy and Management (Hons.) from the University of Melbourne in 2001, Maria began her career as an adviser for the Victorian Government. Her passion for writing and communication eventually led her into the corporate world of PR and events and, by the age of 30, she had established her own company.

With more than 25 years of experience working across the public, private and community sectors, Maria is an expert in PR, events and social media strategy, having serviced international clients, tourism boards and major luxury hospitality and travel brands.

Since moving to Rome in 2011, Maria has become an award-winning food and travel journalist contributing regularly to Fodor's, Condé Nast, *CNN*, *USA Today*, *The Sydney Morning Herald*, *The Age* and *The Australian*. She has interviewed some of the world's greatest chefs and spent thousands of hours talking to and learning from passionate and dedicated food lovers the world over.

Her HeartRome brand and social media network have a global following that exceeds 50,000 and have been featured in *BBC Travel*, *The Washington Post*, *Grazia*, *ELLE* and *Vogue*, among others.

Maria has spent her entire life travelling the world and eating her way through Italy. International press and Italian food authorities continue to recognise her knowledge and expertise, including

About the author

ELLE magazine, which has featured her as a leading expert on the Italian lifestyle; *Corriere della Sera*, which selected her to speak among the most prominent women in food in Italy; and *La Repubblica*, which named her one of Rome's most influential people in travel.

Her love for Italy is rivalled only by her love of club sandwiches, hotel check-ins and dessert. In Rome, you'll find her walking the streets of Trastevere, at a luxury spa or dining with friends. Maria is the author of *I Heart Rome* (republished as *The Eternal City*) and *How to Be Italian*. *Mangia* is her fourth book.

Published in 2024 by Smith Street Books
Naarm | Melbourne | Australia
smithstreetbooks.com

ISBN: 978-1-9227-5489-9

Smith Street Books respectfully acknowledges the Wurundjeri People of the Kulin Nation, who are the Traditional Owners of the land on which we work, and we pay our respects to their Elders past and present.

Publisher: Paul McNally
Managing editor: Avery Hayes
Editor: Jane Ormond
Recipe testing: Caroline Griffiths
Food photography: Mark Roper
Food styling: Deborah Kaloper
Food preparation: Caroline Griffiths and Amanda Menegazzo
Design concept and layout: Vanessa Masci
Proofreader: Penny Mansley

Printed & bound in China by C&C Offset Printing Co., Ltd.

Book 342
10 9 8 7 6 5 4 3 2 1